ORGANIZED DEMOCRACY

Political Institutions in a Welfare State
– the Case of Norway

BY
JOHAN P. OLSEN

UNIVERSITETSFORLAGET
BERGEN · OSLO · TROMSØ

© UNIVERSITETSFORLAGET 1983
ISBN 82-00-06442-5
Cover design: Harald Nystad
Printed in Norway by
Reklametrykk A.s, Bergen

Distribution offices:

NORWAY
Universitetsforlaget
Postboks 2977, Tøyen
Oslo 6

UNITED KINGDOM
Global Book Resources Ltd.
109 Great Russell Street
London WC1B 3NA

UNITED STATES and CANADA
Columbia University Press
136 South Broadway
Irvington-on-Hudson
New York 10533

TIL MIN VANDRINGSKAMERAT

CONTENTS

ORGANIZATIONAL FACTORS IN POLITICAL LIFE

AN INTRODUCTION

It has become a cliché to say that Western democracies are in difficulties. The post World War II optimism on behalf of representative democracy has turned into a worry over crises of governability, representativeness, rationality and legitimacy. And the enthusiasm for democratic structures and processes has been challenged by the assertion that problems are caused by the way political institutions are organized. Political institutions have not, it is argued, adapted to new tasks and contingencies.

This book considers the possibility that political institutions have modified in significant ways since 1945; that our models so far have not been able to comprehend the changes; and that the interpretation of institutional behavior as pathological might reflect a theoretical misunderstanding of what is sensible under present circumstances rather than a mistake in behavior (Eulau 1967; March 1978, 1981a). If so, we need a theoretical framework which helps us better to understand the role of organizational factors in political life.

Such concerns are linked to a 2000 year old search for a theory of governmental forms and today they are more relevant than ever. Contemporary western polities are organized democracies. Policy making takes place within complicated networks of organized, public and private, actors. Thus, insight into the conditions for, and effects of, alternative forms of organization and coordination is vital for the analysis of how representative democracies work. Required is a "new institutionalism" focussed on how, and to what degree, behavior and outcomes are molded by political institutions.

We examine a few possible contributions of theories of decision making in organizations and some more general ideas about formal organizations.[1] While there is no coherent body of empirically based theory which links the performance of representative systems to organizational variables (Scharpf 1977), it is possible to identify some clusters of ideas about how organizations function and how choices are made (March 1981a).

Organization theory suggests a middle way between the formal-legal tradition of political science and an environmental-deterministic view. The formal-legal approach emphasizes the uniqueness, sovereignty and autonomy of the state. Political institutions can best be understood by knowing the formal organization and the legal rules that govern their operations (Eckstein 1979). The environmental-deterministic argument, on the other hand, is that it is unnecessary to study institutional structures and processes to predict behavior and outcomes. Knowledge about economic, technological, demographic, and cultural constraints is adequate (Huntington and Dominguez 1975).

In contrast, organization theory focusses on the interdependence of institutional and environmental factors. Theories of organizational decision making have become increasingly contextual in character (Cohen, March and Olsen 1972; March 1981a; March and Olsen 1976), but it is also observed that organizations are sometimes able to control, modify or ignore their environments (Child 1977, Nystrom and Starbuck 1981).

Formal organizations are dedicated to rationality, discipline and predictability through the coordination of resources and human beings, but organization theory cautions against expecting too much of human beings and human institutions. Specifically, limitations of understanding, capacity and authority should be considered.

Bounded rationality makes calculation and experiential learning problematic, and theories of decision making in organizations are concerned with how individuals and institutions try to act in a rational way in an uncertain, ambiguous and unstable world. Furthermore, time and attention are scarce resoures. Most participants in most decisions are part-time participants – their involvement depends on other demands on their time. As a consequence we need theories of how attention is allocated; what difference it makes who participates in a decision; and how relations between political institutions are affected by differences in their capacity to attend to many issues simultaneously.

Political models describing organizations as conflict systems, coalitions or negotiated orders have to some degree replaced the view that organizations are rational structures established to maximize agreed upon purposes (Bacharach and Lawler 1980; Cyert and March 1963; March 1962; Pfeffer 1981). Hierarchical command, voting and rules are only a few of the many ways conflict is coped with, and the directive capacity of political leaders is constrained by a need to achieve the cooperation of many actors. It is unrealistic to assume that some participants act in a rational way to defend interests (e.g. elected politicians), while others do not (e.g. bureaucrats); that some phases of a decision making process are "political" (e.g. the formal choice) while others are not (e.g. implementation); or that citizens try to influence political institutions in one way (e.g. voting) and ignore a variety of other possibilities.

The complications of understanding, capacity and authority modify the simple, instrumental view of decision making in political institutions. They also re-activate the old debate about the role of intention, reflection and choice in the *development* of political institutions (Mill 1861; Scott 1981). The belief that organizations can be designed and implemented to achieve preconceived goals (H. Wheeler 1975; Zoffer 1976) still lives side by side with the observation that it is difficult to establish a firm theoretical basis for institutional design; that political leaders seldom attend to such concerns over an extended time period; and that they often do not have the authority to prevent opposition or defeat. Frequently it is reported that organizational structures are difficult to change through arbitrary intervention (March, 1981b; March and Olsen 1982; Sait 1938; Sartori 1968).

Concurrently with pointing out the constraints on purposive-rational behavior, organization theory has called attention to the symbolic-expressive aspects of political institutions. Most models of politics view policy making processes as a vehicle to produce substantive outcomes. What matters is who-gets-what. There is little interest in value-rationality, symbolic-expressive behavior, or symbolic gratifications. Alternatively, such phenomena are viewed as manipulation, falsification, and substitutes for policy benefits (Edelman 1964).

Organization theory, however, suggests that the significance of symbolic aspects is much more comprehensive. Politics is (also) an interpretation of experience – a fundamental process through which peoples' models of the world, their values, beliefs, affections and emotions, are influenced. Through this process political reality is constructed: visions of the good society, a sense of purpose, direction, identity and belonging are developed. Typically, behavior which is viewed as pathological within a purposive-rational framework makes sense when it is viewed as part of a ritual or ceremony, and linked to the creation of meaning rather than to the production of substantive decisions. Organizational forms and procedures are mechanisms for legitimating participation and outcomes. They may give reassurance that things are done appropriately, in particular in situations where it is difficult to demonstrate how a specific decision accomplishes objectives.

Thus, organizational structures affect the legitimacy of a political system, as well as its governability, representativeness, and rationality. A dilemma for representative democracies is that an organizational form with a positive effect on one of these values may have a negative effect on other values, making them more salient and more difficult to achieve. Each organizational form mobilizes a certain bias (Schattschneider 1960) – each constrains, channels, and provides incentives for various behaviors.

The institutional complexity of representative democracies reflects functional differentiation as well as patterns of power. Organizational forms compete as well as supplement each other. They have their ups and downs with changing tasks, values, power-distributions and contingencies. And given the comprehensive agendas of modern welfare states a simple institutional solution is unlikely. A task for students of organizations is to specify the biases which different organizational forms mobilize and to test predictions about the conditions under which different forms will be used.

Can theories of decision making in organizations be of any help in analyzing the alleged crises of political institutions in western democracies? Probably; but the aspirations of this book are modest, indeed. No attempt is made to present a theory of organized democracy. But a few preliminary observations of political institutions in a contemporary welfare state indicate the potential value of organization theory to political analysis.

Based on Norwegian data the following chapters attend to some important questions in the debate about the present institutional malaise: (a) Do citizens' initiatives, that is, collective behavior organized outside established political institutions, signify a legitimacy crisis and a breakdown of representative processes? (b) Has the Parliament ceased to be a significant political force and is the territorial-electoral system inadequate to maintain the representative quality of the state? (c) Is the executive unable to perform the role as the organizing center of the political system, providing policy initiatives and integration, and giving direction to the public bureaucracy? (d) Has the bureaucracy become the most serious challenge to democracy rather than its servants, providing a rational basis for policy making and implementation? (e) Are representative democracies heading for a corporatist era and a grand coalition of higher civil servants and representatives of the strongest organized interests in society? (f) Are representative democracies likely to collapse in the near future rather than to continue on the basis of incremental reforms and peaceful coexistence?

The answers suggested give little support to a portrayal of democratic institutions as crisis-ridden. The institutions have problems, but sometimes the problems are in our models rather than in our institutions. In such a spirit, can the Norwegian experience be used to generate more general insights about political institutions and processes? Does it hold any lessons for democratic theory?

Eckstein (1966:3) reported that when writing a monograph about Norway he was frequently asked why anyone should want to study Norwegian politics and what the relevance of such a small country could be. Among the reasons given by Eckstein was that such a study could help counteract the great power fixation of the literature. Norway was interesting because it had fared comparatively well in terms of political stability and welfare provided citizens. And smallness could be an asset when the scale of the system is a key variable. Later, Heisler and Kvavik (1974) have concluded that Norway is the archetype of the "European polity" and Logue (1979) has argued that developments in Scandinavia will reveal a good deal about the dynamics of the welfare state. It has become clear that the access to data is better in Norway than in most countries. And, while an elaborate political-administrative apparatus is needed to govern even such a small country, the limited size makes it easier to get an over-all-view of the complex interaction between institutions and organized actors.

The questions of relevance can only be decided by the readers. But if this book has some value it is likely to be traced back to one of the three groups which have inspired it. First, students of decision making in organizations, with James G. March, Stanford University, as the natural intellectual and social center. Second, students of comparative politics and administration, organized around Ezra Suleiman, Princeton University, and Richard Rose, University of Strathclyde. Professor Rose was the first to suggest that I put this book together, and since he probably has the world record in number of political science books written or edited, I took him seriously. Third, my colleagues in Bergen, who more than any other group I know believe that students of organizations and students of politics can learn more from each other than what is the case today – a belief closely linked to the fact that in Norway organization theory has developed in departments of political science rather than in business schools.

---

[1] March (1981a) provides a synthesis of this literature. See also Cohen and March 1974; Cohen, March and Olsen 1972; Cyert and March 1963; Egeberg 1981; Feldman and March 1981; Glenn 1975; Lægreid and Olsen 1978; March 1962, 1978, 1980, 1981b; March and Olsen 1976, 1982; March and Sevon 1982; March and Simon 1958; Olsen 1970, 1972a, b, 1978; Olsen and Sætren 1980a; Roness 1979, 1981; Simon 1957; Starbuck 1965, 1976, 1982.

1

CITIZENS' INITIATIVES AND THE ORGANIZATION OF REPRESENTATION*

A BREAKDOWN OF THE REPRESENTATIVE PROCESS?

The idea that the political institutions of Western European democracies are crisis ridden gained increasing support during the 1970s. The argument went that there is a deepening crisis of confidence in the major institutions of representative democracy and that the problems are inherent in the actual structure of the institutions. Their ability to make binding, collective decisions is reduced and there is a breakdown in the representative process (Bell, 1976; Berger, 1979; Crozier, 1982; Crozier, Huntington and Watanuki, 1975; Freedman, 1978; Habermas, 1975; King, 1975b; Lindberg et al., 1975; Offe, 1972; Rose, 1980; Schaar, 1981; Sullivan, 1979; Vidich and Glassman, 1979; Weiler, 1981; Wolfe, 1977). The failure of political parties is especially critical, and for Berger (1979) the question is "whether the political parties are now at a point that lies along a curve of indefinite downturn and disintegration, or rather, whether the point we have now reached is the bottom of the curve".

The warning of declining representational capabilities, a widening gap between expectations and performance, and a possible, or inevitable, downfall of democracies has been derived from normative-ethical arguments over the nature of just authority; from analyses of fundamental norms of discursive processes; and from empirical studies of behavior and opinion. *One* way the crisis is supposed to reveal itself is through the mushrooming of collective political behavior outside the established institutions of governance and representation.

The term "citizens' initiatives" refers to collective political behavior organized outside standard established institutions. They have elements of goal oriented and strategic behavior, but they are unstable coalitions. The time perspective is limited – typically an initiative focusses on a specific issue or situation and dissolves when a decision is made or circumstances change. The ad hoc-character is reflected in their organizational structure. Citizens' initiatives lack the characteristics of formal organizations, e.g. standard operating procedures and rules, role differentiation linked to careers, clear membership criteria, and permanent

13

staffs of their own. We need to distinguish citizens' initiatives from formal organizations, like political parties and interest organizations, and from homogeneous mass behavior, panics, crowds, mobs, riots, and armed revolts (Weber, 1978: 1377; also Gamson, 1975; Oberschall, 1973; Olsen and Sætren, 1980a; Tilly, 1975, 1982). We also need to understand whether citizens' initiatives have organizational properties which make this form of political expression and organization attractive to some groups, some issues, or under some circumstances.

It has been argued that such citizens' initiatives prove that the governors are out of line with the governed. Institutions systematically exclude some cleavages, issues, values, and participants. Protesters find themselves confronting closed doors and deaf ears (Benewick and Smith, 1972; Carter, 1973; Hvinden et al., 1974; Lowery and Siegelman, 1981; Offe, 1972; Rodenstein, 1978). And Berger (1979) claimed that protesters are in fundamental opposition to representative institutions – there is a profound loss of confidence in the possibility of using the state to good ends.

This chapter examines the idea that citizens' initiatives signify a legitimacy crisis, and that the occurrence of such protests is closely linked to the organization of representative institutions. It also examines some other possible explanations for the use of one form of participation rather than another, while retaining the focus on how the use of citizens' initiatives may depend on the organizational properties of government, of the institutionalized forms of participation and representation, and of the citizens' initiatives.

First, the legitimacy crisis-hypothesis and its implications are discussed. Next, these implications are used to examine some Norwegian data, which suggest significant limitations on viewing citizens' initiatives as a result of reduced legitimacy. Third, an alternative interpretation, based on organization theory, is suggested. Political parties, interest organizations, and citizens' initiatives are seen as organizational forms which supplement rather than preclude each other. Each form has a comparative advantage with respect to different democratic values. Together they provide a repertory of organized, collective action that at least under some circumstances increase the representational quality of the state and facilitates long term change and survival.

THE LEGITIMACY CRISIS-HYPOTHESIS AND ITS IMPLICATIONS

The right to open, organized opposition is a foundation of democratic systems (Dahl, 1966, 1973), and an orderly polity is based on an interplay between authority and partisan conflict (Weber, 1978). Most political

14

struggles most of the time are regulated by institutions, laws, and conventions which change only slowly. A legitimate political order means that citizens accept the normative validity of political institutions. They command consent without the use of massive coercion. But within such an order there is room for conflict between material and ideal interests.

A political order routinely defines appropriate alternatives of organized opposition behavior, but the normative status of citizens' initiatives in contemporary democracies is presently unclear. Interpretations vary from perceiving such behavior as a threat to representative democracy to viewing it as the fulfillment of a more direct democracy. Typically, conclusions are closely linked to the authors' favorite theory on how relations between governors and governed should be organized and to the issues currently activating protests (Bjørklund, 1981; Olsen and Sætren, 1980a). The variation in interpretations also reflects the heterogeneity of such protest behavior and choices about which phenomena are included in or excluded from, the analysis.

The legitimacy crisis-hypothesis assumes that citizens' initiatives are fundamentally different from institutionalized forms of opposition; that using this form implies a denial of the normative validity of established institutions and that differences in acceptance of the moral justification of the political order predict variations in participation in citizens' initiatives; and that the use of citizens' initiatives threatens the survival of representative democracies. These are all problematic assumptions which should be tested empirically.

Actually, little is known about the basis of legitimacy in contemporary democracies. It is widely believed that we need to make a distinction between a system's instrumental performance and the perceptions and beliefs of citizens of the appropriateness of the exercise of authority (Lipset, 1963; Weber, 1978). Legitimacy depends on previous performance, on loyalty (Hirschman, 1970), and on diffuse support (Easton, 1965). Democratic, political processes have an inherent value, not only as a means to achieve preferred policy decisions. However, it is unlikely that legitimacy is based on procedural criteria, like legal-rational authority, alone (Weber, 1978), independent of the contents of decisions. It is also unlikely that the legitimacy today is linked so strongly and exclusively to electoral accountability, and thus to the functioning of political parties and electoral systems, as assumed by some political theorists (chapter 5; Rokkan, 1966). For example, it seems likely that citizens view protest activity organized outside political parties and interest organizations as entirely legitimate. It is also conceivable that citizens view such protest behavior as compatible with working through parties and interest organizations.

In addition, little is known about the relative importance of legitimacy for obedience and support in contemporary democracies. Every regime attempts to cultivate a belief in its legitimacy, but obedience normally follows from a complex mixture of motives and beliefs. The transition from a political order arising out of tradition, coercion, or of expediency to one based on a belief in its legitimacy is gradual (Rothschild, 1977; Sullivan, 1979; Weber, 1978). Thus, it is difficult to predict the behavioral implications of reduced legitimacy.

It is also difficult to determine the point at which protests eventually turn into a legitimacy problem, and how much the legitimacy of a system can be challenged before seriously threatening the system. No regime enjoys the full support or compliance of all its citizens and few regimes are fully legitimate or coercive (Rose, 1969). In democratic systems there will always be a disloyal opposition which explicitly rejects the regime, which is not committed to legal means of gaining power, and which does not reject the use of force (Linz, 1978). The breakdown of democracies is a long and complex process. When it occurs many of the actors and spectators do not realize or intend the consequences. The transition to a new regime is often possible only because so many of the participants are unaware of the ultimate implications of their actions and have analyzed the situation incorrectly (Linz, 1978:80–81). An implication is that we have to consider the attitudes, perceptions and beliefs of participants in citizens' initiatives, but we also have to analyze the potential effects of such initiatives independent of the personal views of the parties involved.

Thus, the appropriateness of the concept of legitimacy is not obvious when it comes to exploring the possible relationships between citizens' initiatives and representative institutions and behavior. The approach used here to test the legitimacy crisis-hypothesis is to specify some of its possible implications and to use them to examine some Norwegian data. Specifically, we consider characteristics of the participants that are activated in citizens' initiatives, the issues that are raised, the methods used, and the responses from government. What should we observe if citizens' initiatives were a result of a legitimacy crisis?

If Western European democracies are haunted by a legitimacy crisis we would expect a fairly large number of people to be active in citizens' initiatives. Sometimes it is predicted that the activists would be those with few resources – the poor and disadvantaged (Carter, 1973). But other groups may be in a better position to delegitimize a regime (Rothschild, 1977), and we would expect a crisis to be more serious if key groups like the armed forces, the bureaucracy, the owners of capital, the intelligentsia, or the clergy are activated. Weber suggested that myths of who deserves to be in power are questioned when status and power structures in society are changing (Weber, 1978:1450). Increasing individual or group resources make it impossible to treat people as purely passive objects of government. They will demand personal freedom and independence (Crozier, 1982) and activate themselves outside established institutions if their interests and demands are not accommodated within such structures. But decreasing status or power may also sharpen consciousness and identity, and as the size of a group decreases the activity level of those remaining may increase (Madeley, 1977). This would be the case, for instance, if the moderates leave an organization while the militants stay (Hirschman, 1970). It would also be the case if aspiration levels adapt more slowly than representative structures. First, resources and support decline, but the group losing power will be comparatively favored in established institutions. Then, the position in the representative institutions is weakened, but aspirations and the memories from an earlier «golden age» persist, thus citizens' initiatives may be used.

If the occurrence of citizens' initiatives is linked to long term changes in status and power, we would expect such protests to be organized around some relatively stable "community of fate" (in terms of material or ideal interests), rather than an ad hoc consensus on a specific issue. A result would be that participation is characterized by some continuity, rather than being a one-shot affair. We would also expect little overlap between participation in citizens' initiatives and in established institutions, except for cases where activists use representative institutions for propaganda purposes.

Different policy issues tend to generate different configurations of interests and participation (Dahl, 1961; Eckstein, 1960; Lowi, 1964, 1972), and thus different problems of representation. As the range and scope of the state's activity increases, there is a disproportionate increase in the need for legitimation (Habermas, 1975:71). A growing agenda also generates more complex cleavages and more viable coalitions, which in turn create technical problems for representative institutions. However, if citizens' initiatives result from a legitimacy crisis, we would expect the morality of political institutions rather than their efficiency or partisan considerations to be in focus.[1] It would be a way to redefine morals, create justifications and expectations; to search for meaningful choices and for standards by which to rank alternatives (Dahrendorf, 1979). We would expect citizens' initiatives to claim that the representative institutions are morally bankrupt and to challenge them on the basis of personal or group norms concerning the operation and structure of the polity. While ad hoc in character, we would expect citizens' initiatives to share some vision, and to be committed to a new political, social, economical, or cultural order. For instance, Wolfe (1977:252) predicted that in late capitalism the major political issues will not take place within the parameters of liberal democracy, but over them. A legitimacy crisis would reveal itself in anti-institutional citizens' initiatives directed against the state itself, political parties, public bureaucracies, and established interest organizations (Berger, 1979).

A legitimacy crisis would also be reflected in the methods used by

17

protesters. Citizens' initiatives may communicate information about preferences and beliefs or apply pressure on government to conform to certain viewpoints (Nie and Verba, 1975). We would expect a legitimacy crisis to express itself in the use of civil disobedience and violence, e.g. blocking streets or malls, occupying offices or buildings, damaging property, using guns or explosives; rather than signing petitions, peaceful marches, public meetings or demonstrations. Political violence is effective in limiting the functionability of representative institutions. It is both an indicator and a contributing cause of the breakdown of democratic regimes (Linz, 1978).

One criterion for distinguishing between democratic and totalitarian forms of government is their respective propensities for tolerating action outside the established institutions as a means of political expression (Drewry, 1972:25). Democratic regimes are assumed to be more able to learn, to absorb, and to accommodate challenges. However, rulers generally treat challenges to their legitimacy and to the legitimating principles of the regime as more serious than other kinds of challenges (Rothschild, 1977). If their legitimacy is threatened, we would expect institutional elites to be more likely to launch a massive counterattack.

Political violence in particular compels a democratic regime to face the dilemma of confrontation or lenient response. For instance, should the first outbreaks of violence be stopped, and if so, by which type and amount of force; or should the protesters be offered negotiations and thus recognition. Confrontations might create martyrs and contribute to further mobilization and challenges. Reluctance to use coercion, or ineffective use of force, on the other hand, might be seen as a sign of weakness, resulting in a power vacuum which is decisive in the transfer of legitimacy to the opponents of the regime (Linz, 1978:23, 56).

In a crisis situation we expect the government's ability to differentiate between citizens' initiatives to be reduced so that flexible responses become less likely. Empirical indicators may be the use of massive repression, a declaration of emergency, the abdication of responsibility, government instability, difficulties in forming new governments, and a loss of belief in their own legitimacy among institutional elites. We would expect attitudes towards citizens' initiatives to be highly polarized, i.e. participants will hold strongly positive attitudes, institutional elites will be strongly negative. Coalitions between participants in citizens' initiatives and parts of the institutional elites would be extremely rare. The outcome of challenges to regime legitimacy will depend on the level of societal support for those who want to introduce alternative political arrangements. The attitude of ordinary citizens may be strongly affected by the interpretations given by the media and by opinion leaders. A legitimacy crisis becomes acute if opinion leaders who have stayed on the side line give their support to those challenging representative institutions.

In the next section these expectations will be considered in the light of citizens' initiatives in Norway.

THE CASE OF A SCANDINAVIAN WELFARE STATE

The modern political history of Norway is characterized by peaceful coexistence and revolution in slow motion. A modern welfare state has been built without agonizing conflicts (chapter 6; Torgersen, 1970). Heisler and Kvavik (1974) viewed Norway as the archetype of the "European polity"-model: a state which has institutionalized a stable political process characterized by little politization, public debate, or mass appeals; a decline in the role of parliaments, ideological parties, and elections; the delegation of authority to administrative sub-systems and to experts; the cooptation of the organized interests affected by public policies, giving them considerable control over distinctive issue areas; and an emphasis on compromise and trust. Martinussen (1977) called Norway a "distant democracy". Lijphart (1977: 111) claimed that the Scandinavian countries have moved further in the way of depolitization than any other Western country. And Logue (1979) argued that the success of the Scandinavian countries has been built on increased organization, coordination, complexity, and dependence on experts. Now, these countries may be victims of their own success, and developments in Scandinavia supposedly reveal a good deal about the dynamics of the welfare state.

The image of technocratic politics and deferential citizens is in some important respects deceptive. For instance, a mass mobilization blocked Norwegian membership in the European Economic Community. The opponents succeeded in getting a referendum. Both sides mobilized through citizens' initiatives. And a majority voted "no" in spite of the fact that a "yes" vote was advocated by most of the political "establishment", including a large majority in the Parliament, the leaders of the two major parties, the employers' and business associations, the Federation of Trade Unions, and most of the Norwegian press. Only the farmers' and the fishermen's organizations, together with some trade unions opposed membership (Gleditsch and Hellevik, 1977; Valen, 1973).

In January 1982 a citizens' initiative against the construction of a hydroelectric power plant on the Alta River in the northern part of Norway, dissolved after three years of resistance. The construction of a road to the site of the planned power plant was blocked; there was a hunger strike; the prime minister's office was occupied; delegations were sent to the Pope in Rome and to the United Nations in New York. Explosives were also used – although these acts were denounced by the

19

leaders of the citizens' initiative. Three times the Storting, by large majorities, decided to commence construction. The result was the largest police operation since World War II. One thousand policemen were sent to Alta and 900 protesters were arrested in an operation that cost 90 million Norwegian kroner (Dagbladet (Oslo), January 13, 1982).

Such highly visible protests are only the top of the iceberg. In spite of a multiparty system and a well developed network of interest organizations and voluntary associations, citizens' initiatives are used fairly often. Here we present a few observations based on a newspaper study, several questionnaires, and some case studies. The newspaper survey consisted of a systematic listing of all citizens' initiatives covered by five major newspapers from different parts of Norway during the first six months of 1974 and a study of two of the same newspapers for the same period in 1954. The questionnaires were administered to a representative sample of the population, 15 years of age or older (1975, N = 2202); to civil servants in the ministries (1976, N = 784); and to employees (1976, N = 536) and elected officials (1976, N = 475) of a sample of economic-producer organizations (Olsen and Sætren, 1980a). Hernes administered a similar questionnaire to members of public committees and boards (N = 2142; Hernes, 1982; Hernes and Voje, 1980).

Respondents were presented with a list of citizens' initiatives, based on the newspaper survey. Information was collected on whether a person had participated, the issues activating him/her, the forms of participation, and the attitudes towards citizens' initiatives as a supplement to political parties and interest organizations. The organizational and bureaucratic elites were also asked about the frequency of citizens' initiatives in their issue areas, their contacts with, and the perceived influence of, such initiatives. Because the questionnaires were part of a comprehensive study of political power in Norway, it was possible to link information about citizens' initiatives to a wide variety of data on the respondents' participation in political and organizational life, their social characteristics, and their attitudes, perceptions, and beliefs.

Participation in citizens' initiatives is extensive in Norway. 48 percent of the population reported that they had been active at least once (Olsen and Sætren, 1980a). Participation is also highly resource dependent. Citizens' initiatives are not tools for people with few social resources and far removed from representative political institutions, to offset their powerlessness. Pensioners, housewives, and manual workers are least active. Those who are not members of political parties or interest organizations rarely participate. In most cases, participation coincides with one of two types of resources – either social ones, like a high formal education or an occupation which gives some leadership training; or political resources, such as experience from public office, activity in political parties or interest organizations. Citizens' initiatives, however, also mobilize a group which frequently discusses politics and ardently follows the news, without having many political or social resources.

Participation depends on changes in power and status, as well as on absolute resources. The changes in the relationships between the sexes and generations are reflected in that women are as active as men, and young people as active as the middle aged. In this respect citizens' initiatives contribute to equalizing the imbalance in other forms of participation. Religious groups (Madeley, 1977), farmers (Haga, 1978), and fishermen (Knudsen, 1979) provide examples of high activity in citizens' initiatives following a decline in strength.

There is a strong interdependence and overlap between citizens' initiatives and routine political processes. With few exceptions, initiatives are reactions against decisions made by representative institutions, and most often they have a partisan aspect. Citizens' initiatives provide an opportunity of appeal to the public for the losers in representative politics. For instance, those who identify with the Labor Party, strongest in the electoral arena for the last half century, use citizens' initiatives least often. The same tendency is seen for those who identify with the political parties which are strongest in economic-producer organizations and thus in the corporative-functional channel of representation. Most economic-producer organizations are led by people from (or sympathizing with) the Labor Party, The Conservatives, and the Center (former Agrarian) Party. Supporters of the Left Socialists' Party and other smaller parties on the left wing, the Christian People's Party, which often stands alone on some central moral issues, and the Liberal Party, with a platform emphasizing ecological concerns, resort most frequently to citizens' initiatives.

Some citizens' initiatives are based on a set of binding values. The struggle for the preservation of natural resources and the environment has developed into an ecological political view and an eco-philosophy, a philosophical system whose basic premise is ecological balance (Næss, 1964). Protesters have also sometimes referred to international law, to international treaties, to solidarity across nations, or solidarity with oppressed ethnic or social groups. But ideological consistency is an elite phenomenon. The most explicit criticism of the representative system – and thus the ideological profile which comes closest to the one suggested by the legitimacy crisis view – was found among a minority of recently hired civil servants in the ministries. These were people just out of university, who got their degrees in the late 1960s and early 1970s, and who planned to leave the ministries soon.

The more general tendency is for initiatives to be issue-oriented, ideologically heterogeneous, unstable coalitions. Participants agree on specific issues, but disagree about many other things. Each initiative comes to mean many different things to different participants, thus they

21

may make for strange bedfellows. Absolute or relative deprivation, or a general lack of confidence in government, are not significant factors in explaining participation in citizens' initiatives. Participation is seldom linked to a general perception of being a loser in the political competition for material benefits – as an individual, as a member of an interest organization, or as a member of a local community. Neither is participation based on a general rejection of representative institutions or to a preference for direct democratic forms, like referenda. Indeed, those who argue that political parties should have more power are more active in citizens' initiatives than those who think political parties should be less influential. The characteristic attitude expressed by participants is that Norwegian society is basically democratic, but that the system has failed in certain policy areas or in specific decisions (Gleditsch, Hartmann, and Naustdalsli, 1971; Kolbenstvedt, Strand, and Østensen, 1978; Tangenes, 1978). For most participants the activity is limited to a single initiative or to a single policy area. A small group of individuals (13 percent) is involved across a wide variety of issues – citizens' initiatives is their style of political expression and organization.

These conclusions are supported by the data on the participation of organizational and bureaucratic elites in citizens' initiatives. Participation outside established channels and institutions is by no means alien to these groups (table 1.1). But there are some important differences – elected and employed leaders in economic-producer organizations participate more than do civil servants. And they are more active the higher their formal position, the more resourceful their organization, and the more the organization is integrated in public policy making. For civil servants in the ministries we find the opposite pattern – those active are young and they hold positions at the bottom of the hierarchy. For all groups activity is linked to participation in political parties and in a variety of organizations and associations. It is also linked to exposure to citizens' initiatives in the issue area in which they work, but this effect is much stronger for organizational than for bureaucratic elites.

The observations support the idea that participation in citizens' initiatives is encouraged by integration in organizational networks (Curtis and Zurcher, 1973; von Eschen et al., 1971) rather than by conditions of "mass society" (Kornhauser, 1959). Elites have skills, status, and contacts that make them attractive for citizens' initiatives (Edwards and Booth, 1973). But as institutions, ministries restrict such participation more than do interest organizations. Organizational elites are more exposed to citizens' initiatives, and as we will see, it is more difficult for them not to become involved and even to take leadership.

A detailed analysis of the different types of initiatives indicates considerable variations as to programs and goals (Olsen and Sætren, 1980a).

Table 1.1: *Rates of participation in various types of citizens' initiatives, by the population, elected officials and employees in economic-producer organizations, civil servants in the ministries and representatives in public committees (percentages).*

| | Population (1975) | Economic-producer organizations (1976) | | Civil servants in the ministries (1976) | Representatives in public committees (1977) |
		officials	elected employees		
Local environment/ community well being	10	18	17	15	25
School/education	13	15	9	5	16
Environmental protection	8	14	10	10	13
Public funding for local development	7	14	7	2	7
Language issues	5	3	2	3	7
For joining the EEC	8	23	26	–	}33
Against joining the EEC	15	21	16	–	
Against free abortion ...	13	7	3	2	6
Wages, prices and taxes	4	13	5	3	7
Fishing limits	3	5	2	1	4
Women's liberation, equal rights	4	6	5	6	12
For free abortion	6	5	5	6	9
People's Peace Prize	3	7	3	2	5
Foreign policy issues	4	11	8	9	12
Percentages participating in at least one citizens' initiative	48	65	58	33	60
Total number of respondents	(2 203)	(476)	(536)	(784)	(2 142)

Sources: Olsen and Sætren (1980a) and Hernes and Voje (1980) (the latter provides numbers for representatives on public committees).

– : question not asked.

Still, a trend is discernible. While each initiative is an ad hoc phenomenon, some of the broader conflicts are familiar from Norwegian political history. The citizens' initiatives of the 1960s and 1970s in several respects represent a continuation of the historical tension between a central nation-building culture and two countercultures – one based on the protection of traditional values, especially an orthodox evangelistic world view, against the evils of modern urbanized and secularized life;

23

the other based on a radical vision of, and desire for, major changes in Norwegian society (Rokkan, 1970; Valen and Rokkan, 1974).

In the struggle against Norwegian membership in the EEC these two countercultures joined forces against the post World War II economic and political establishment and succeeded in the face of vastly superior resources (Gleditsch and Hellevik, 1977; Valen, 1973). In other issues, such as abortion and women's liberation, and the moral base of public education, the two groups normally confront each other, as they also often do on foreign policy.

The ecologically oriented initiatives receive a more heterogeneous support, and this is particularly true for regionally based protests and for community groups reacting against the obstruction of their immediate environment. Regional initiatives often mobilize people from different parties and organizations against central authorities or other regions (Tangenes, 1978). Participants in community initiatives are mobilized less as a matter of principle, than because they are directly affected by some public policy. Examples would be city renewal (or lack of it), traffic regulations, or issues related to schools or kindergartens (Kolbenstvedt, Strand, and Østensen, 1978).

Economic cleavages, economic production and distribution, and the defense of class interests, have not been significant subjects of citizens' initiatives since 1945. As has been the case in most countries (Berger, 1979; Inglehart, 1977, 1981), citizens' initiatives have protested against a state that was affluent and expansive. Protests have focussed on the quality of and direction of life in an advanced welfare state more than on economic production and the distribution of material benefits, which has been the major concern of representative institutions. Issues of life style, morals, and fundamentals of community life have the greatest mobilizing power; especially when they have a dramatic and symbolic character.

The differences in capacity for mobilization for different groups are surprising, given the widespread assumption that citizens' initiatives is a form of expression primarily for the political left and people with postmaterialist values. Typical examples of citizens' initiatives so disposed are the protests against Norwegian participation in Western military and economic cooperation, against nuclear weapons, for free abortion, and for women's liberation. None of these initiatives have, however, mobilized half as many participants as did the initiatives against free abortion. Groups mobilizing in defense of nationalism, rural populism, traditional values, and against what they perceive as the moral turpitude of a decadent urbanized and secularized culture without norms and binding moral obligations (Øystese, 1980), have in general remained very able to activate their supporters.

The notion that citizens' initiatives is predominantly a medium for left-wing or postmaterialist groups may partly be ascribed to the large number of repeat performances by their supporters. Most of those who rallied against free abortion or for or against EEC-membership have not participated in other protests, while about half of the participants in left-wing or postmaterialist initiatives have been involved in a wide range of issues. The notion may also be linked to the types of participants activated. Typically, radical initiatives have more support among the elites, while for instance the anti-abortion initiative is recruiting a higher percentage of those with only elementary education than of those with a university degree. Furthermore, the idea may arise from the fact that radical groups often make use of demonstrations, while the traditionalists more often resort to collecting signatures. Demonstrations do, of course, receive more media coverage. Finally, Norwegian traditionalist groups have a long tradition of mobilizing their supporters in citizens' initiatives, and they may simply be more successful than their counterparts in other countries. At least that seems to be the case compared to the other Scandinavian countries (Damgaard, 1980; Gidlund, 1978; Gundelach, 1979).

Interpreting citizens' initiatives in the light of two stable "countercultures" may underestimate the heterogeneity of citizens' initiatives. Often initiatives are organized around issues with strong symbolic and dramatic content, arousing strong feelings of moral outrage, but ambiguous enough to allow alternative interpretations. Participation may be primarily expressive – an end in itself rather than a means to achieve a policy goal. Thus, the principle of demonstrating may be more important than policy achievements (Parkin, 1968). In almost all cases the moral base of public policies is involved. Very few participants, however, are mobilized by a vision of an alternative political order and major changes in representative institutions. At stake are the morals of single decisions or single policy areas. Participation is linked to expressing support for certain principles, parties or organizations. Initiatives are not attempts to achieve major changes in the political community, the territory of the state or the regime. As a matter of fact, the most comprehensive mobilization – against EEC-membership – took place in defense of the established system and against transferring authority to institutions outside the country.

These aspirations are reflected in the methods used by protesters and in the response by authorities. By international standards the level of revolt in Norway is modest. Most initiatives appeal to government and to public opinion. They communicate beliefs, preferences, values and sympathies. They hope to gain support by evoking norms of fairness, equity, and justice. Appealing to the media, however, creates a dilemma. Citizens' initiatives get the most attention if they are new and unusual. When such protests become a part of routine politics, the media coverage declines. Particularly, this is the case when it is observed that initiatives are taken in order to get the attention of the media (Tor Strand, Bergens Tidende, December 11, 1981). One possibility, then, is to escalate the efforts, at the risk of exceeding what the political culture of a country defines as legitimate. In Norway those limits are rather narrow. For instance, the Alta confrontation made it clear that the political culture gives little support to initiatives which involve violence and where lives may be lost. Therefore, civil disobedience is used fairly infrequently, and physical violence is extremely rare (Hagtvet, 1981).

For the majority of the participants the level of involvement is low. 79 percent of the participants signed petitions, 25 percent donated money, and a similar number participated in mass meetings, 33 percent took part in demonstrations, and 20 percent performed typical leadership activities, like organizing, recruiting members, making speeches, and writing in the newspapers. The resource threshold for assuming leadership is high, as illustrated by the fact that the percentage of civil servants taking on such tasks is twice as high as for the population as a whole, and among employees and elected officials of economic-producer organizations it is almost three times as high. Most citizens' initiatives are coalitions of skilled and experienced leaders who shoulder the costs of simultaneously organizing an initiative and trying to influence a specific issue; and followers who participate without heavy costs.

The methods used by protesters do not invite massive government use of force. The Alta case is an exception. Confrontations occurred after a prolonged (more than ten years) decision making process, with postponements and reconsiderations by the Storting (Parliament). The Minister of Justice labelled the protests "collective crime" directed against democratic institutions (Press conference, March 21, 1980). The early confrontations delayed the Government's presentation of a bill containing some of the most controversial watercourse development plans until after the general election in 1981 (Minister of the Environment, press conference, August 25, 1980). But the police operations were peaceful, and a poll revealed that the government had the support of a majority of those who had an opinion (Dagbladet (Oslo), May 16, 1980; Aftenposten (Oslo), October 10, 1980). The situation was different in the EEC-issue because the elected representatives were so obviously out of line with the majority of the population. However, the process employed – a referendum – is a legitimate part of Norwegian democracy, even if seldom used (Nilson, 1978).

Cooptation has been the most common strategy in issues such as sexual equality and women's liberation. For instance, in 1967 only 7 percent of the members of public committees and boards were female, but following active public policies for involving more women, the figure in 1980 was 34 percent of those recruited that year (St. meld. no. 7, 1981–82). Government policies included financial schemes and the establishing of new administrative agencies, among them an ombudswoman for sexual equality. And women have improved their representation in political parties, in the Storting, in local government, and in the civil service (Hernes, 1982; Skard, 1980). Other groups have also increased their representation, and the new laws on public administration and public planning propose wider participation for affected groups (Baldersheim, 1979; Stokkeland, 1976).

There have been few confrontations over nuclear policy like those observed in other countries (Nelkin and Pollak, 1981). This is so because the Norwegian government, partly due to the close proximity to the Soviet Union, has decided not to have nuclear weapons on Norwegian territory in peacetime; and because the availability of oil and electrical power has so far obviated nuclear power plants (Andersen, 1980). Environmentalists have to some degree institutionalized support in the Ministry of the Environment (Lægreid and Olsen, 1978). Christian groups have achieved amendments to some laws they viewed as interfering with individual and religious freedom (Olsen, 1981; Øystese, 1974). But they have not been able to amend the abortion law. On the contrary, the public has become more pro-abortion since the law was introduced.

The main observation is that the government has distinguished between different types of citizens' initiatives and adopted a strategy of flexible response. When confronted with intensive minorities and civil disobedience, the main reaction has been a willingness to compromise (Olsen, 1981; then Prime Minister Odvar Nordli, Debates in the Storting, 1979–80:167).

The effects of citizens' initiatives are, however, difficult to measure, and surprisingly little effort is focussed on careful evaluation of actual consequences. Citizens' initiatives attract attention from the mass media. Their leaders receive almost as much publicity as do institutional elites. But the media are of little help when it comes to clarifying whether citizens' initiatives make any difference, and if so, in what way (Olsen and Sætren, 1980a, 1980b). The newspaper survey turned up nothing about the effects in 69 percent of the cases. Of the remainder, 26 percent claimed that demands were met; for 27 percent they were partly met; for 31 percent the initiative did not succeed; and for 16 percent the authorities had not yet responded (Olsen and Sætren, 1980a:217). Kolbenstvedt, Strand, and Østensen (1978) reported a similar tendency. And Strand (1978) argued that citizens' initiatives may help detect weaknesses in the administrative system and thus increase its efficiency. But in spite of the success some citizens' initiatives have had in influencing specific decisions, few civil servants in the ministries and few leaders of the economic-producer organizations attach much political significance to this form of political expression and organization (Olsen and Sætren, 1980a).[2]

Focussing on the immediate impact on policy making may, however, be a mistake. Citizens' initiatives have important symbolic-expressive aspects. They may affect perceptions, identities and loyalties (Gerlach and Hine, 1970; Lipsky, 1968). Waves of public sentiment may be used to create or erode support for a political party or representative institutions. The EEC issue is an example. The Liberal Party split in two and the Labor Party lost both voters and members. Still, the long term effects are uncertain, and the effects on political loyalties seemed to vanish within a few years (Valen, 1978). A decade after their defeat in the EEC-referendum, the Labor Party and the Conservative Party received two thirds of the votes in the general elections. The long term effects on interest organizations seem to be even more modest (Martinussen, 1978; Valen, 1978).

In general, citizens' initiatives have not much altered the way most Norwegians feel – a common sense of identity and a fairly high legitimacy of representative institutions. The functioning of representative institutions has not been interrupted; institutional elites have not lost faith in their legitimacy; around 80 percent of the population take part in elections; around one fifth of the adult population are members of political parties, and the number has grown slightly recently; 70 percent are members of interest organizations or voluntary associations; the popular support of representative institutions has been stable since 1945; and public support for extremist groups or parties is very small (Bratbak, 1982; Hernes and Martinussen, 1980; Lafferty, 1981; NOU 1982:3; chapter 2).

Citizens' initiatives are not viewed as a threat to the representative, political process. Nearly half the population favor such initiatives as a supplement to political parties and interest organizations, only 10 percent considered it a disadvantage. Bureaucratic and organizational elites are less positive. 26–30 percent find advantages, 15–19 percent primarily disadvantages, while the majority argued that there are both advantages and disadvantages. Attitudes are less dependent on principles than on the issue at stake (Bjørklund, 1976, 1981), and successful protests tend to influence attitudes among participants (Offerdal, 1974): there is a positive relationship between being active in and positive to citizens' initiatives. But the correlation is modest and there is no polarization of attitudes between participants and non-participants.[3]

Citizens' initiatives also receive support or sympathy from groups within representative institutions. Even in the Alta case, where the level of confrontation was unusually high, the protesters received the support in principle, if not in the methods used, from some political parties, representatives of the Storting, local governments, and administrative agencies. A lower court also criticized the state and supported the protesters on some counts, but the Supreme Court unanimously ruled in favor of the state. And clearly citizens' initiatives are most successful when they are able to build a coalition with groups within the representative system, so that they have spokesmen in a variety of political arenas (Egeberg, Olsen, and Roness, 1980; Olsen, 1981).

The attitudes may indicate that citizens' initiatives, as a form of political expression and organization, are more legitimate in Norwegian society than assumed by the legitimacy crisis-perspective. Leaders (sometimes) view initiatives as a nuisance but seldom as a threat. And during the 1960s and 1970s citizens' initiatives increased their legitimacy, in Norway as elsewhere (Barnes and Kaase, 1979; Dexter, 1978; Gidlund, 1978; Marsh, 1978). It became evident that most protests focus on particular government policies or decisions, not on the overthrow of the political or socio-economic system (MacFarlane, 1971). In all the countries studied there is a positive correlation between political participation inside and outside representative institutions (Barnes and Kaase, 1979:152). But while citizens accept initiatives outside representative institutions as legitimate, political theorists tend to stigmatize (or celebrate) it as anti-system oriented. There is a time-lag between practical politics and political theories – as observed earlier for the assessment of the legitimacy of political parties and interest organizations as participants in the political process.

The data indicate that the legitimacy crisis-perspective is of little value when it comes to explaining participation in citizens' initiatives in Norway. There is also little reason to believe that Norway is unique. Many of the same observations are made in other European democracies (Barnes and Kaase, 1979; Damgaard, 1980; Gidlund, 1978; Gundelach, 1979; Marsh, 1978; Mouritzen et al., 1978). Taylor and Hudson (1972) showed that from 1948 through 1967 Norway ranked sixtieth of 136 nations in terms of protests and demonstrations, and was at the bottom of the list in terms of riots, use of arms, and deaths from political violence. The next section offers elements of an interpretation of citizens' initiatives in such countries, where issue-oriented, unstable coalitions have fairly high legitimacy as a part of the ordinary political process. The fact that so many political endeavors are organized outside political parties, interest organizations, and representative institutions indicates that government and the channels between government and the people do not capture some important concerns in society. We focus on some organizational properties of citizens' initiatives, parties, and interest organizations which may shed some light on the use of different forms of participation.

POLITICAL ORGANIZATION AND DEMOCRATIC VALUES

The myth of the newness of citizens' initiatives probably helped attract the attention of the media and create "big splashes" even when there were few participants (Nie and Verba, 1975: 26–27). But there is nothing new about citizens' initiatives as a form of political organization and expression. Some of the issues, demands, and techniques of the 1960s and 1970s were new, but as a form it is older than political parties and interest organizations (Weber, 1978: 904–910).

It is not the case that citizens' initiatives are used only by those who are excluded from representative institutions (Eldersveld, 1958; Milgram and Toch, 1969). Rather, at any given time and place there is a limited standard repertory of performances – forms of collective action that the population knows how to carry out in an organized way. Each form is well suited, and may have a comparative advantage, for certain tasks and certain groups under certain circumstances; each may be completely inadequate for other tasks and groups or under other circumstances. Organizational forms may supplement rather than preclude each other when it comes to express and act upon shared preferences; to document support in terms of numbers and determination; and to carry symbols of the identity of participants and the causes they support (March and Simon, 1958; Tilly, 1982).

The major test of a democratic polity is that it succeeds in making binding, collective decisions and in remaining a political community (Wolin, 1960). This test will be more difficult to pass in periods with an expanding governmental agenda; improved political competence among citizens; and uncertainty about basic values and beliefs. Such periods require a variety of organizational forms.

Weber predicted that the acquisition of political power in a mass democracy would create role differentiation, professionalization and bureaucratization of political organizations. A major concern was how to save any remnants of spontaneity, individualism, entrepreneurship, and how to provide the polity with new direction and a sense of purpose (Weber, 1978:1447). For Scandinavian political parties this prediction has largely come true, as it has for the major interest organizations. They have formed peak-organizations and have become integrated into the public policy making apparatus. Political organizations have lost much of their character of political movements, and thus of mass mobilization and enthusiasm. Decision making has to a large extent been delegated to leaders (chapter 5).

Representative institutions have more and more become dominated by purposive-rational behavior with little room for value rationality, emotions, symbolic-expressive behavior and thus for symbolic gratification.

The floor debate in parliaments has become less important (chapter 2), and a major characteristic of the corporative-functional policy making system is its intimacy and lack of openness to public view (Moren, 1974). In Mill's words, politics is focussing on the "business side" of political life, with little interest in processes of identity formation and change (Mill, 1951). Mill's criticism of the utilitarians is in many ways relevant for the development of representative institutions in the Scandinavian (and some other) countries the last half century. Primary emphasis has been placed on political structures and processes as a means to produce substantive outcomes. Cleavages, identities, and powers have to a large extent been taken as given. There has been little interest in the symbols of politics, how politics is linked to the discovery, clarification, and elaboration of meaning, and to the interpretation of experience and existence. Many have "forgotten" that politics is part of a process by which a polity maintains and changes social values; develops visions and a sense of identity and direction, and thus ideas about what constitutes a good society and how alternative institutions may be imagined to contribute (March, 1978, 1980, 1981a; March and Olsen, 1976, 1982; March and Sevon, 1982; Wahlke, 1971; Wolin, 1960).

The development was an institutional response to the economic crisis of the 1920s and 1930s and the confrontations and class conflict. For a long time it made the political system more governable, provided coordination, predictability, stability, and responsibility. But at the same time representative institutions and political organizations tended to become organizational palaces. That is, organizations characterized by a high degree of structure, but also by rigidity and inertia (Hedberg, Nystrom, and Starbuck, 1976; Starbuck, 1982; Starbuck, Greve, and Hedberg, 1978). Such organizational structures do not facilitate innovation; the discovery of new socially attractive goals; experimentation with new ideas, identities or allies; or the testing and changing of power and status relations. They tend to deprive the political process of the renewal generated by public disputes and political competition, and by inputs from groups not represented (Heisler and Kvavik, 1974).

While organizational palaces promote important values like governability, orderliness, purposive-rationality, predictability, and accountability, they may be an impediment when societies change abruptly in unexpected directions – when there is a need for immediate response and quick transformations. Under such circumstances the need is for organizational tents (Hedberg, Nystrom, and Starbuck, 1976; Starbuck, 1982; Starbuck, Greve, and Hedberg, 1978). Organizational tents do not have clear and stable structures of authority, division of labor, and responsibility. They put more emphasis on flexibility, initiative, creativity, and immediacy. Their loose and unstable structures make it possible to move quickly, and to say and do things that would not be

31

permitted by the standard operating procedures of organizational palaces.

Organizational palaces and organizational tents also suggest different structures of the polity and different models of governance. A representative democracy based on political parties and territorial elections suggests a *hierarchical structure*. Members of the electorate choose the officials by a majority voting procedure, after which the officials seek to govern in the name of the electorate and through a bureaucracy. The party winning the election gets a mandate and the authority to carry out its program. Officials are held accountable through the elections, and dissatisfaction leads to their removal. In its pure form the model assumes a concentration of power in an omnipotent legislature, with well-defined objectives and an apprehensible technology through which the bureaucracy can implement policies (Hayes and March, 1970; Lipset and Rokkan, 1967; Pennock, 1979; Rokkan, 1970).

In contemporary welfare states parliaments do not have the capacity, authority or understanding necessary to fill this role. Their dependence on bureaucrats and experts is well known. The vast network of organized interests makes it unrealistic to base governance on majorities of votes alone. Elections often give little indication of what the electorate wants on specific policy issues. And the more functions government performs, the less likely that public opinion will converge and that a mass of voters will be able to agree on a coherent program. Disciplined parties will find it increasingly difficult to be programmatic, and typical reactions are to emphasize persons more than programs, to avoid certain issues, or to relax party discipline (chapters 2 and 3; Pennock, 1979; Rokkan, 1966). A result is that political parties have been deprived of their hegemony as the intermediary between the people and the government. And Pennock (1979: 299) argued that it would be a great mistake to assume that political parties and electoral systems provide the only, or even the chief, link between citizens and government.

The integration of the major interest organizations into government has moved countries like Norway towards a more *specialized structure*. The bargaining structures established assume effective organization of interest groups. Integrated participation by organized interests is most likely where there is interdependence between a small number of governmental agencies and organized interests. Thus, integrated participation prevails where societies segment into functionally autonomous sectors, especially sectors characterized by small numbers of well defined, stable interests, so that for each policy topic it is easy to specify stable rules about which organizations can participate, which problems and solutions are relevant, and which rules of the game are legitimate. Integration also assumes that interests are disciplined enough so that

32

leaders can commit their followers with respect to the outcome of the negotiations (Hayes and March; chapter 5).

Integrated participation has costs for the interest organizations. Spontaneity is traded for certainty; ideological identity for compromises; freedom from responsibility for recognition; and control by members for effective representation. Thus, integrated participation is attractive only for some organizations, for some policies, in some situations (chapter 5).

Where spontaneity, ideological identity, freedom from responsibility for public policies, and membership control are important values, organizations may prefer particularized, informal, ad hoc contacts. In such cases they themselves can determine the timing, target, substance, and method of participation (Nie and Verba, 1975). Where interests are badly organized, unstable, or unclear the polity may tend towards undifferentiated or open structures.

In an *open structure* policy making processes are accessible to anyone. Those attending may bring with them any concern, problem, or solution. And the participants themselves decide how to proceed in order to reach a decision. Each decision is likely to involve a different constellation of individuals or groups, and the outcome is dependent upon who is attending at any given moment and what are on their minds at that time. Any decision is susceptible to being transformed into a "garbage can" – a discussion of the concerns of anyone currently an active participant. The definition of a choice changes as participants wander in and out of choices (Cohen, March, and Olsen, 1972; Hayes and March 1970; Heclo, 1978; March and Olsen, 1976; Schattschneider, 1960).

Open structures are fertile ground for citizens' initiatives. They provide an occasion for symbolic-expressive behavior – dramatic scenarios, uncompromised goals, strong symbols, moral indignation, and simple slogans – in a world otherwise dominated by the compromises of professional politicians, bureaucrats, and experts. Issues like the Alta-development and the EEC-membership encourage a public debate about the moral basis for the political community and for representative institutions – questions receiving little attention in routine political processes. Such confrontations also elucidate the limits within which demonstrators have to stay in order to generate public sympathy.

Open structures also provide an opportunity for making government accountable on specific issues. Citizens may support a party or an interest organization in spite of their position on a specific issue, and citizens' initiatives may allow the expression of more complex interest structures. Organizational tents may be useful when issues generate unconventional cleavages, so that conflicts go through political parties, as well as interest organizations and public agencies. They are also useful for people in relatively transitory positions, such as students. They are helpful when political attention fluctuates rapidly, and for issues not captured by

33

established operating procedures in government, political parties, or interest organizations.

Political leaders may use citizens' initiatives as trial baloons where they are reluctant to commit their party, their organization, or themselves. For instance, the Secretary General of the Norwegian Society for Conservation of Nature said that his organization could not support civil disobedience. If it does, it may lose financial support from the state, representational rights in public policy making, as well as the support of members and the public (Torbjørn Paule, Aftenposten (Oslo), July 29, 1980). But if a citizens' initiative is successful in its quest for public support, organizations and parties may later adopt its points of view. There is also a contagion or diffusion effect – one successful initiative enhances the chances of others (Bjørklund, 1976; Gidlund, 1978; Gundelach, 1979; Jørgensen, 1973; Kuby and Marzahn, 1977). Leaders may accept the high costs of organizing initiatives because they can get support on specific issues, which they cannot expect in general elections. And of course, they may hope that in the long run support on specific issues may pay off in terms of new members or voters.

Citizens' initiatives also provide an opportunity for citizens who do not want to be professional politicians or who do not want to have a long term commitment to politics. Political theorists usually disapprove of such "privatism" which includes preferences for career, leisure, family, or consumption rather than participation in public life (Habermas, 1975: 75). But it may be argued that contemporary societies provide many arenas for self-fulfillment, and we have to expect people to have different trade-offs between participation in those arenas. Thus, citizens' initiatives provide an opportunity for part-time participation.

Modern welfare states combine hierarchical, specialized, and open structures, and political parties, interest organizations, and citizens' initiatives are all legitimate forms of participation. But the relative importance of such forms of collective, political action changes over time. This study suggests some possible generalizations. The political process will be more sensitive to contextual fluctuations and short run changes in political attention the more individual political resources citizens have. Experience from public office, political parties, interest organizations, a managerial occupation, a higher formal education, and exposure to media and international events provide such resources which tend to make structures more open.

The more comprehensive the role of government, so that authorities have to strike a balance between a more complex matrix of competing interests (Richardson and Jordan, 1979), the more ambiguous the definition of "the public interest", and the less certain the technologies for achieving public goals. And under conditions of ambiguity and uncertainty, fewer people will be willing to delegate decisions to representatives or experts. They will be less willing to accept hierarchical or specialized structures.

Hierarchical and specialized structures are most likely in periods where moral, status, and power structures are fairly stable. We have studied a period where these factors were somewhat destabilized – a period characterized by some as the end of the social democratic consensus for many European countries. A grand program had been realized and had lost its fire. It had also commenced to produce its own contradictions (Dahrendorf, 1979). It was a period with slack resources, which encouraged expectations for more than material benefits and "the business side" of politics. It was a period that invited experimentation with identities, solutions, and allies; and it generated a demand for symbolic-expressive behavior that representative institutions were unable to meet, or to meet in time.

The effects of open structures and citizens' initiatives on the representative quality of the state will depend on the distribution of political resources in society, and on the ability and motivation to use the opportunities offered by open structures. Often such structures benefit those who can afford, and are willing, to meet frequently and for long hours (Christensen, 1976; Dahrendorf, 1979; Kreiner, 1976; Rokkan, 1970; Seidman, 1980).

In the Norwegian case the main observation is that the opportunities provided by open structures are used most by those with many social and political resources. But the effects on representativeness are mixed – citizens' initiatives tend to make the system more representative along some dimensions, less representative along others (NOU 1982:3, table 4.18, p. 124). For instance, the male-female balance is more equal than for any other type of political participation. like holding public office, participating in political parties and interest organizations, making individual contact with public authorities, or writing in newspapers. But in terms of the participants' level of formal education, citizens' initiatives make the system less representative. That is especially true compared with participation in political parties and interest organizations, which in Norway traditionally have had a strong class base and fairly equal participation across groups with different levels of formal education (Rokkan and Campbell, 1960).

Citizens' initiatives also have a partisan effect which may counteract the bias introduced by the development of a corporative-functional channel of representation. The integration of interest organizations in public policy-making was not opposed by political parties, and there is a strong interdependency between the territorial-electoral and the corporative-functional systems. For instance, approximately half of the leaders of economic-producer groups studied reported that they had also held office in a political party or represented a party in public office. Because three parties are overrepresented, relative to their popular support in public elections, the corporative-functional channel upsets the balance created by the one man-one vote principle. But since the other political parties are overrepresented in citizens' initiatives, this bias is modified to some degree. This observation illustrates the partisan character of citizens' initiatives and the interaction between different forms of political organization.

The effects of citizens' initiatives in terms of the chances for a breakdown of, or the long term survival of, democracies in Western Europe, depend on the characteristics of citizens' initiatives as well as the characteristics of the other available forms of political organization. Like Barnes and Kaase (1979) we find little evidence of an imminent breakdown, nor a process of long term decline, because of reduced legitimacy. The main tendency in Western Europe has been for government to regard civil disobedience and other political behavior outside established institutions with more tolerance (Spitz, 1954). Experience shows that representative institutions and the code of law are more robust and tolerate more deviations, than often imagined (Eckhoff, 1976). Thus, many have come to accept the potential value of disorderly politics to a larger process of orderly change. They have come to view citizens' initiatives as a normal, or even a necessary part of democratic systems (Marsh, 1978: 15, 233).

Citizens' initiatives will not replace political parties or interest organizations. Together they will provide a repertory of possible forms of organized, collective behavior. The use of the different forms will have its ebbs and flows depending on societal conditions; the problems, tasks, and choices facing the polity; and the comparative ability of different organizational forms to cope with those problems and situations (chapter 2). Thus, the solution is not to reorganize political parties and interest organizations along the lines of citizens' initiatives. Political parties and interest organizations became organizational palaces because that enabled them to fulfill some important functions. But that same development also increased the need for organizational tents.

CRISIS IN INSTITUTIONS OR IN OUR MODELS?

The legitimacy crisis-interpretation of citizens' initiatives illustrates an old tradition in the social sciences: when institutions do not work as the preferred models say they should, blame is put on the institutions rather than on the models. The opposite conclusion is more likely to be appropriate. Normally political theories track political practice, and often the time lag is significant. We have to ask whether the crisis exists in our models of political organizations and institutions (Eulau, 1967; March, 1978).

The legitimacy crisis-hypothesis underestimates the institutional complexity, the many institutional defense lines of, and the complex basis of legitimacy of contemporary democracies. A representative system is both a forum for conflict and a consequence of agreement. In particular, it assumes some shared understanding of why there should be collective decision making; why participation should be regulated by rules; and why one set of access rules should be used rather than another. Representative structures specify participation rights and duties; access for issues, problems and solutions; and procedures of problem solving and conflict resolution; all of which reflect relatively stable distributions of inter-dependencies, competences, values and resources (March and Olsen, 1976: 40–42). Representation is a device for limiting citizen participation in government as well as for limiting the power of governors (Eulau, 1967). The hierarchical and specialized structures of a representative system cause a particular policy issue to become relatively independent of the broader context within which it arises. Citizens' initiatives challenge such structures and make policy making more contextually dependent. By doing so, citizens' initiatives provide flexibility, and thus supplement the established (and more rigid) institutions and facilitate long term changes.

Legitimacy is achieved through majority decisions in representative assemblies. But it is also achieved by making collective decisions through plebiscites; by entrusting decisions with the courts or with experts; by geographical decentralization or by allowing self governance for functional groups. Likewise, the legitimacy of a system may be strengthened if moderately concerned majorities (sometimes) accept the view of intense minorities whose feelings and preferences are expressed through a high activity level. Too often, theories of representative democracies ignore this institutional complexity. They assume that legitimacy can (and should) be based solely on political parties and the electoral system – a very unlikely alternative in modern welfare states.

In the representative democracies of Western Europe there is a multitude of forms of participation, representation, and governance which reflect functional differentiation as well as patterns of power. Prescriptive and descriptive theories of representative democracy have so far not been able to capture this complexity. To rethink our models of political organizations and institutions, as well as the relationships between organizational forms, democratic values, and moral principles is a pressing task. Doing this, we should evaluate organizations not only as vehicles for making and implementing choices. We should also study their ability to help us interpret experience and develop a collective sense of direction, purpose, identity, and legitimacy. The main question is old and at the core of the study and practice of politics: how do different organizational forms affect a political system's ability to make binding, collective decisions and at the same time remain a political community.

Notes

* This chapter is a slightly edited version of a paper presented at the Western European Studies Conference on "Representation and the State: Problems of Governability and Legitimacy in Western European Democracies", Stanford University, October 11–16, 1982. I want to thank James G. March, Harald Sætren and Reidun Tvedt for comments and help.

[1] We distinguish three interrelated, but separate modes of evaluation of political institutions (Hayes and March, 1970; Sears, 1975). Protests may focus upon:
(a) the moral, political order and thus raise basic normative questions of governance like who should be included in the political community; what are the proper tasks and ends of government; what are the proper rules and procedures for problem solving and conflict resolution; who should rule and what are the proper roles for representatives, bureaucrats and citizens?
(b) the ongoing partisan struggle and the ways in which groups try to fulfill their interests within the political order, for instance, when they challenge incumbent authorities and their policies while accepting the political community, the regime and its central symbols.
(c) the technical efficiency of the system – the degree to which institutions render decisions efficiently, given a political order and a constellation of interests and power within this order.
The separation of these three aspects is empirically difficult when long-term efficiency and partisan considerations are in fact components of the legitimacy of a system.

[2] For a similar observation in Sweden, see Gidlund (1978). It is unlikely that the bureaucratic and organizational elites deliberately misreport their perceptions. If citizens' initiatives were a threat, they might be motivated to dramatize rather than to underreport the consequences. A simple interpretation is that citizens' initiatives are not important participants in Norwegian policy making. Another possibility is that they are crucial in a few policy areas but unimportant in the great majority of areas. Also, it is possible that the elites focus on immediate policy impact and thus underestimate the long-run effects citizens' initiatives might have on opinions, identities, loyalties, etc.

[3] Of the population 33 percent had been active and held a positive attitude; 17 percent were active and negative; 21 percent passive and positive; and 28 percent passive and negative. Among the organizational elites the group of active and negative was larger, among the bureaucratic elite it was smaller. A possible interpretation is that the positive and passive may be people who perceive a need for citizens' initiatives but do not have the necessary individual resources to participate; or they do not presently perceive a need, but want to keep the possibility of mobilization open in the future.
The active and negative are primarily people who are exposed to or challenged by citizens' initiatives. They would prefer that decisions were made within established institutions, but they cannot afford to stay passive when decisions are moved out of representative institutions by others.

2

THE UPS AND DOWNS
OF PARLIAMENT*

POLICY MAKING, INTERPRETATION, AND ORGANIZING

Parliamentarism has been justified as an organizational form well suited to link governors and governed and to represent the people in the process of government. The complexity of political systems, however, makes it problematic to claim that a single institution under all conditions is the most effective representative of citizens. The parliament's most important resource base, authority and legitimacy, depends on its comparative ability to detect, articulate and represent public concerns or the concerns of powerful groups.

Such concerns may be attached to policy content. The significance of the parliament then depends on its ability to make choices that affect who-gets-what in terms of substantive outcomes – the distribution of goods and burdens in society. We include general policies, the allocation of collective benefits/burdens to a constituency, and services of particularistic benefits/burdens for individuals or smaller groups (Eulau and Karpe, 1977: 244). Prolonged effectiveness in problem solving and conflict resolution gives legitimacy to an institution or procedure (Lipset, 1963). The claim that parliaments have lost power and political significance is most often based on the argument that they are not effective participants in policy making processes.

However, such concerns may also be attached to peoples' models of the world – their values, beliefs, affections and emotions. The significance of the parliament then depends on its ability to influence how political processes and outcomes are interpreted and how political reality is constructed. Few facts are able to tell their own story without some comments to bring out their meaning (Mill, 1956: 25). "Policy making processes" are also processes of interpretation and symbolic-expressive behavior. They are opportunities for public statements and appeals, and for exhibiting proper behavior (March and Olsen, 1976).

In this perspective the significance of the parliament is less dependent upon its ability to initiate, modify or veto policies than upon its ability to convey signals, moods and impressions and to make others take its interpretations into account. If it is successful, the parliament may affect the degree and type of political community, i.e. the rules, ordered relationships and shared loyalties which provide a framework for coping with conflicting interests. It may affect the relevance of issues and cleavages, and the support for specific institutions, groups or individuals. It may create or ruin trust, confidence, reassurance and compliance (Easton, 1965).

Sometimes symbolic-expressive actions are viewed as falsification and manipulation. Image crafting substitutes for performance and policy benefits (Edelman, 1964). But the relevance of symbolic-expressive behavior for the study of legislatures is much more comprehensive. (We use expressive to refer to *effects* and not to the intention of the actors or their opinions of what they are doing.) There seems to be a basic need to find meaning and order in confusing and ambiguous situations, and we should not underestimate the importance of influencing the world through influencing beliefs and normative structures (March, 1980), affections and emotions. Institutions are surrounded by a body of justification, glorification, mystification, dogma, ceremonies, and rituals, and political success depends on a certain conformity with such normative structures (Meyer and Rowan, 1977). Authority and legitimacy may be established by convincing participants and on-lookers that decisions are made in appropriate ways, as defined by organizational or societal ideologies.

The importance of symbolic-expressive behavior and of processes of interpretation are documented by studies of decision making in formal organizations (Cohen and March, 1974; Cohen, March and Olsen, 1972; Feldman and March, 1981; March and Olsen, 1976; Olsen, 1970). It is also well known that legislative behavior is not only concerned with decision making (Wahlke, 1971). Generally, the rationale supporting the Westminster model postulates that the influence of parliament normally comes not so much through the approval, rejection, or alternation of bills as through the deterrence effect of bad publicity arising from parliamentary scrutiny and debate (Franks, 1971).

John Stuart Mill (1962) viewed the parliament as radically unfit for functions like governing, law making and administration, because such functions would take skills which could only be achieved through long study and experience, and decisiveness which could be found in a small body but not in a voluminous assembly. The parliament should function as the nation's Committee of Grievances and its Congress of Opinions; it should cultivate the minds of the people; act on opinion and moral convictions; watch and control government and compel full exposition and justification of policies by throwing the light of publicity on the acts of government. Bagehot (1966) stated that expressive, teaching, and information functions are more important than legislative functions. Crick (1964) viewed the work of the parliament as a continuous election campaign, and Hennis (1971) argued that the main function of the parliament is to influence public opinion and thereby determine the results of the next election. Wahlke (1971; Wahlke et al., 1962) emphasized the parliament's role in building consensus and sustaining the political order. Eulau and Hinckley (1966) underlined the task of drawing the lines of cleavages sharply enough so that issues may be crystallized and clarified, as well as the legitimation of decisions made elsewhere and the provision of catharsis for anxieties and resentment. Weber (1946) claimed that the main function of the parliament was to recruit and train political leaders. Blondel (1973) observed that meeting detailed demands and providing specific services, often of a psychological character, are among the oldest undertakings of legislatures.

Yet Polsby (1975: 274) argued that there is a drift in the purpose and character of the deliberative process, from the reaffirmation of norms in the service of group solidarity to the consideration of alternatives in the service of rational problem solving. Rationalization, intellectualization and "disenchantment" of the parliamentary process would be consistent with Weber's general prediction (Weber, 1968). However, there are countertendencies. The more complex the public agenda, the more vague the performance criteria, the longer it takes to get feedback, and the more interdependent choices are, so that it becomes difficult to evaluate the contribution of a specific choice autonomously, the more important the symbolic-expressive aspects of policy making. The verification of "right" decisions becomes heavily procedural and normative (Feldman and March, 1981: 83). Increased complexity makes governance and coordination by policy, plan or rule more difficult, and increases the significance of coordination based on a continuous stream of information and interpretation (March and Simon, 1958).

A potential dilemma for parliaments is that their effectiveness as policy makers and as interpreters may demand different configurations of agendas, personnel, internal structures and procedures, and transaction structures and procedures. Policy making and interpretation sometimes reinforce each other and create a solid base for authority and legitimacy and thus for organizing. Other times there may be tension between them, and organizations may put up a structural and procedural facade that matches prevailing ideologies, but also shields behavior and leaves core technologies of the organization free (Meyer and Rowan, 1977).

The policy-making effectiveness of parliaments depends on present contingencies which can be coped with only by the introduction of structural differentiation and elements of hierarchy and specialization. A parliament's effectiveness as interpreter is dependent upon history. Folk theories of parliaments change slowly, and the present popular theory of the Norwegian Parliament – the Storting – is based mostly on late 19th century conceptions. A dilemma for the Storting is that the folk theory at the same time emphasizes its role as a significant policy-making institution and as the stronghold of the political amateur.

The axiom of parliamentary systems, that the parliament should make the most important political choices, has had a strong position in Norway. The Storting played a key role in writing and defending the 1814 Constitution when the Danish-Norwegian state was dissolved, the Norwegian state was founded and a new Swedish-Norwegian union established. Throughout the political conflicts during the last part of the 19th century the Storting came to symbolize a successful defense of national values and a victorious struggle for lay governance of a well established civil servants' state. Democracy came to mean governance by the Storting; and the norm is still that real, not only formal, power should be in the hands of representatives elected by the people. But today it is often claimed that the Storting has lost power and that its power position should be restored. Typically reformers of the Storting argue that its declining power is linked to:

- The organization of its agenda: The Storting is misallocating its time and energy; it deals with trivial matters more than with fundamental principles related to major problems facing society.
- The recruitment of personnel: The Stortings's lack of power is due to the quality of the people manning and running it and to its inability to attract and recruit the most competent people.
- The organization of internal work and decision making procedures: Standard operating procedures are too cumbersome and time consuming, and inadequate for intelligence, consensus and majority building, and leadership.
- The organization of transactions with the environment: Instead of being the center of authority, the Storting has become isolated. It has not accommodated new values, priorities, and groups in society. And it has not controlled the Cabinet and the corporative-functional structure of policy making where major decisions are made by higher civil servants and leaders of organized interests.

We discuss these complaints and assumptions on the basis of Norwegian experience and some recent ideas about decision making in formal organizations. The main argument is that variations in the political significance of the Storting do not follow a pattern of steady decline from a peak during the 1880s. Rather, the data suggest an ebb-and-flow perspective. The Storting is a part of a larger institutional network, and its significance depends on its comparative ability to cope with problems and opportunities. The Storting's ability to cope is constrained by characteristics of the parliament as a general organizational form – a fairly large assembly of representatives elected on a territorial basis has some inherent strengths and weaknesses. But its abilities are also influenced by

the specific configurations of agendas, personnel, structures and procedures that it develops or designs.

THE HERITAGE: ALL POWER IN THE HALL
OF THE STORTING AND LAY RULE

Norwegians have great tolerance for discrepancies between the written
constitution and political praxis, and we learn more about the role of the
Storting by reading political history than by reading the constitution.

The forming of the institutional identity of the Storting and the
introduction of the parliamentary system in 1884 were integrated parts of
making the modern Norwegian state and breaking up the union with
Sweden (Danielsen, 1964; Kaartvedt, 1964). It was also part of a democratization process. Parliamentarism was introduced in Norway 33 years
before it arrived in Sweden (Verney, 1957), and the Storting became an
institution for propelling newly enfranchised groups, and especially the
peasants, into politics (Rokkan, 1966). Thus, the interest base of the
winning coalition was different from those in many Western European
countries. The winners were not a growing industrial and commercial
middle class created by an expanding capitalist system, but rather a
coalition of peasants and urban intelligentsia. The result was that the
legitimacy of the Storting was closely connected to the idea of lay rule.
The ideal was the political amateur who brought common sense to policy
making, had a fairly short career and thus other vocations besides
politics, worked for modest compensation without much professional
staff, deliberated and voted as one of a collegium of equals, and organized transactions with the environment by a parliamentarian chain of
governance (Grumm, 1971; Weber, 1946).

Working and decision making procedures reflected the struggle
between the constitutional powers. The pattern was to constrain the
cabinet from governing by vigorous initiatives and detailed control. The
Storting worked as a "shadow cabinet" by means of a strongly politicized
presidency and active committees (Danielsen, 1964). The slogan was "all
power in the hall of the Storting", and in 1884 the Cabinet was reduced to
"a committee of the Storting" (Seip, 1963:14, 1981: 181–187).

In many ways the Norwegian situation invites an idealized, nostalgic
notion of a golden era, which may both prevent insight and provide
unrealistic expectations and disillusionment (Clark et al., 1980: 307;
Loewenberg and Patterson, 1979: 282). However, the fact is that the
Storting made government more representative by revolting against
those whom John Stuart Mill believed should provide decisiveness (the
king and the cabinet); and against those who should provide skills and

knowledge achieved through long study and experience (the civil service). While the Storting never became an omnipotent institution, it had a leading and governing role, especially in periods dominated by a few major issues related to building a modern Norwegian state and society. But it did not take long before criticism arose. The Storting lacked decisiveness and insight, as well as representativeness. And it was claimed that parliamentarism was an outdated organizational form.

For instance, Halvdan Koht (1909), later to become a minister of foreign affairs and professor of history, in 1909 argued for more lay governance, saying that "it is a historical law, that every institution has its bloom and then dries up . . . Then it not only loses its own vigor, it also threatens the growth of the new (institutions) coming up". The Storting had lost its representativeness. It should be replaced, or at least supplemented, by direct democracy like plebiscites.

Arguments for less lay governance were also often based on a biological metaphor predicting a sequence of institutional birth, maturation, and death. Fridtjof Nansen in 1911 described the Storting as an institution breeding laymen and dilettantes in a period needing strong leadership and policies based on expertise. Such leadership could only be provided through a strong Cabinet (Winsnes, 1942).

The system's representativeness and its ability to act came into focus during the second large mobilization in Norwegian politics – that of manual labor. While peasants were mobilized through the electoral system and the Storting, the labor movement had its breakthrough in opposition to this system. It was based on a strong and active party membership organization in close cooperation with the Federation of Trade Unions and a large number of affiliated associations. As late as 1928 the Labor Party was still, in principle, revolutionary. Its representatives in the Storting were viewed as instruments of the party and of the labor movement at large. Consistent with Marxist ideology, the Storting was viewed as a propaganda forum for building up its strength outside the Storting. Since the beginning of the 1930s, however, the Labor Party has developed into a parliamentarian reform party. It has worked in close cooperation with the trade unions and has contributed to integrating organized interests into public policy making, supplementing the territorial-election channel with a corporative functional channel of representation and policy making (Christensen and Egeberg, 1979; Egeberg, 1981; Hallenstvedt and Moren, 1975; Kvavik, 1976; Moren, 1974; Rokkan, 1966; chapter 5, this book).

In the period between the two world wars Norway also experienced a series of unstable governments. Their short tenure was due to the fact that they were not supported by a majority in the Storting, while at the same time the Storting was intervening in policy making – often, and in great detail. The perceived seriousness of the situation was reflected in the joint program of all political parties in 1945, demanding "a more simple, united budgetary process and a parliamentarian praxis that would strengthen the Cabinet's position and responsibility". The consensus of the post World War II period also meant more demand for expertise and a restoration of the civil service to considerable prestige and influence (Highley et al., 1975).

None of these developments have changed the basic image of the Storting as a central policy making institution and the stronghold of the political amateur. But it has become obvious that the system depends on a delicate balance between representativeness, leadership and expertise. The relative importance of these values changes over time. For instance, high internal conflict or tension make representativeness more relevant. External threats and a need for rapid decisions increase the demand for decisiveness, unity and coherence. Consensus or complex issues call for expertise and neutral competence. While the three values are with us all the time, fluctuations in their perceived importance affect the relevance and effectiveness of institutions and organizational forms (Jacobsen, 1964; Kaufman, 1956).

The observations support an ebb-and-flow perspective on the significance of the Storting rather than a biological metaphor predicting linear decline. As an institution the parliament has played a bewildering role in form, spirit, and authority for more than 500 years (Beard and Lewis, 1932), and it seems to be one of the most enduring and applicable inventions of political man (Loewenberg, 1979: 19). The Storting's significance depends on its comparative ability to cope with problems and situations through processes of policy making or interpretation. How then, should the Storting allocate its energy and attention in order to remain a significant political institution? How does it spend its time?

THE SEARCH FOR AN "IMPORTANT ISSUE"-AGENDA: A BLIND ALLEY?

The more decisions made on behalf of the state, the smaller the share of those decisions can be attended to and given a thorough consideration by a single institution. One of the most important decisions the Storting has to make is which tasks it should perform and which it should entrust to others. Representatives view the power of the Storting, as well as the well-being of the democratic system, as depending on the Storting's ability to give priority to significant societal problems and not to get immersed in details (Forh. i St., 1977: 4027, 4055; Innst. S. nr. 277, 1976–77; Grøndahl, 1979).

The priority problem is real. Since 1945 the public sector has grown faster than the energy provided by representatives. The size of the

Storting has changed little. In 1919 the number of representatives was 150 and in 1972 five more seats were added. The Storting may stay in session for an unlimited period within its four year term, but the length of sessions has been rather constant since World War II. Yearly sessions were introduced in 1869; in 1945 fall sessions became obligatory, and the Storting meets from the beginning of October to the end of June, interrupted only by short vacations.

In principle the Storting controls its own agenda. How does it allocate its time? Sisson and Snowiss argued that allegations concerning the decline of legislatures are often based less upon analysis of the functions which such institutions can and do perform, than upon misinformed judgements about what they should be doing or what they have allegedly done during heady moments of the past. Thus there is often little systematic data about how parliaments allocate their time (Sisson and Snowiss, 1979: 44). This is also the case in Norway. The data are sparse but some general trends are discernible. While the total number of decisions made on behalf of the state has grown dramatically since 1945, the number of issues dealt with by the Storting has grown modestly, and primarily due to an increasing number of questions (table 2.1). Are these issues important? In what way?

Table 2.1: *Number of issues in the Storting. Annual average in four-year periods, 1945–81. (Budget issues excluded.)*

	Laws	General Issues	Questions*	Total
1945/46–1949	133	247	85	465
1950–1953	95	313	213	621
1954–1957	85	297	317	699
1958–1961	102	293	284	679
1961–1965	83	286	281	650
1966–1969	72	299	330	701
1969–1973	100	325	369	794
1973–1977	92	393	475	960
1977–1981	86	363	438	887

* Includes three types of questions which to different degrees allow the mover to explain the question and others to participate in a debate.

Source: The President's speech at the dissolution of the Storting (St. tid.) and unpublished statistics from the office of the Storting.

Most often "importance" is linked to the policy making powers of the Storting – budgeting, lawmaking, and controlling the executive. An important-issue-agenda would include decisions concerning large amounts of money, laws regulating central societal activities, and controls protecting civil rights and preventing bureaucratic infringements. If the role as interpreter is more important than the policy making role, an "important agenda" may look different. Any issue that has a flare of drama or the entertainment value that may attract public attention and convince voters will do, independent of its substantive content.

The number of hours spent on budgeting has probably decreased. Since 1945 it has been nearly an axiom that the Storting should not change the total amount of the budget (Stavang, 1964: 40), and it has become clear that it is difficult to have much impact after the budget has been presented in the Storting (Highley et al., 1975). Budgeting routines have been rationalized. Work procedures are less detailed; almost all decisions concerning a specific ministry are handled at the same time and by the same committee; the number of budgetary recommendations has decreased from a yearly 200–300 prior to 1968 to 20–21 thereafter (Rommetvedt, 1980). A result is that since 1969 the plenary assembly of the Storting has used approximately 100 hours a year on the budget and general debates about finances (Statistics from the Office of the Storting, 1981: table 5.4) – much less than it used to. Rommetvedt (1980) shows, however, that the number of dissents in budgetary decisions has increased since 1973. This may indicate that the opposition is using more time on budgetary decisions.

The time spent on lawmaking in the plenary assembly has been fairly constant.[1] There have been yearly fluctuations, but measured by the number of new laws, reforms of existing laws, and by number of pages in the Law Gazette, the average level of activity is not very different from what it was during the period between the two world wars (fig. 2.1). From 1968–70 to 1978–80 the number of laws proposed by the Cabinet to the Storting actually fell from 170 to 148 (Ot. prp. 1968–69, 1969–70, 1978–79, 1979–80) – a tendency which has its counterpart in a strongly increasing number of administrative regulations (Aubert, 1976).

The data are less clearcut when it comes to controlling the executive branch. The Storting takes it as given that it has the right to intervene and control the administrative apparatus. Yet it is agreed that the Cabinet should organize the executive branch and that the Storting should curb its tendency to intervene. A result is that intervention follows assessment of individual issues and situations. There is little interest in discussing general principles of legislative-executive relations (Andenæs, 1978; Eckhoff, 1978; Roness, 1979), and the Storting committees most involved with the control of the executive branch are ranked lowest in status and influence (Hellevik, 1969; Hernes, 1971; Skard, 1980). There are no public hearings; parliamentary investigations are rare; and the Storting does not give formal approval of executive, bureaucratic or judicial personnel.

Fig. 2.1: *Legislative activity 1865-1979. Annual average in different periods.*

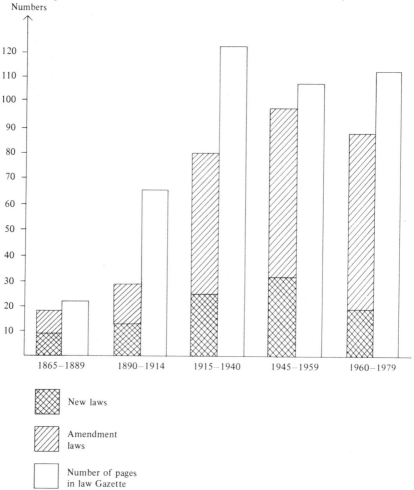

New laws

Amendment laws

Number of pages in law Gazette

Sources: Aubert (1976: 118, table 2); St.tid.

At the same time representatives use more time than ever in the administrative process helping citizens and local governments, firms, and associations without strong administrative apparatuses to cope with the intricacies of the welfare state (Kielland, 1972: 190). This activity includes contact with civil servants and ministers as well as questions in the Storting.

A weekly question hour was introduced in 1949 as an experiment in order to increase the influence of the representatives, and it has been used frequently ever since. It has become an instrument of the opposition, but most questions are related to topics of great concern to local constituencies. A general complaint has been that the question hour too often focusses on trivia. It has been argued that representatives ask questions when they have little else to do (Greve, 1964: 124), and ministers and civil servants complain because many of the problems raised could easily have been solved by picking up a telephone rather than presenting a formal question.

These observations are not surprising given recent studies of decision making in formal organizations. "Important choices" often turn out to be heavily constrained so that there is only one way out, or they take the form of pragmatic adaptation, incremental compromise and evolutionary drift as people cope with the environment by means of available resources (March, 1980). Emphasis on formal choice, making a law, a budget or an appointment, also assumes a simple administrative process – i.e. preparing and implementing choices are unproblematic. If, however, one views policy making as unfolding through a series of interrelated actions and events, and if one assumes that much discretion is linked to preparing and implementing formal choices, the ombudsman and errand boy functions may give considerable leverage.

The Storting is a political institution, and from a policy making perspective it would be unlikely to spend much time on consensus decisions, even if they involve large amounts of money or important laws. The Storting is most significant as a policy maker in situations of moderate conflict where it can function as a court of appeal for disagreeing agencies or organized interests (Grimsbo, 1973; Lægreid and Olsen, 1978). And in conflict situations the Storting may be a corrective to an otherwise functionally highly specialized and spatially partly blind policy system producing unintended aggregate effects at the local level (Strand, 1978).

From a policy making perspective it may also be smart to be unpredictable. The Storting can intervene only in a small fraction of all public decisions. But it can threaten participation and let other policy makers know that the price of non-intervention is some attention to the concerns of the Storting and some anticipation of its reactions (Friedrich, 1937; March and Olsen, 1976: 51). Even a random sampling procedure with adequate sanctions for not attending to the interests of the Storting could be more effective in keeping others alert than the predictability of a firm hierarchy of decisions.

The observations make even more sense when they are linked to the Storting's role as interpreter. Consensus issues can call attention to the participants' relatedness and joint interests through the expression of shared feelings and attitudes, but they are of little use for parties who want to signal their distinctiveness. Heavily constrained decisions with large substantive stakes may be unfit as social dramas, public appeals, and for spreading information which may win votes, give reassurance or develop trust. "Small decisions", that is, decisions in which the substantive stakes are small, are often used for such symbolic-expressive purposes (Olsen, 1972a). They are redefined and linked to important principles of justice, equity or honesty. Sometimes the symbols of the process dominate and policies are made with an implicit understanding that they will not be implemented (Aubert, 1969; Sætren, 1983).

The more important its role as interpreter, the more likely that the Storting will spend time on issues that allow representatives to show good will to their constituency and to glorify their parties. Publicity is also the key to why representatives present formal questions rather than take informal contact. Sometimes publicity speeds up a decision, but sometimes the symbols of attending to the concerns of constituencies are more important than the substantive issues at stake.

Thus talking may not be the main weakness of parliaments (Loewenberg, 1971: 1). Rather it may be the most proper business (Mill, 1962: 112), because it allows representatives to exercise ideals and norms that cannot be reached in a given situation, but which are of great importance to constituencies or to the political culture at large. In this perspective "importance" is not an intrinsic aspect of a decision, but a result of a political process of interpretation. Thus the quest for an "important issue" agenda may be a blind alley. While a planning logic of politics pictures policy making as heroic, rational choice and emphasizes the importance of establishing a hierarchy of more and less important decisions, politics may also be viewed as in principle unpredictable. One sees, develops a sense of proportions, and discovers guidelines of conduct only after getting engaged in the battle (Heaphey, 1975; Østerud, 1979). Choice processes are often highly contextual; they may become "garbage cans" for issues and participants (Cohen et al., 1972; March and Olsen, 1976), so that they change significance during the process. For instance, most cabinet crises in Norway in this century have not been struggles over large substantive stakes. They have rather been linked to issues that in a specific situation were redefined and given great political significance.

Our preliminary conclusion is that the available data – sparse as they are – do not prove that the Storting is doing a good job organizing its agenda and allocating its time. But it is problematic to claim that there is a gross misallocation. Such claims are based on debatable assumptions about the proper tasks of the Storting and the nature of public policy making. And they are difficult to discuss in the abstract rather than in relation to personnel recruited, and to intraorganizational- and transaction structures and procedures used, to which we shall now turn.

PERSONNEL – THE SURVIVAL OF THE AMATEUR

Polsby argued that policy making capacity is linked to a professionalization of the legislature and a shift away from the representational values of representatives as amateur citizens embedded in their local communities (Polsby, 1975: 297). However, we also consider the possibility that recruitment patterns may be more effective as symbols conferring legitimacy than by their effect on output (Stø, 1974; Trice et al., 1969). We expect the emphasis on policy making capabilities to result in the selection of representatives with special "technical" qualifications, and the emphasis on interpretation and symbolic-expressive functions to encourage (in the Norwegian context) the selection of representatives with social characteristics more like their constituencies and with strong ties to their local communities. Professionalization would imply higher economic and status rewards: recruitment of more professional, managerial, and technical skills, and more formal education. Members of the Storting would become more like other national elites and less like their constituencies. Experience from other national institutions would increasingly replace experience from local institutions. Professionalization would also increase the tenure of representatives.

In this perspective the Storting illustrates a case of slow professionalization – an institution in which the political amateur still plays an important role, a fact linked both to Norwegian political history and to the present system of nominations.

The 155 members of the Storting and their substitutes are chosen for four years through direct, proportional elections in 19 multimembered (4–15 seats) constituencies which follow the borders of the counties. The turnout usually exceeds 80%. Nominations are organized by political parties in a decentralized way without formal approval by the national parties. While voters have little knowledge about candidates, the conventions are sensitive to the party image created by the slate. They try to make it representative in terms of sex, age, geography, organizational affiliations, and political opinions in order to appeal to voters (Valen, 1974; Valen and Katz, 1964).

The system gives the periphery a certain overrepresentation at the expense of the center. Up till 1952 the Constitution provided that there should be twice as many rural as city representatives, making the weight of rural and city votes grossly unequal (Groennings, 1962: 164; Kvalø, 1968). Also removed in 1952 was an eligibility rule demanding that representatives should live in the district they represented, in order to create strong bonds to the constituency.

The tendency in the legislation organizing elections is a moderate change away from the traditional control of the Storting by rural areas and opening up for a modest professionalization. The same tendency is

51

seen in the economic compensations – from a traditionally strong emphasis on modesty and thrift with public money, especially when it comes to paying representatives, economic compensations and status have been rising ever since 1945 (Forh. i St. 1970: 60–117; Innst. O. III, 1970–71; NOU 1977:34). In 1981 representatives were paid approximately 27,000 dollars plus a per diem depending on how far from Oslo they live.

Table 2.2: *Members of the Storting 1814–1977 by occupational, geographical and professional background and by time periods. New members in each period.*

	1814–1860	1861–1900	1901–1921	1922–1940	1945–1957	1958–1969	1970–1977
Occupation:							
Civil Servants	36	19	15	8	15	13	17
Teachers	3	8	10	9	7	15	23
Lower public employees	11	10	10	9	10	6	11
Farmers/fishermen......	20	26	27	27	23	17	11
Liberal professions	4	9	12	13	11	11	7
Business leaders/ self employed	26	25	23	21	14	15	12
Employees in parties/ private associations ...	0	0	1	4	7	14	5
Manual workers	1	2	3	9	10	6	7
Housewives/students	0	0	0	–	4	5	8
Birthplace:							
Oslo	4	8	4	8	7	7	14
Other cities	35	29	32	24	22	27	27
Rural areas	61	63	64	67	71	66	58
Education:							
Primary School	40	23	15	21	15	5	4
Below university level ...	15	40	49	52	60	58	54
Lawyers	20	19	16	9	10	8	4
Other, university level...	25	19	20	18	16	29	36
Number of persons	(914)	(587)	(335)	(322)	(236)	(198)	(113)

Source: Archives, Norwegian Social Science Data Service, Bergen.

Changes in legislation and incentives have not caused dramatic changes in recruitment patterns. The Storting has never been dominated by an aristocracy and it does not recruit a socio-economic elite. Neither does it fully resemble the people in socio-economic composition, yet it does so more than most legislatures. More than half of the representatives in the period since 1945 grew up in a family in which the main breadwinner was a manual worker, peasant or fisherman. Looking at the representatives' own occupations, the representation of peasants and fishermen has been cut in half since 1945, and at the same time teachers below the university level has become the most numerous group (table 2.2). The representation of industrial leaders have for a long time been declining (Enerstvedt, 1967). Table 2.2 also illustrates the comparatively weak position of academics in the Storting.

Rural areas are still somewhat overrepresented, and removing the eligibility rule has had little impact. In 1957 slightly more than 1% of the 1,620 candidates studied (Valen and Katz, 1964: 60), lived outside their district, and almost all of them only temporarily. In the period 1945 to 1977 69% of all elected representatives were born in the district they represented, the capital ranking lowest with 39% (Norwegian Social Science Data Archives).

In sum, for most members, being elected to the Storting means increased status and income and more interesting work. They have socio-economic backgrounds that make it unlikely that they will bring professional, technical or managerial skills relevant to policy making. The strong representation of teachers, together with groups like journalists (Wale, 1972), may indicate that symbolic-expressive and representational values are important.

Table 2.3: *Organizational and political experience of the members of the Storting, 1969–1977. Percent.*

	1969	1973	1977
Party representative	77	86	92
– on county level	53	56	64
– on national level	29	38	44
Representative in interest organization, total.....................	69	75	77
– on national level	29	37	32
Local councillor........................	87	87	86
Member of the council at the county level	33	37	41
Alternate member of the Storting..........	43	41	45
Member of public comittees	43	45	45
Cabinet member	5	6	6
Number of persons	(150)	(155)	(155)

Source: Skard (1980:75, table 11).

Inspection of the political and organizational background of representatives modifies the picture. Experience in the party (membership) organization is nearly compulsory. So is experience in local government and in interest organizations. A considerable number have experience as an alternate member of the Storting or in public committees (table 2.3). This recruitment pattern secures representatives with considerable political and organizational training and socialization. Ties to local politics are strong – but less so than before World War II – and being elected to the Storting makes it more likely that one gives up offices in the party at the local level and gets office at the national level (Hernes, 1971: 47).

The significance of the capabilities, predispositions and loyalties representatives bring with them depends on the Storting's ability to train, socialize and discipline representatives. In most organizations this ability increases the longer the tenure of the individuals, but tenure data are more difficult to interpret in legislatures than in bureaucracies. External control over entrances and exits prevents massive deviations from local concerns, and long tenure may simply indicate that a representative has not become socialized by the Storting.[2]

If, however, professionalization is linked to long tenure, the data again indicate a modest professionalization. Hellevik (1969) found that of 407 representatives elected since 1945, 3% had served in all six periods between 1945 and 1969; 6% had served in five periods; 9% in four periods; 16% in three; 24% in two; and 42% had served in only one period. The long-run trend in this century had been toward reelection of incumbents, but it was broken in 1945 when the first elections in nine years were held. Later the pre-war trend continued till 1961 when the number of reelected dropped to close to 60% (fig. 2.2).

Fig. 2.2: *Reelected and new members of the Storting: 1900–1977. Percent.*

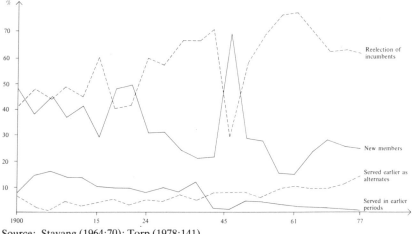

Source: Stavang (1964:70); Torp (1978:141).

54

Members of the Storting think personal characteristics are important (Hernes, 1973: 1). And a study of the 1814 to 1969 period shows that high social status makes it more likely that a representative will achieve a position with a certain rank in the Storting. However, the trend is for social status to mean less (Hernes, 1974). The importance of organizational affiliations also seems modest. For instance, representatives who had held office in interest organizations were not more active than others when it came to raising questions and interpellations of interest to those organizations (Hoel, 1972). Members of the Storting tend primarily to view themselves as representatives of their parties and their districts (Hernes, 1971: 194, 317). And we will later show that their thinking and behavior are linked to the tasks and positions they get in the Storting.

Some preliminary conclusions may be suggested. Professionalization has been modest and the image of the amateur citizen-representative plays an important role. The data do not support a general conclusion that the significance of the Storting is declining because the qualifications of representatives are declining. Representatives may not bring with them many technical and professional skills, but they should be well qualified to bring to national politics concerns, perspectives, and information from the local level. At the same time long party careers are likely to modify a purified parochialism. Some groups are clearly under-represented (women, manual workers, the youngest and the oldest), but recruitment patterns reflect fairly well the groups active in politics. They should symbolize lay governance and thus contribute to legitimacy and trust. This image of a lay tradition is even more evident in the Storting's reluctance to establish a staff of its own.

Staff

When yearly sessions were introduced in 1869 the staff of the Storting included two persons, and "no other institution has been so worried about losing power to hired staff as the Storting" (Danielsen, 1964: 163–164). Still there has been a certain growth. In 1981 the Storting employed 264 persons, 60 more than four years earlier, and for the first time administrative personnel outnumbered clerical personnel. (We exclude the Storting's Ombudsman for Public Administration and the Auditor General.) (Dok. nr. 8, 1975–76; Forh. i St , 1976–77: 2827–2863, 4653–4666; 1978: 1588–1625; Innst. S. nr. 2, nr. 120, 1977–78; Innst. S. nr. 179, nr. 446, nr. 447, nr. 448, 1976–77.)

Many leading parliamentarians do not accept the idea of a Storting staff in competition with the public administration (Forh. i St. 1978: 1616, Bratteli, 1772–74: Dørum; Hansen, 1978). Still, there is dissatisfaction with present arrangements. In 1976 only 8% of the representatives were satisfied with the secretarial help they got. Only 15%, however, argued that each representative should have a secretary of his or her own – an idea that was characterized as unrealistic by the chairman of the committee which prepared the issue and the spokesman for the recommendation to the Storting (Forh. i St., 1978: 1591; Innst. S. nr. 446, 1976–77).

Thus, the Storting denies itself services that are taken as given in most sectors of society. It is possible that this is due to a fear of losing power. But it equally likely is the attitude that an expansion of the staff would violate established symbols of lay governance and saving money for taxpayers. Debates in the Storting indicate, however, that there are differences between generations in this question, and that leaders now taking over may be less reluctant to expand staffs.

It is not clear what an expansion would imply. It is argued that one of the most critical factors conditioning the capacity of a legislature to respond to the growing responsibility is staff (Balutis, 1975: 23; Campbell and Clark, 1980; Fox and Hammon, 1977). But it is also argued that staff is a mixed blessing, and that the effects depend not only on the size of the staff, but also on its location, training, careers, mobility, and loyalties (Baerwald, 1979; Loewenberg and Patterson, 1979: 161; Salisbury and Shepsle, 1981). There are gross variations across countries in the use of staff, but few studies of their operations and effects.

ORGANIZING WORK AND DECISION MAKING

There is a growing interest in finding organizational forms that make the Storting effective in spite of its more difficult tasks and more complex environment. Standard complaints are that procedures are out of date and conditions for work inefficient; few representatives attend assembly meetings and the use of written manuscripts makes debates dull; and the information distributed to the environment is inadequate. However, complaints have been combined with a reluctance to change those conditions – in spite of the fact that the Storting controls its own rules, procedures and budgets. We interpret this reluctance as a reflection of the multipurpose character of the Storting and the fact that different functions demand different organizational arrangements.

A central idea in liberal democratic theory is that the will of the people crystallizes through rational discourse and voting in the plenary assembly. But policy making significance depends on the ability to exploit the benefits of division of labor. Use of committees increases the parliament's capacity for attention and produces more experience and specialized knowledge. In most legislatures committees are the work horses. But specialized committees also tend to make specialized policies, with a lack of overall coherence (Bentham, 1838; Loewenberg and Patterson,

1979: 210). One may expect the plenary assembly to provide integration, or the job can be done by political parties, a board of presidents, or a special committee, like the Finance Committee.

We also recognize that organizational arrangements have meaning and importance regardless of their immediate policy impact. More than pronouncements of goals and intention, organizational forms signal commitments; and considerations of "due process" are strongly linked to legitimacy (Kaufman, 1977; Meyer, 1979; Meyer and Rowan, 1977). The Storting's role as interpreter will primarily depend on what is going on in the plenary assembly. To rephrase Wilson (1956), the plenary assembly is the Storting on public display whilst the Storting in its committee-rooms (and party caucuses) is the Storting at work. In Norway the tendency since 1945 has been towards "modernization" of organizational structures and procedures, i.e. rationalization, specialization, standardization, and formalization. Although the development has been more reluctant and slow than in many other countries, it has probably made the Storting more fit for policy making functions. It may also have made it less fit for symbolic-expressive functions.

The decline of the floor debate

The Storting has a somewhat special one and one half-cameral structure. All representatives are elected to the Storting, but questions related to legislation are dealt with in two separate chambers: the Odelsting (with three fourths of the representatives) and the Lagting. In 1980–81 the Storting sat for 111 days, the Odelsting for 28 and the Lagting for 20 days, for a total of 547 hours. The number of sitting days has varied little since 1945, but there is a slight tendency towards fewer plenary meetings.[3]

The frequency of meetings does not necessarily indicate policy making significance. This fact was strongly stressed in the 1945–1961 period of "the parliamentarism of Hønsvald". Named after the parliamentary leader of the Labor Party it signified a situation in which the destiny of the cabinet, as well as other major decisions, were to be made in the Labor Party caucus, not in the assembly (Greve, 1964: 396; St. tid. 1959: 753, Hønsvald). The declining policy significance of the floor debate is, however, not only linked to a one party majority situation. Since the 1930s, proposals from standing committees have been more and more frequently accepted without changes (Vassbotten, 1935); today it is unlikely that something surprising might take place on the floor. If a representative should be convinced by the arguments of the opponents, it is unlikely to be reflected in the ways votes are cast.

There has also been a rationalization and formalization of debates. Traditionally there was little practical need for and strong principles against the use of closure. Debates proceeded without interruptions or obstruction. But since 1945 debates have become more firmly regulated. There are general rules for how often and for how long a speaker may take the floor, and in all major debates a list of speakers, and how many minutes each speaker will have, is drawn up through agreements between the president and the party leaders in the Storting (Danielsen, 1964: 177–99; Greve, 1964; Langslet, 1970; Skard, 1980: 172; Forh. i St., 1965–66: 1832–1833, 2723–2749; Innst. S. nr. 2, 1950: 24–62; Innst. S. nr. 65, nr. 133, 1965–66).

A result is that representatives take less interest in the floor debate. Often only a handful are present in the hall until a vote eventually is taken. The main speakers will be the leaders of the party caucuses, ministers, committee chairmen and the spokesman for a special issue. Since all representatives are spokesmen for some issues, the distribution of speaking frequency is moderately skewed, except for the fact that smaller parties are strongly overrepresented in the floor debates.[4]

Another result of the regulation of debates has been increasing use of written manuscripts. Speeches tend to be monologues, all too often loosely coupled to what the preceding speaker said (Skard, 1981: 77–86). Thus debates may be unfit for the functions assumed in liberal democratic theory – discovering the right solution and making choices. But they may also be unfit as vehicles for political competition in which different parties might expose each others weaknesses, exhibit their own unity and strength, or appeal to cleavages and differences that could contribute to the result of the next election. Strictly regulated debates lack the flare of political drama that might attract public attention.

Norwegian mass media have traditionally taken great interest in what is going on at the parliamentary arena. It is still the best covered part of the political process, but the journalistic style is increasingly to comment rather than to report. The introduction of live TV from the hall of the Storting also changed the situation. Now people could see the nearly empty hall – the place where the most important decisions were supposed to be made (Arbeiderbladet (Oslo), June 24, 1981, editorial). Representatives have become more concerned with this symbolic effect, and they are likely to move into the hall, at least when the TV-cameras are on: a reminder of the importance of symbols and rituals in modern politics. A result is that there will be less time for policy making in committees and party caucuses.

Division of labor: Committees

Delegation to committees has a long tradition in the Storting. Increased work load produced specialization which produced continuity (Danielsen, 1964: 153–54, 161–62). Today, members of the Storting are distributed on 12 standing committees, nominated by and with proportional representation from the parties. Each representative is a member of one standing committee. Committees have no formal authority, but they prepare all decisions for the Storting and most of the time their recommendations are followed (Danielsen, 1964: 117; Hernes, 1977: 289). The work load varies widely, but work methods are basically the same. Some committees meet each day, others a couple of times a week (Skard, 1980: 52). Most of the working material comes from the Cabinet as propositions or reports which the president distributes to the committees. Work methods are thorough, time consuming and informal. No minutes are kept and meetings are not open to the public. There is little rhetoric – members try to find "practical solutions" and compromises across party lines. Other members of the Storting, ministers, civil servants, experts and others who may contribute something, may get permission to be present and to speak. A committee has the right to get documents, but civil servants are not required to meet in a committee (Forh. i St., 1976–77: 4656–66; Innst. S. nr. 439, 1976–77).

Do committees provide the specialization and expertise needed to make the Storting capable of independent opinion so that they need not only follow recommendations from the Cabinet? The committee system provides specialization. But at the same time it creates a hierarchical element in the Storting that to some degree counteracts specialization.

Some committees are viewed as more important than others, and their ranking changes only slowly (Danielsen, 1964: 151; Hernes, 1971; Selle, 1981). Representatives differentiate between the status, the national importance, and the party importance of a specific committee. However, some committees (Protocol, Administrative Affairs, Judiciary) have for some time been ranked low on all criteria. The differential evaluation creates incentives for mobility and an internal career system (Hellevik, 1969; Hernes, 1971, 1973, 1977; Skard, 1980).

Hellevik (1969: 136, 138) observed that in the period 1950–69, in a new Storting 31% were new representatives, 42% would continue in the same committee, and 27% would come from another committee.

Of those holding offices (chairman, vice-chairman, secretary) in a committee from 1945 to 1980, 44% had been a member of the same committee. 32% came from another committee, and 24% were new members.[5] The Shipping and Fishery committee tops the list with 8.8 years of prior membership for chairmen. At the bottom we find the least attractive committee (Protocol, 3.0 years) and one of the most attractive ones (Finance, 3.2 years). On the average, committees had 7.5 chairmen from 1945 to 1980, and the tendency is that tenure gets shorter. This illustrates the effect of a committee hierarchy: those committees which representatives try to avoid and those which are attractive and therefore take some time to get to, have the shortest tenure.

This moderate specialization may partly be caused by the hierarchy of committees; partly it may reflect shifting majorities in the Storting and deliberate attempts by political parties to counteract specialization and to increase the general political-economic orientation and capability of its representatives (Bratteli, 1979; Hansen, 1981; Forh. i St., 1978: 1608, Willoch).

One consequence is that seniority in the Storting is less important than in many other national assemblies. For instance, it explains very little of the perceived influence of representatives (Hernes, 1973: 20). A person with a high standing in a major party may become a committee chairman in his/her first term, an illustration of the fact that the committee hierarchy provides party leaders with a system of rewards and penalties.

The specialization tendency is also constrained by the limited administrative apparatus established around the committees. Until 1977 committees would "borrow" administrative secretaries from the ministries – only one committee had a permanent position for a secretary. Then it was decided that each committee should have a secretary of its own (Innst. S. nr. 446, 1976–77). This slow development is partly due to the fact that representatives have given priority to clerical personnel over expert administrative help. And they have preferred to use expert help for party caucuses and for a law office in the Storting, rather than for the committees (Innst. S. nr. 446, 1976–77; Forh. i St., 1971–72: 2252, Bjorvatn; 1978: 1588–1625; Hansen, 1981). It is wrong, however, to interpret the lack of administrative resources as an indication of committee irrelevance. The committee structure symbolizes the relative importance of issues and groups in society. In principle it is supposed to reflect the most significant societal problems and to parallel the ministerial structure (Forh. i St., 1979: 2716–2718). Organized interests in society are eager to be represented in "their" committees and they often succeed (Hernes, 1977: 290). We return later to the external interest bases of committees. Here we consider three factors that indicate the degree of specialization: the degree of intra-committee conflict, the degree of inter-committee intervention, and the degree to which the committee structure organizes the participants' attention and use of time.

The committees' ability to reach compromises is important because unanimous recommendations will almost always be accepted by the Storting, making it a more specialized decision-making system. And most of the time committees in the Storting reach consensus. Rommetvedt (1980: 47–52) studied 13,315 recommendations sent to the Storting and the Odelsting in 1945–1977. Of these 17% included dissenting votes, comprising 23% of the 3430 recommendations to the Odelsting (issues related to law-making) and 15% of the 9885 recommendations to the Storting. The number of dissents have been fairly stable, but in the last period studied (1974–77), there was a rapid growth to 32% in total, and 46% in the recommendations to the Odelsting. These figures do not include budget decisions, but in the study of 6289 budget recommendations Rommetvedt found a similar trend.

Achieving consensus is thought to be facilitated by the low public visibility of committee decision making. Representatives argue this makes it easier to reach "reasonable compromises" and "correct decisions". And there is little enthusiasm for making committee meetings more open or for leakages from committee meetings (Hansen, 1981; Hernes, 1971: 21).

Specialization also assumes a high degree of non-interference between committees. Non-interference has been linked to norms of reciprocity (Fenno, 1973); but in the Norwegian case, data indicate that attention may be a more conspicuous factor. Norms demand that representatives should use more time outside their committees than they do, but non-intervention is facilitated because it is difficult to find time to read, understand, and take part in decisions in other committees. The large majority of representatives spend most of their time in their committees; these are the issues they are most acquainted with; and they perceive their own influence as strongly related to decisions made in the committee. There is a marked difference in the level of knowledge and influence inside and outside committees (Hernes, 1971: 352, 382, 509).

In sum, the data support an organizational perspective that assumes we have to know an individual's position or role in the Storting in order to understand a representative's thinking and behavior; and we need to know the Storting's standard operating procedures in order to predict the destiny of external initiatives (Polsby, 1975; Wahlke et al., 1962). The division of labor originally set up for coping with a diversified and large flow of issues has come to have a critical impact on decisions. Transformation of resources in the Storting often implies interactions of a complex nature, but the basic trend is that statuses outside the legislature are declining in importance (for instance as a base of influence) and there is a corresponding increase in the importance of one's role in the Storting and its subunits (Hernes, 1971, 1974: 163, 167, 1977: 291, 305).

The committee structure provides moderate specialization. It organizes the representatives' use of time and attention. But several factors counteract excessive specialization, and the functioning of committees cannot be understood unless we consider the interaction between committees and party caucuses. A major reason for non-interference is that committee members know the general attitudes and feelings in their party caucuses and take them into account. Party loyalty is a key factor in the process of integration in the Storting.

Integration: The board of presidents and the party caucuses

Moderate specialization creates moderate stress on the integration capacity of the board of presidents and the party caucuses. Each *ting* elects a president and a vice president, and together they constitute the board of presidents. The formal status of the President of the Storting is high – he ranks second to the King in authority. But the formal powers are modest. Presidents direct the debate and see to it that the rules of procedure are observed. They may take part in debates if they vacate the chair, they have a tie breaking vote, and they may give committees permission to meet and to travel between sessions.

Between 1945 and 1981 there were seven presidents of the Storting. 34 persons held 54 offices in the three *tings*. Only five of them held more than one office, and only two of the presidents of the Storting held any other office. Thus there is no hierarchy. Positions are controlled by the parties, and position in the party is more important than seniority in the Storting. On the average presidents are appointed in their fourth period in the Storting, but it is also possible to become president in one's first term.

Formal powers and career patterns indicate that the board of presidents is not the political nerve center of the Storting, and it is not (Skard, 1981: 63–66). Still, the board of presidents meets once a week and is a site for making compromises rather than exposing conflicts. Since 1961 the opposition has held three of the six positions – a move hoped to facilitate cooperation after the Labor Party lost its majority (Lyng, 1973).

Party caucuses are more important for organizing decision making and work in the Storting and for creating majorities. Parties control large parts of what is of interest to representatives, a fact contributing to unity and discipline (Hernes, 1973: 25, 1977: 286; Laasko, 1981). All important matters are discussed there before they appear on the agenda of the assembly. The importance of party caucuses is also illustrated by the location of staff resources. While staffs are still small, party factions have since 1963 been provided money for hiring secretaries (Forh. i St., 1978: 1588–1625; Innst. S. nr. 446, 1976–77). Given the coherence of Norwegian parties the party situation in the Storting is crucial.

Since 1921 fourteen parties have been represented. Only four parties have been there all the time, and the Labor Party has been dominant. When it lost the 1981 election, it had been in power since 1935 – except for a six and a half year period. From 1945 to 1961 the Labor Party had a majority of the seats but not of the popular votes. When there is disagreement in the Storting, 90–95% of the time party members vote together (Bjurulf and Glans, 1976). Voting discipline is especially high when the majority is narrow. Voting also depends on issues. In defense and foreign policies there has been a high degree of unanimity in the

Storting for most of the period since 1945. On issues following the right-left dimension, like tax policies, parties demonstrate their ideological position and their distinctiveness. On issues related to distributions of benefits or costs throughout the territory, geographic background is often more important than party membership (Bjurulf and Glans, 1976: 243). Loyalty to a party creates a system of who should say and do things. The system defines the party leader, the committee expert or the issue spokesperson as the one who should act. Statements from others are often defined as solo play and not appreciated. The system makes representatives function in a certain way and makes it more difficult for them to (always) say what they really mean (Grøndahl, 1979; Stavang, 1964).

Each party organizes itself with a chairman, a vice chairman, and a board. Both the caucus and the board have weekly meetings. Their functions vary somewhat with the size of the party faction. The meetings in the party caucus provides a site for discussion between representatives in the Storting and other party leaders. The rules for who can attend vary somewhat, but in general ministers, undersecretaries, the political secretaries of ministers, the board of the party (membership) organization, representatives from the youth and women's branches of the party, top employees of the party (both the parliamentarian and the membership organization) and representatives from the party press, will be present. "Outsiders" are allowed to speak, but except for ministers, seldom do so.

Only Storting representatives are allowed to vote in caucus and board meetings, but decisions are seldom made by voting. There is a "sense of the meeting" and minorities are expected to give in.[6] These meetings have an important information function, decisions are made on controversial issues, but in general the party caucus of a major party is so big that it will have some of the same limitations as the plenary meeting of the Storting. It will not be able to deal in detail with most decisions. The party faction in committees has to be trusted on most issues, especially as long as that faction agrees among itself. Representatives report that their influence in the party caucus is highest when issues linked to their committee or their constituency are at stake. But they do not see themselves as totally powerless in other decisions. If they try to affect decisions in other committees the first move is to work on the party faction in that committee, the next to use the party caucus (Hernes, 1971: 514).

Party loyalty makes integration fairly easy when one party holds a majority. The parties' right to bind representatives is accepted, especially in the socialist parties, but only a small minority say that representatives have to vote against their will (Hernes, 1971: 516; Larsen and Offerdal, 1979: 183, 190). When no party has a majority parties are torn between the desire for policy compromises through coalition formation and the need for preserving party identity and distinctiveness. Policy-cooperation among parties is smooth and friendly. The style is one of sharing rather than winner-take-all, and compromises are struck on the distribution of presidencies, committee chairmanships, and committee seats, as well as in the "pairing"-practice, where a representative who has to be absent arranges that a representative from an opposing party also stays away. The loss of the majority made the Labor Party invite other parties for consultations, and informal consultations were used to the degree that party leaders were criticized because they committed their parties and tied up party caucuses and committees (Greve, 1964: 405).

There is a striking contrast between this willingness to cooperate within the Storting and the unwillingness to make cooperation formal and to signal it to the environment. Since 1918 there has been only one majority coalition government in Norway.[7] Non-socialist parties have had great difficulties cooperating in elections in spite of common goals and ideologies, and in spite of very likely policy benefits. The assertion of distinctiveness and the preservation of unity has proved to be fundamental barriers to cooperation, and the closer in debate, the more parties have tried to establish that they were different (Groennings, 1962: 160, 289, 307).

The Labor Party has no less need for asserting its distinctiveness. That party has never taken part in a coalition government. Actually, Norwegian parties invest heavily in the belief that their platforms present a clear political alternative to the voters, and that elected representatives will try strenuously to realize the program (Valen and Katz, 1964: 92). To mobilize voters and to keep up party activists' enthusiasm, parties forego policy benefits in order to preserve their identity. This is typically done in situations of greatest visibility: formal coalition building and electoral cooperation. In a way, if conflict did not exist, it would have to have been invented. While Mannheim (1949) argued that bureaucrats had a tendency to turn politics into administration, politicians may have the opposite tendency, especially in small, homogeneous countries like Norway.

We conclude that the Storting has developed a matrix-like organization with the party caucuses and the committees as building blocks. Consistent with the parliament-of-laymen tradition, representatives rely on expertise and technical information from outside. The structure reflects the multipurpose character of the Storting. It may not be ideal for policy making or for interpretation, but it does attend to both functions. Problems of reorganization should be viewed in this light – it is difficult to strengthen the policy making capacity of the Storting without reducing its effectiveness as interpreter.

TRANSACTIONS WITH THE ENVIRONMENT

The significance of a democratic legislature depends on its ability to organize effectively both its transactions with constituencies and with other power centers. Here we focus on three arguments for the decline of the Storting: (a) the Storting is an agent controlled by the Cabinet and/or a party; (b) the Storting's irrelevancy and isolation – and the dominance of the corporative functional policy making system; (c) the Storting's loss of representativeness, of legitimacy and support in the population at large, and thus of power.

A centralized environment: The Cabinet and the party

The environment may be viewed as dominated by one central actor – the Cabinet or a party – outperforming the Storting both as a policy maker and as interpreter. This is an inversion of the constitutional sovereignty of the Storting. The constitution does not recognize political parties and it gives the Cabinet few powers – ministers have to vacate their seats in the Storting, the Cabinet cannot dissolve the Storting, and the Cabinet is collectively and individually responsible to the Storting.

Probably a bi-polar model where the Storting confronts the Cabinet or the party, historically important as it is, today conceals more than it reveals. Relationships are characterized by interdependence and integration more than domination or separation. The Cabinet knows it has to explain and defend its actions in the Storting and achieve a majority there. The Storting knows that it cannot govern on its own. Members of the same party speak about "their people" in the Cabinet, Storting or party. The membership organization and the party caucus are well-integrated and there is a mutual process of influence between the two sub-systems. In practice influence depends on the type of decisions and on the contingencies of those decisions (Valen and Katz, 1964: 89).

Of special importance is the party situation. The concern about weak Cabinets and an interventionist Storting turned into the very opposite complaint when the Labor Party won a majority in 1945. Then it was argued that the Storting had disappeared as a political force. The Cabinet had become a committee of the party and the party caucus in the Storting was left with a broken back. Norway was pictured as a one party state. The description is controversial (Seip, 1983)[8], but it reflects a situation in which the Labor Party lived up to its tradition of emphasizing the importance of the membership organization and accepting the national convention as the highest authority; in which the value of party discipline and unity was highly recognized; in which the most influential people were located in the membership organization, the Cabinet, the Federation of Trade Unions, and in the party newspaper in the capital, rather

65

than in the Storting; and in which top leaders had their basic training and socialization in the membership organization and in the labor movement at large, rather than in the Storting.

Things have changed. After a new series of minority governments there is a return to arguments that were familiar in the period between the two world wars. For the Cabinet the minority position creates fatigue and a longing for the support of a united majority in the Storting. For the party a minority position produces too many compromises, making cleavages between parties less clear and appeals based on a clear identity difficult. And again the Storting is accused of being too interventionist and not allowing the Cabinet to do its job (Aftenposten (Oslo), 24.3. 1980, Nordli; Forh. i St., 1977: 4066, Hansen).

The style of compromise is illustrated by the fact that since 1945 only two minority governments have resigned after a vote of non-confidence. Successful votes against individual Cabinet members are equally rare (cf. chapter 3). A Cabinet sometimes accepts a defeat on a specific bill in the Storting and there is an agreement that the defeat will not make the Cabinet resign. But more often a compromise is worked out. Either there are careful consultations before a proposal is presented in the Storting, or a committee takes informal contact with the minister to find a solution both parts can accept. It has even been discussed whether a committee should be required to consult the minister in such cases (Forh. i St., 1977: 4029, Borten). Interdependencies are dealt with in two different ways – reflecting the needs for specialization and for integration. On the one hand there are several collective meetings between party leaders in the Storting, the Cabinet, the party, and (for the Labor Party) the Federation of Trade Unions. These are weekly routines. On the other hand, there are highly specialized contacts between ministers (undersecretaries and political secretaries) and "their" committee, "their" party faction in the committee, and individual representatives (cf. chapter 3).

The well developed contact patterns are contrasted by a moderate mobility between the Storting and the Cabinet. While Huitt (1968) argues that the crucial element in the parliamentary model is that the executive is selected by the legislature from among its own members, the Norwegian parliamentary system has none of these characteristics. The party caucus in the Storting most often has moderate to small influence when a Cabinet is formed. And since 1945 only 41% of the Cabinet members served in the Storting before they were appointed (cf. chapter 3; Bratbak, 1981b).[9] This pattern has been interpreted as a consequence of the weak position of the Storting (Stavang, 1964). The pattern may also reflect that different characteristics are needed in the two positions. It may also be the result of strategic calculations and the constitutional rule that ministers have to vacate their seats in the Storting. A party, and especially a minority party, will not want to take all of its most experienced representatives away from the Storting – some are needed to defend the Cabinet.

The Norwegian system is one in which neither party leaders, Cabinet members or Storting representatives feel all-powerful or powerless. The parties are central actors, but they have limited resources to follow the day to day business of government. Ministers judge their contacts with the Storting as very important. Their schedules depend on the agenda of the Storting, and often they have to cancel other meetings in order to be available in the Storting. They feel a need to visit the Storting as often as they can in order to avoid surprises, and they rely on "their" committee faction and the leaders of the caucus to sound out problems. Ministers who do not have any one committee to report to (like Commerce and Shipping) view that as a handicap. Confrontations on the floor of the Storting are frustrating for ministers. Some report that they never become well-acquainted with the Storting. "I am scared to death each time I go there," one minister without experience from the Storting complained.[10] Members of the Storting are also sometimes frustrated because they feel that they lack time, information and influence. But on the average they feel that the Storting has a major impact on Cabinet policies, even if they are aware that there are many other influences (Bull, 1980: 290; Hernes, 1977; Kielland, 1972).

In sum, we think it is a mistake to interpret Storting-Cabinet-party relations in terms of confrontation and domination. Perspectives are influenced by the position one has, but there are also shared interests and common ideology, and much coordination takes place through anticipated reaction and mutual adjustment. The return to minority governments has strengthened the role of the Storting, and experiences with minority governments have created an agreement to improve working conditions for the opposition in the Storting (Dok. nr. 8, 1976–77; Forh. i St., 1977–78: 1588–1625; Innst. S. nr. 446, 1976–77). Finally, the bipolar model also has to be rejected because it simplifies the environment of the Storting too much. The Storting does not face a centralized environment dominated by one actor, but a highly specialized environment in which public agencies and organized interests in society are major actors. It is often argued that both elected and appointed politicians have lost power to these two groups.

A specialized environment: Civil servants and organized interests

Increasingly task of policy making is to discover the limits set by those who prepare and implement a policy and those who are affected by it (Richardson and Jordan, 1979: 137, 141). Weber (1946: 232–33) argued that the most serious challenge facing contemporary societies was to maintain control over the expanding bureaucracy. And Rokkan (1966) called attention to the "two tier" system developed as the territorial channel of representation was supplemented by a corporative-functional channel. Organized interests are generally thought to be getting more involved with the administrative apparatus and less with the Storting. The corporative-functional channel, whose main participants are top civil servants and representatives of organized interests, in combination with experts from institutions of research and higher learning is viewed as more effective. Decisions are made more rapidly and precisely and with less "noise" and play for the gallery (Hallenstvedt and Moren, 1975; Kvavik, 1976; Melander, 1974). Is, then, the corporative-functional channel better adapted to present policy making needs, and has the Storting become isolated from this arena? We consider some observations that indicate that this may not be true.

The corporative functional policy making system has some general limitations. It works best under conditions of fairly high consensus and mutual acceptance and understanding. It provides compromises, predictability, recognition of the participants, and effective bargaining among leaders. But it is not useful for making appeals to the public and signaling ideological identity; it ties up the participants and makes spontaneous acts difficult; it makes the participants responsible for public policy; and delegation of bargaining rights to leaders make membership control more difficult. In general its importance dwindles when the level of conflict rises. It is organized around economic cleavages, and economic-producer organizations have around 90% of the representatives from organized societal groups. Thus, the system does not attend to some other major cleavages in Norwegian society and does not provide access for some other major organized groups.

The system is highly specialized. Representation is linked to a multitude of councils, committees and boards at the ministry, department or agency level. The system has built-in countervailing forces and opposition. Civil servants compete with each other for power, resources and prestige – defending their jurisdictions and domains. The societal groups represent a variety of interests.

The low degree of participation by members of the Storting in these councils, committees and boards, often viewed as a sign of powerlessness, is interpreted differently by the Storting. Absence prevents overload: the Storting needs some shock absorbers and it needs someone else to prepare decisions. If civil servants or public committees do not function adequately, which includes their consulting those affected by policies, the relevant Storting committee will be "drowned" by inquiries. Absence also prevents seduction: a common observation is that members of the Storting who take part in a committee or in the board of a specific institution become strong defenders of that cause or institution. Non-participation is thus a way of preventing an early commitment before decisions are presented in the Storting (Forh. i St., 1959–60: 2468–2483; 1976–77: 4025–4077; Innst. S. nr. 277, 1976–77; NOU 1972: 38; Follesø, 1975; Grønlie, 1973).

The low participation level does not signify that the Storting is isolated from organized interests or from the civil service. Storting committees are frequently visited by organized groups and civil servants, and individual representatives have considerable contact (Hansen, 1978; Gudmund Hernes, Dagbladet (Oslo), June 13, 1981; Melander, 1974; Skard, 1981). Leaders of interest organizations also report considerable interaction with individual members of the Storting and with committees (cf. chapter 3; Egeberg, 1981; Gaasemyr, 1979).

Still, it is true that contacts with the administrative apparatus are more frequent than with the Storting. This pattern may reflect variations in institutional capacity of attention more than political importance. For instance, leaders of interest organizations report even less contact with the Cabinet than with the Storting, but that observation has never been interpreted as signifying a decline in the Cabinet's power. Contact patterns also reflect that some issues are routine and that the Storting or the Cabinet are contacted only when compromises cannot be reached.

Contact between representatives and the civil servants is more formalized, more modest, but growing. In the ministries the norm is that a civil servant should report to the minister when he or she has met with a member of the Storting. Contact with Storting members is organized hierarchically – top civil servants interact most frequently. For members of the Storting contacts are most often linked either to the representatives' committee or to issues of special relevance to the constituency (cf. chapter 3; Lægreid and Olsen, 1978).

Linkages to institutions at the local and regional level may also provide representatives with a countervailing power to the influence of corporative-functional coalitions. Such coalitions tend to structure programs on uniform national and professional standards, not tailored to the special needs of a particular region or community (Seidman, 1980: 324; Strand, 1978). When a geographic area is used as the basis for organizing policies, the influence of functional specialists and functionally organized interests tends to become reduced. Representatives in the Storting are the specialists on preferences and reactions of constituencies – in a way they are the "spatial specialists". And during the 1960s and 1970s local government grew considerably faster than central government (Kjellberg and Hansen, 1979). Central government has come to rely increasingly on local government to implement new programs, a tendency we believe will strengthen the role of the Storting. Confrontation between the corporative-functional and the territorial-electoral system is, however, unlikely. The two channels provide two types of specialization, but there is considerable overlapping, interaction, and integration between them. In

Norway the links between political parties and organized interests have traditionally been strong. For example, 46% of the elected leaders in nationwide economic-producer organizations report that they have held party office (Egeberg, 1981; Gaasemyr, 1979; Rokkan, 1966).

In the Storting this situation is reflected in a set of dualistic attitudes. Statements about influence and power are highly dependent upon the context in which they are made. Civil servants may be seen as too powerful, but they are also viewed as the defenders of objective competence, and the opposition in the Storting may view civil servants as a counterweight to the power of the governing party (Jacobsen, 1960; Forh. i St., 1980: 2670, Willoch). Representatives may complain because interest organizations are too powerful and because centrally negotiated income policies exclude the Storting from political influence. But at the same time the free bargaining rights of organizations are defended; there are complaints if the government does not consult organized interests before a decision is made; and it is recognized that interest organizations are the only alternative to information from the public administration (Forh. i St., 1959–60: 2468–83; 1979–80: 2449–2524; 1980–81: 426–443; NOU 1980: 7: 151; Skard, 1981: 103).

Party affiliations modify representatives' geographical and functional identifications (Hernes, 1971: 260), and most of the time representatives do not see party, functional and geographical interests as contradictory. Neither do they see themselves as isolated and powerless in relation to policy making in the corporative-functional system, nor do civil servants and organizational leaders hold this view. The Storting is seen as a significant, but not an omnipotent institution (cf. chapter 3 and 4; Lægreid and Olsen, 1978). Even when Storting representatives are not present, their opinions are taken into account when decisions are made in the bureaucracy, the major interest organizations, and in the corporative-functional channel.

In the long run, however, the relative power of the Storting depends on the legitimacy and support it has in the public at large. Next we shall consider the possibility that the Storting has become (over)adapted to a particular environment – i.e. stable cleavages and stable organized interests, making it difficult to adapt to new situations, issues and groups.

An undifferentiated environment: Voters and citizens

A highly specialized organization well adapted to a specific environment may outperform generalist organizations at a given point in time, but may fare less well over a longer time period to the extent that the environment has undergone change (Hannan and Freeman, 1977). Representative institutions are assumed to be able to learn and adapt because they have to appeal to the public. Bentham (1838: 130) argued that the fittest law for securing the public's confidence is that of publicity. Traditionally the Storting has been an open institution. An important aspect of the lay tradition is that ordinary citizens should have an opportunity to be heard by their representatives. The system is still open – for those who take the initiative – but openness primarily creates access for representatives from institutions, parties, and organized groups. And a majority of the representatives say that they have a special duty to defend non-organized and weak groups (NOU 1980: 7: 170). Do they get into contact with such groups?

Institutionalization of regular office days in the constituencies is still in its beginning. But most representatives maintain close ties. Only 15–20 representatives, primarily the youngest ones, have brought their families to Oslo. The Storting does not have meetings Mondays in order to give representatives a better chance to talk to their constituents. There are approximately 90 committee site visits annually, lasting 4–5 days. And political parties urge representatives to travel. One party demanded that at any time half of their representatives should (in principle) be on the road (Hansen, 1981; Skard, 1981; Statistics from the Office of the Storting, (June 25) 1981).

Still, most citizens have to be reached through the mass media. Members of the Storting are well covered, especially in newspapers at the regional and local level, but they have to compete with other institutional elites. The tendency is towards more personification and popularization, and the Storting has become concerned about its ability to inform the public (Hernes, 1978; Olsen and Sætren, 1980b; Skard, 1981; Innst. S. nr. 446, 1976–77). But there is also concern about leakages. While back-benchers may view leakages as benefiting democracy, party leaders complain because it is impossible to keep information secret (Kielland, 1972: 101; Korvald, 1978; Nordli, 1978).

Do citizens listen to what representatives say, do they trust what they hear, and do they support the Storting as an institution? General surveys are few but they are fairly consistent. The Storting is viewed from a certain distance, but on the average people believe it is an important institution, that it is working well and that it deserves to be trusted; and some argue that it should have more power (Aftenposten (Oslo), March 3, 1979 and June 7, 1980; Martinussen, 1977; Norsk Gallup, January 1976; NOU 1980: 7: 192; Valgundersøkelsen, 1969). Responses to such general surveys are, however, often difficult to interpret, and we may learn more from what people do than from what they say.

Peoples' "zones of indifference", that is, the areas in which they accept communications from the Storting and government as authoritative, have become more restricted (Barnard, 1938). The debate over whether Norway should join the European Common Market, in particular, put more stress on the parliamentary system than any other issue since 1945. In a plebiscite a majority of the people voted against joining, while a great majority in the Storting, as well as in other elites, wanted Norway to join. This discrepancy evoked questions about the ability of the party and electoral systems and the major interest organizations, to capture the moods and the interests of the people (Gleditsch and Hellevik, 1977; Valen, 1973).

As shown in chapter 1, the use of citizens' initiatives – collective behavior focussed on a single decision, and channeled outside established institutions, parties, and interest organizations – has become more commonplace. And these actions have primarily been organized around issues that have attracted little attention in the corporative-functional channel: sexual equality, environmental problems, the quality of neighborhoods, and questions related to moral and style of life rather than to economic production and distribution (Olsen and Sætren, 1980b).

This mobilization was a reminder that fairly large parts of the population did not like the way the political system was functioning, and during the 1970s citizens' initiatives became a major competitor to the Storting as interpreter, if not as policy maker. But except among tiny minorities, the general legitimacy of the representative system was not at stake. And with one or two exceptions there have not been any major confrontations between police and demonstrators. Citizens' initiatives have been warning signals rather than challenges, and in most cases the representative system has answered by coopting issues and groups (cf. chapter 6).

In sum, the data do not support the views that the Storting is omnipotent; that it is dominated by some single actor; or that it is isolated from policy making and the real power centers or from the people it represents. It is an important institution, but it is only one part of a network of institutions, competing and cooperating in processes of policy making and interpretation.

REFORM AND THE SEARCH FOR A ROLE

What are the implications of this analysis for the chances of reorganizing and strengthening the Storting? The concept of a sovereign parliament is an important part of political history and of the democratic creed, but today there is no base for such a power concentration. However, our interpretation is that during the last part of the 1970s the Storting became a more rather than a less significant institution. The increased significance was something that happened to the Storting, more than something achieved through deliberate efforts. The Storting has not recruited a new breed of more assertive and better skilled representatives, and there has not been major changes in agendas or internal organization. The Storting is a multipurpose institution and its agenda-building follows a political logic, where the importance of issues are defined through a political process of interpretation. Changes in structure may have made the Storting more fit for policy making and less fit for symbolic-expressive functions. But recruitment patterns seem better adapted to the latter function than to the former. Maybe the real strength of the Storting under changing environmental conditions is that its agenda, recruitment and internal organization are not perfectly adapted to any single function or aspect of the environment.

Primarily we link the increased significance of the Storting to changes in its environment. Some general societal changes have increased the "demand" for things the Storting is comparatively good at; at the same time as some of its weaknesses have become less relevant. From an ebb-and-flow perspective we expect this tendency to continue – we expect a certain reparliamentarization of political life in Norway.

For instance, a stagnating economy will slow down the number of political reforms. The number of propositions and reports from the government to the Storting is assumed to be strongly reduced (Innst. S. nr. 366, 1980–81; St. meld. nr. 79, 1980–81). Thus there will be less strain on the Storting's decision making capacity. There will be a change from developing new policies to attempts at reinterpreting the situation – "create more realism", "reduce expectations", "make people understand the foundations of the modern welfare state". This means a change from tasks the corporative-functional system is comparatively good at to tasks the Storting is comparatively good at. So far slack economic resources have buffered differences in values, beliefs and identifications among policy making centers in the specialized corporative-functional system. Economic stagnation will increase the chances that agencies and groups are unable to compromise and that they will appeal to the Storting. There will be more demand for coordination and collective decisions and less patience with highly specialized and selective policies. Issues will be less linked to technical problems and more linked to what the Storting is good at – finding political compromises. As the agenda changes from selective to collective policies, the decision-making legitimacy of the Storting increases and the legitimacy of the specialized corporative-functional system decreases (Egeberg, 1981). Coordination problems are often seen most clearly at the local and regional level, where specialized policies may create aggregate effects not predicted or desired. A mobilization of local and regional institutions (as compared to functional coalitions) tends to strengthen the Storting.

General demographic changes make it likely that more people with higher formal education and professional and technical skills will be recruited. This may increase the policy making capacities of the Storting, and speed up the process of "modernization", i.e. more staff, better working conditions, and better compensation. But more emphasis on formal education and professional and technical skills also tends to decrease experience from local politics, and it may reduce the Storting's capacity as experts on local needs, interests and perspectives. Representatives with more formal education have better opportunities outside the Storting and outside politics, and they may therefore be more difficult to discipline. This will reduce party control, make the individual representative more important, and create a strain on the Storting's ability to coordinate and integrate policies.

Finally, there will be less political stability. Among the post-war generations, class and cultural identifications are much weaker than among older generations, and party loyalty has decreased (Knutsen, 1981; Valen, 1981). The competition for votes becomes more relevant, and no party is likely to get a majority in the Storting in the immediate future. One-party majority governments tend to strengthen the government, and minority or coalition governments make bargaining and majority building in the Storting more relevant.

The three first decades after World War II were characterized by strong economic growth and slack resources, political stability, and a political consensus. In such times there are high demands for leadership and for expertise, giving the Cabinet and the corporative-functional decision making system a comparative advantage. As these conditions have changed, the strains on the government have increased and the corporative-functional system has stagnated (here measured in terms of number of public committees, boards and councils) (St. meld. nr. 7, 1981–82). At the same time there has been more concern about the representativeness of political institutions, making citizens' initiatives a more significant competitor to established institutions.

Is there, then, any room for deliberate intervention and reorganization? The question of the extent to which forms of government are a matter of choice is central to political theory and to organization theory; but there is little agreement about how it should be answered. While some view organizational forms as a result of design and choice, others interpret them as a result of organic growth processes (Bailey, 1835; March and Olsen, 1982; Mill, 1962: 1–17; Scott, 1981).

We believe the degrees of freedom for deliberate intervention and reorganization are modest. Uncertainty about the effects of reorganizations makes it more likely that the Storting will adapt to culturally defined forms and change only as these definitions change. Moreover, experience shows that the political payoffs from reorganization often are small. The symbols of reorganization may arouse political interest, but the implementation process is difficult to control (Roness, 1979).

But we also think that the development of democratic institutions depends on our ability to use – at the margin – alternative organizational forms intentionally. In order to make realistic estimates of the acceptability and feasibility of change, we need to understand why the Storting operates the way it does now (Froman, 1968), the multipurpose character of the institution, the culturally defined constraints that may not coincide with task requirements, and the power and interest bases of the Storting, as well as other institutions that perform representational, interpretational and policy making functions; and we need to determine the comparative advantages of these institutions.

We believe representative assemblies should use more energy on procedural rather than substantive planning (March and Simon, 1958). Focussing on substantive decisions tends to transfer an increasing number of control tasks to the Storting. Because of limited capacity, control may be more formal than real. A focus on procedural planning means intervention in the organization of choices (Cohen et al., 1972; March and Olsen, 1976). It includes creating decision sites, establishing access rules for people, problems, and solutions, and providing rules for the way in which decisions should be made. Procedural planning means controlling certain premises for future decisions rather than controlling the decisions themselves (Forh. i St., 1977: 4062, Førde).

The implication is that the Storting should be more concerned with its role as Organizer in addition to its roles as Interpreter and (substantive) Policy Maker. Organizing, and a concern for the form of the polity, is a classical political function, i.e. it affects all citizens and gives rules for the political life of the community, decisions where the representative assembly more than any other institution, should have legitimacy.

Notes

* This chapter is a revised version of a paper which was written together with Per Lægreid, and presented at a conference on "The Role of Parliamentarians in Contemporary Democracies", Centro de Investigaciones Sociológicas, Madrid, Spain, December 15–16, 1981.
  We want to thank Julia Ball, Søren Christensen, Tom Christensen, Michael Cohen, Rolf Danielsen, Heinz Eulau, Susan Hammond, Karen Havdal, James G. March, Vivi Olsen, Hilmar Rommetvedt, Per Stavang, Reidun Tvedt, Mariann Vågenes and the participants of the Madrid conference for advice and help.

[1] As we will return to, the Storting splits into two chambers in matters related to law-making. Since 1945 the number of days used by the two chambers has declined somewhat. Over the last few years the two chambers have been sitting for 80–90 hours.

[2] In their study of 82 city councils in the San Francisco Bay area Eulau and Prewitt (1973) showed that amateurs who viewed their participation as a temporary civic duty rather than as a career, were less responsive to their constituencies than those who pursued long careers. Thus the organization of career possibilities may prove more effective than rotation in office from a democratic point of view – an observation in opposition to much democratic folklore.

[3] The peak was in 1963–64 when the Storting was sitting 137 days due to a cabinet crisis. During the last few years the Storting has been sitting beyond 6 pm only 30 days, and beyond 11 pm 6–7 days (Statistics from the Storting, June 25, 1981).

[4] For instance, in 1979–80 a total of 171 took the floor in the Storting (including ministers and alternate members). 28 persons took the floor ten times or less. In the other brackets the numbers were: 11–20 times: 63; 21–30 times: 36; 31–40 times: 13; 41–50 times: 17; 51–60 times: 2; 61–70 times: 4; and 70 times or more: 8 persons. In the group active more than 50 times there are five ministers, one spokesman for the Labor Party, four other party leaders from the major opposition parties, and all the four representatives of the two smallest parties. The average number of speeches for representatives from the Labor Party was 17 and from the two smallest parties 93 and 127. One representative from the Socialist Left Party was taking the floor 175 times during that year. (Data compiled from Forh. i St. by Mariann Vågenes.) See also Aasland (1963).

[5] Data compiled by Mariann Vågenes from Torp (1946–1981). This material shows that among representatives 1945 to 1980 a little less than 4% had been members of four committees; 12% had been in three; 35% in two, and a little more than 45% in only one committee. Only 1% had held office in three or more committees, 16% in two and 83% in only one committee.

[6] We use information given by the leaders of the secretariats of the four major parties in the Storting. The leader of the Labor Party secretariat estimates that there have been 10–15 votings during the 300 meetings he has attended. The other informants suggest similar or even smaller numbers.

[7] In addition all parties participated in a short term government immediately after World War II (Strøm, 1982).

[8] The description in Seip (1963) is controversial because it undercommunicates that the Labor Party all the time had to compete with several other parties and could easily have lost its majority; because it ignores some successful interventions in policy making by the party caucus; because it does not take into account that party leaders and the Cabinet often compromised in order to avoid negative reactions inside and outside the Storting; and because the Cabinet always takes into account "the mood" in the Storting (Berg and Pharo, 1977; Andenæs, 1964). There are also variations across parties, i.e. in the non-socialist parties the party caucus in the Storting has traditionally been comparatively stronger than the membership organization (Kamsvåg, 1980).

[9] This number does not include the 1982 Conservative government, where 10 out of 17 ministers had previous experience from the Storting.

[10] Interviews with ministers, undersecretaries and political secretaries in the Bratteli government (1973). Also, Rønbeck (1979).

3

THE CABINET AND
THE LIMITATIONS OF
EXECUTIVE LEADERSHIP*

A central theme in Western political thought is how to reconcile the need for leadership and order, and thus a state strong enough to prevent anarchy, with the need to tame Leviathan, to provide representativeness and to prevent a monolithic, all-powerful state. The solution written into the Norwegian Constitution of 1814 was in the spirit of Montesquieu. Functions and powers were separated. The king was given executive leadership, with the right to select his advisers, the Cabinet, and to appoint his servants, the administrators. The introduction of parliamentary government in 1884 gradually converted the Cabinet into an executive committee of the Storting and the king into a ceremonial leader. Since the executive derived its authority from the representatives of the people, it was to be dependent in a large part on national elections and on laws, budgets, and other instructions from the Storting. Transactions with the administrators and those affected by governmental interventions would be dominated by legal-rational authority.

The concept of a parliamentary chain of governance has been – and is – the prevailing interpretation of executive leadership in Norway. But there are alternatives. Interpretations oscillate between theories that assume the fate of the nation is decided by a powerful executive elite and the view that executive leaders are the prisoners of and bookkeepers for broad technological, economic, demographic, and cultural forces. A single metaphor is unlikely to capture the complexity of modern political systems. This chapter offers an interpretation of Norwegian executive leadership based on ideas and observations from empirical studies of decision making in and between formal organizations.

EXECUTIVE LEADERSHIP AND PROBLEMS
OF POLITICAL CAPACITY, UNDERSTANDING,
AND AUTHORITY

Leadership may refer to formal roles, to types of activities, or to the results of those activities. The executive leaders discussed here are selected on the basis of their formal roles. They are politically appointed leaders – including the prime minister, the other Cabinet ministers, the under secretaries of state, and the political secretaries – all of whom have to leave office when a Cabinet resigns. To what degree such politically appointed leaders actually lead is the crucial empirical question: whether they run the ministries, make the most important policy decisions, and affect the course of history. This chapter considers the relations within the executive branch of central government. The key questions here are the *degree* to which politically appointed leaders are able to give direction to the large administrative apparatus acting in their name and *how* they give this direction.

The point of departure is the common observation that public agendas have changed dramatically in recent decades. An enlarged and more complex agenda may produce a strong executive, or a demand for one, making the executive the organizational center of the political system (Seligman, 1968: 107–113). Yet the increased volume, complexity, and interrelatedness of governmental tasks have in important ways reduced the opportunity of executive leaders for rational calculations and political control. The expanded agenda strains executive capacity because of limitations on time and energy; makes it difficult for executives to understand their own goals and the relations between means and ends; and raises problems of executive authority in relation to other elected or appointed political leaders, to administrative staffs, and to organized interest groups.

An interpretation of executive leadership must take into consideration that time, energy, and attention are scarce resources. It is also necessary to acknowledge that the expanded public agenda makes assumptions about omniscient rationality problematic. Executive leaders often have to act in an ambiguous and uncertain world, without a consistent, well-defined ordering of preferences. Government cannot refuse to deal with problems to which no one knows the answer. Finally, the expanded public agenda is closely interrelated with increased demands for representation and participation. The Cabinet is at the top of an electoral hierarchy, but it cannot expect other actors to accept its policies for that reason. And it can rarely force through policies solely on the basis of its electoral power. Thus it is necessary to ask how much power and authority results from winning elections and entering executive positions.

Executive institutions, their structures, personnel, procedures, and policy making will be viewed as organizational responses to the expanded agenda of public policy and as attempts to cope with the problems of capacity, understanding, and authority.

What, then, are the major factors favoring executive leadership in influencing events and behavior? The exercise of leadership depends on whether other centers of power recognize the authority and power of executives as legitimate, and on whether these centers can be called in to back up executive decisions (Stinchcombe, 1968: 158–160). Executive leadership in Norway is based on party support, and it makes a difference whether the support comes from a majority or a minority party, a well-disciplined or a fragmented party, a single party or a coalition of parties. It also makes a difference whether executive leaders have a strong or weak position within their party or coalition. Executive leaders also need support from and legitimacy among organized interest groups. Thus the organization of the interest group system, like the organization of the party system, is important.

The recruitment of executive leaders and the way they function are expected to reflect executive dependencies and coalitions. While it has been difficult for social scientists to specify the effects of different recruitment processes on the functioning of executive institutions (Headey, 1974: 269; Heclo, 1973; King, 1975a: 184), organized interests want their people, or people sympathizing with their interests, in executive positions. They also want to monitor and influence executive processes. Thus, one expects well-developed and fairly stable networks of communication between executives and their dependable allies.

In this chapter I consider the possibility that executive leadership depends on constitutional rights and that the number of politically appointed executives is important. Also considered is whether their ability to give direction to the administrative apparatus is affected by their experience, tenure, and unity. Experience in directing other large-scale organizations may also be valuable. The shorter the tenure of executives, the more likely that they will be guests instead of masters in the ministries. But it is also possible that the longer their tenure, the more likely ministers are to identify completely with "their" ministries, civil servants, and clients. Executive teams may be well or poorly organized. The less united they are, and the more energy they use to fight each other, the less likely that executive influence will be a dominant force. Finally, I study staff resources, their location, and the degree to which there are competing sources of expertise. The ability of the executive leaders to formulate goals and to initiate, implement, and assess policies depends on the size and competence of their staffs. But at the same time large staffs may take over, alienating leaders and making them prisoners of the pet projects of the staffs. I also ask to what degree the influence of executive leaders depends on their role perceptions and their philosophy of governance. Do they expect to make a difference, and how much?

THE ANATOMY OF THE EXECUTIVE

From November 1945 till 1979 there were ten Cabinets and seven prime ministers in Norway (table 3.1). The Constitution specifies a lower limit on the size of the Cabinet – a prime minister and at least seven other members. As of October 1979 there were sixteen members in addition to

the prime minister, each heading a ministry.[1] Each ministry was divided
into departments and divisions with a total of 2,730 positions, clerical
personnel included. The prime minister had a small staff, but he did not
head a ministry. Approximately fifty persons – ministers, under secretaries of state, and personal or political secretaries of the ministers – were
party appointees and leave office when the Cabinet resigns (table 3.2).
The under secretary is next in command to the minister, while the
political or personal secretary is a personal helper of the minister with no
authority over the career civil servants.

Table 3.1: *Norwegian Cabinets November 1945–1979.*

Prime minister	Duration	Party base	Support in the Storting	Reason for resigning
Gerhardsen	Nov. 1945–Nov. 1951	Labor Party*	Majority	Personal decision by the Prime Minister who said he was tired.
Torp	Nov. 1951–Jan 1955	Labor Party	Majority	Demand within the Labor Party for stronger leadership.
Gerhardsen	Jan. 1955–Aug. 1963	Labor Party	Minority after 1961	Vote in the Storting related to accidents in the Kings Bay mines.
Lyng	Aug. 1963–Sep. 1963	Conservatives, Liberals, Center Party, Christian Peoples Party	Minority	Vote in the Storting when the Cabinet presented its program.
Gerhardsen	Sep. 1963–Oct. 1965	Labor	Minority	Elections giving nonsocialist parties a majority in the Storting.
Borten	Oct. 1965–Mar. 1971	Concervatives, Liberals, Center Party, Christian Peoples Party	Majority	Internal problems in the coalition, especially related to the European Common Market issue; decision made in the parties.
Bratteli	Mar. 1971–Oct. 1972	Labor Party	Minority	Resigned after a majority of the people voted against Norwegian membership in the European Common Market in a referendum.
Korvald	Oct. 1972–Oct. 1973	Center Party, Christian Peoples Party, some Liberals	Minority	Resigned after the elections.
Bratteli	Oct. 1973–Jan. 1976	Labor party	Minority	Decision within the Labor Party, partly to solve general leadership problems in the party.
Nordli	Jan. 1976–Febr. 1979	Labor Party	Minority	Health, and political problems.

* A Labor Party Cabinet (Nygaardsvold) was appointed in 1935. In 1945 the Cabinet
returned from London and retired June 25, 1945. From June to November Gerhardsen
led a Cabinet in which all political parties were represented. The Labor Party won a
majority in the elections that fall.

Tabell 3.2: *Norwegian ministries: number of administrative staff and budget proposals.*

	1939–40	1947	1957	1967	1977
Administrative staff					
Ministries[1].......	10	11	14	14	14
Departments................	31	47	55	64	81
Divisions....................	105	184	212	216	304
Civil Service positions........	765	2 159	2 010	2 047	2 730
Politically appointed positions ...	10	22	29	33	50
Budget proposals (millions of					
Norwegian kroner)[2]..........	381	1 268	3 624	10 825	47 877

Source: Roness (1979: 41, 58, 65, 74).

[1] Prime Minister's office excluded.
[2] Refers only to budget proposals from the ministries. Expenses for the royal family, the Cabinet, Storting, auditor general, Supreme Court, state banks, state firms, pensions and insurance, and extraordinary appropriations are excluded.

The prime minister: political organizer but no superstar

The rights and the duties of the prime minister are not well specified in the Constitution or in any other laws and instructions. The counter-signature of the prime minister is required on Cabinet decisions. He has one extra vote if the king is not present in the Council of State, a rare event. He has a right to have any information from all ministries. But the prime minister has no hierarchical authority over the other members of the Cabinet. He cannot issue orders or change their decisions; neither can he dissolve the Storting or call elections (Bloch, 1963; Castberg, 1945; Debes, 1978; Innstilling om den sentrale forvaltnings organisasjon, 1970).

Clearly a prime minister cannot base his leadership on constitutional prerogatives. The key to authority and power is a strong position in a political party, as reflected in the tasks of the prime minister, his contact patterns, his recruitment of personnel, and the selection process.

A very important responsibility of a prime minister is to lead the process of transforming a party platform – or, in the case of a coalition government, party platforms – into policy proposals and programs. Norwegian parties take their platforms seriously. The development of new platforms may take more than two years and activate the party organization throughout the country. It is the prime minister's job to remind the ministers of items on the platforms for which they are responsible and to tally the proposals submitted to the Storting and the programs implemented.[2]

Another important part of the prime minister's job is to gather the necessary political support or acceptance for proposals inside as well as outside the Cabinet. A prime minister has to be an expert on the political effects of policies. He has to foresee and warn against political difficulties, to clarify areas of disagreement, and to cool the intensity of conflicts. His job is more often to identify solutions that are politically feasible than to discover the "correct" or "right" solution. He should also discover and make others aware of areas of political gains. The prime minister's attention will focus on maintaining a viable coalition, on preserving and strengthening Cabinet and party unity, as well as on reinforcing the larger coalition with organized interests in society. These tasks and dependencies are reflected in a series of weekly meetings.

Norwegian Cabinets usually meet three days a week. The most important decisions are made in Cabinet meetings on Mondays and Thursdays. These meetings last for two or three hours. Most often there are eight to ten issues on the agenda – sometimes as many as twenty – but a special Cabinet meeting may be called on a particular issue. Present are the ministers, the under secretary of state in the prime minister's office in charge of public relations, and a director general in the prime minister's office who prepares the meetings.[3] Also of importance politically is an informal luncheon on Fridays.

The preparatory Council of State meets for a half to one hour on Thursdays after Cabinet meetings to consider informally the agenda of the Council of State. Brief discussions occasionally occur, especially if issues have not previously been presented at a Cabinet meeting. The Council of State, chaired by the king, is primarily ritual and lasts for half an hour to forty-five minutes (Solumsmoen, 1962–63; Stavang, 1964). Several attempts to reduce the number of decisions that must be made formally by the Council of State have so far met with limited success (Bloch, 1963).

The role of the prime minister in Cabinet decision making is closely linked to his participation in an external political network. These networks are different for prime ministers from the Labor Party, which has never taken part in a coalition government, and for nonsocialist prime ministers, who since 1945 have always led coalition governments.

A prime minister from the Labor Party has four separate weekly meetings with the party faction in the Storting, with the governing board of that faction, with the party directorate, and with a coordinating committee between the party and the Federation of Trade Unions (LO). The political importance of these meetings is emphasized.[4] The routine meetings are followed up by daily personal and informal contacts and by formalized cooperation on important single issues. An example is that when the Cabinet prepared its platform for 1978–1981, the process was closely coordinated with the preparation of similar platforms for the party and for LO. A coordinating group was established, chaired by the prime minister, with representatives from the party, the youth organization of the party, the party faction in the Storting, and LO (Nordli, 1978: 16).

The prime minister's role in the Cabinet may be strengthened by his external contacts, but he does not have a monopoly on interpreting the views of other power centers. Other Cabinet members also have close relations with the party, with LO, and with the party faction in the Storting. The centrality of the prime minister in these networks has varied.

For prime ministers in coalition governments the situation has been different. The parties protect their autonomy and have not developed a unified communication system between the Cabinet and the Storting. The party factions have seldom had joint meetings, and each minister, the prime minister included, has met only with his own party faction in committees. After 1969, when several coalition party leaders left the Cabinet to return to the Storting, parliamentary leaders participated more actively in the Cabinet's preparation of cases. But then again in the Korvald period leaders of party factions in the Storting were more seldom activated (Lyng, 1978: 92; Solstad, 1969; Vassbotn, 1971: 124–125).

Thus, there are important differences in the organizational frameworks within which prime ministers operate. But there are also similarities. A prime minister is the chief spokesman for the Cabinet in important debates in the Storting. He will consult with the Standing Committee on Foreign Affairs on major foreign policy or security decisions, and perhaps with the leaders of the party factions. So far, however, the opposition has not used the question period in the Storting to challenge the prime minister. He is seldom questioned, and very rarely by other party leaders.

In addition, all prime ministers are in touch with organized interest groups in society. Incomes policies are discussed in a committee of representatives of the Cabinet and of the major economic-producer interests. The Federation of Norwegian Industries, the Federation of Norwegian Commercial Associations, and the Norwegian Shipowners' Association have special contacts with the Cabinet, even when the Labor Party is in office. Generally, however, economic organizations have been reluctant to accept integrated participation in policy-making processes at the Cabinet level. Instead, they have preferred integration at the ministry level (chapter 5).

We may conclude that a Norwegian prime minister has to act in an environment dominated by formal organizations such as parties, the Storting, ministries, and organized interest groups. Though he is unlikely to achieve a position as superstar in these networks, it is possible for him to affect policy making through political organizing and brokerage. The degree of success depends upon many factors, especially his political career.

All Norwegian prime ministers have been party leaders, but some have had a more dominant position than others. Einar Gerhardsen, who was born in 1897, fits the Weberian ideal of a political generalist with politics as a vocation (Weber, 1946). He had only elementary schooling and was a road worker from the age of seventeen to twenty-four. From then on his career was related to politics. He was Prime Minister for seventeen years and chairman of the Labor Party for twenty years. Gerhardsen was not an expert on issues and never headed a ministry. His strength lay in organizing political choice situations, an ability acquired through practice. His major organizational affiliation was the party.

The strong party base on the learning-by-doing aspects are shared by two other Labor Party prime ministers. Oscar Torp (born in 1893), an electrician with no higher education, was Prime Minister for three years and the head of four different ministries over a twelve-year period. For twenty-two years he was the chairman of the Labor Party. Trygve Bratteli (born in 1910) also started as a worker with no higher education and was Prime Minister for nearly four years. Bratteli was a member of the Cabinet for a total of fourteen years heading the Ministry of Finance and the Ministry of Communications. He was deputy chairman of the Labor Party for seventeen years and chairman for ten years. Bratteli, as of 1979, was the leader of the party faction in the Storting.

The biographies of these three prime ministers illustrate the continuity in the leadership of the party that has been in power for more than thirty-seven years since 1935. Since Cabinet members have to leave their seats in the Storting while serving in the Cabinet, the political work of these three prime ministers has been related primarily to party and Cabinet functions. Their party base was stronger than that of the two pre-World War II Labor prime ministers (Hornsrud and Nygaardsvold), and stronger than that of the present (1979) Prime Minister, Odvar Nordli. Nordli (born in 1927) attended junior college and became an accountant. From his early twenties, Nordli was active in party politics and local government. But he has not been employed by the party and has not been chairman. He became a member of the Storting in 1961, was minister of labor and local government (1971–1972), and leader of the party faction in the Storting (1973–1976) before he was appointed Prime Minister.

None of the prime ministers from the Labor Party has had a university degree. This pattern was broken when Gro Harlem Brundtland, who is a medical doctor, was appointed Prime Minister. All the nonsocialists have, and their careers in the Cabinet and the parties are closely related to long tenure in the Storting. Per Borten (born in 1913) spent twenty-seven years in the Storting, was chairman of the Center (farmers') Party for twenty-two years, and held positions in farmers' organizations. Lars

Korvald (born in 1916) has been a representative in the Storting for eighteen years, chairman of the Christian People's Party for ten years, and active in religious organizations. John Lyng (born in 1905) made a career in the court system. He was a member of the Storting for twelve years, representing the Conservative Party, but was never chairman of the party. Lyng later became minister of foreign affairs for a five-year period and was appointed county governor.

Norwegian prime ministers have long party careers. They know their parties, and the party cadres know them. The biographies reflect the fact that political parties are the main arenas for appointing and removing prime ministers. Only twice has a Cabinet left after a defeat in a general election, once after a referendum, twice after votes in the Storting, and four times as a result of party decisions (table 3.1). The careers of the prime ministers show a tendency away from a one-sided emphasis on the party organization, however; party leadership is usually combined with a career in the Storting or a vocation outside politics. The selection and recall processes today reflect this broader base and involve a wider group of participants than in the 1950s.

In 1945 the Labor Party made Gerhardsen Prime Minister, but the decision to withdraw in 1951 was his own. Many of the major participants have described the process, and they basically agree: The decision to leave was a personal choice by the Prime Minister and he more or less appointed his successor. The decision was described as a coup, a bomb, a shock, and a bolt of lightning; it was judged a disaster for the party. Gerhardsen was strongly urged to continue, but he refused. Central participants in the process have argued that if regular party procedures had been followed, Gerhardsen would not have been allowed to leave. Gerhardsen's argument was that he was tired and that changes in the Cabinet had to come suddenly. "I cannot leave little by little," he argued (Gerhardsen, 1971: 294–302; Larssen, 1973: 99, 102; Lie, 1975: 7, 53–59; Nordahl, 1973: 32–34; Solumsmoen and Larssen, 1967: 97–99).

Gerhardsen returned in 1955 after internal party criticism of the Cabinet under Torp, who did not want to leave (Larssen, 1973: 120–134; Nordahl, 1973: 103–105). Bratteli resigned in 1976 as a result of intraparty decisions. At the national conference of the Labor Party there were two candidates for the position of chairman. The solution was to make one the chairman and the other Prime Minister in the next Labor Cabinet. A party committee was appointed to decide the time of the changeover.

The heads of the nonsocialist coalition Cabinets have been selected through interparty decisions, with the locus of influence in the party factions in the Storting. Borten was chosen by a formal vote in 1965, and his coalition was dissolved from within in 1971 when three of the four parties refused to continue. Parts of the struggle between the party leaders took place before open microphones and running TV cameras (Brunvand, 1973; Finstad, 1970; Lyng, 1978; Sørebø, 1971; Vassbotn, 1971).

Most prime ministers in Norway have been appointed on the basis of the candidate's position in his party and the party's position in the Storting (Hermerén, 1975). The people selected are political generalists; they know Norwegian politics well and are expected to coordinate the work of their Cabinets. The ability to coordinate has been reduced, however, as one-party majority Cabinets have been replaced by minority or coalition Cabinets and as the tenure of prime ministers has become shorter. Also, the administrative resources of the prime minister are very modest. And the prime minister cannot expect the Cabinet members to form a unified group.

The prime minister's office

When Johan L. Mowinckel resigned in 1935 he had been Norwegian Prime Minister three times. In all three Cabinets he was also head of the Ministry of Foreign Affairs. Although as Prime Minister he had no secretariat, apparently he did not feel overloaded (Bratland, 1965: 109). Today such a combination seems very unlikely.

Ever since 1945 the limits on the capacity of executive leaders have been on the political agenda, and many institutional changes have been made in response to this problem (Torgersen, 1948a, 1948b; NOU 1974: 18; St. meld. nr. 58, 1975–76; St. prp. nr. 121, 1955, nr. 111, 1970–71). The prime minister still has little administrative assistance, however. A small office was established in the mid-1950s, with three under secretaries of state, one on economic planning, one on relations with the Storting, and one on relations with the media. Three positions of director general were also established, one of which was later transferred. In 1979 the prime minister's staff counted only nineteen persons, including clerical personnel and chauffeurs. Nor can he count on much assistance from committees. Out of a total of 1,155 public committees and boards, 905 permanent, with 7,200 members, only five permanent and three temporary committees are attached to the prime minister's office (St. meld. nr. 7, 1977–78).

When the idea of an office for the prime minister was raised, it was viewed – in Norway as in other countries – as an indication of the prime minister's desire for power. The office has clearly not become a super-ministry, however (King, 1975a: 224; Debes, 1978: 53). Rather, a public commission has argued that with the present administrative apparatus the prime minister is scarcely able to look after the activities of the ministries. Another committee expressed doubt, however, about whether it is "appropriate" to expand the prime minister's office into a coordinating department (Innstilling om den sentrale forvaltnings organisasjon, 1970: 46; NOU 1974: 18:28).[5]

The lack of administrative resources under direct control of the prime minister is not compensated for by control of the selection of the heads of the ministries. Usually the prime minister is the central actor in the appointment of the executive team, but that does not mean that he can always pick the ministers he wants.

Selecting the team

King (1975a: 197) has argued that while appointments to ministerial office in some countries are formally made by the head of state, in almost all countries the real decisions are made by the head of government. This description is fairly accurate for Norway in the 1950s. It is less adequate for the later Labor Party Cabinets and is wrong for the coalition Cabinets of the 1960s and the 1970s.

Prime Minister Gerhardsen comes closest to this description. Gerhardsen took the initiative and suggested a solution. He discussed it with a fairly small group: the deputy chairman and the secretary general of the party, the chairman of LO, the leader of the party faction in the Storting and the president of the Storting, and with the editor of the Labor Party newspaper in Oslo. Changes were then discussed in the party directorate and in the party faction in the Storting. The Prime Minister listened, but the decision was his own (Gerhardsen, 1971: 280–88; Larssen, 1973: 59–60; Lie, 1975: 303; Nordahl, 1973: 33, 101).

The process, which lasted for a short time only, was one of consulting, not bargaining. It was constrained by the expectation that different regions and organized interest groups – and to some degree women and the youth organization – should be represented. The Prime Minister also had to consider the need for able people to remain in the party faction in the Storting.

While both Gerhardsen and the present (1979) Prime Minister, Nordli, have argued that nominating a Cabinet is not a one-man job (Gerhardsen, 1971: 280–81; Dagbladet (Oslo), November 1, 1975), the process has changed in important ways. During the 1970s, Labor Party Cabinets have been selected through a longer process, with more participants, more demands for group representation, and more publicity. It has become more difficult to govern through selecting Cabinet members. One result has been public demands within the Labor Party for a stronger leadership. The argument is that "too much democracy" and quotas for various interests produce a Cabinet characterized by mediocrity and lack of a clearly defined political orientation.

Changes in selection procedures have been explained by the different styles of leadership of Gerhardsen and Bratteli (Larssen, 1973: 98, 123;

Lie, 1975: 57; Sundar, 1979). While personal style may be important, changes in selection procedures also reflect more fundamental political and social trends. The Labor Party, having lost its majority, needs ministers competent in interparty as well as intraparty bargaining. Because its traditional base – blue-collar workers, fishermen, and farmers – is declining in size, the party has to attract new groups, and in the process has become more heterogeneous. More interests have to be taken into consideration, including special interests more concerned with the choice of a specific minister than with the overall composition of the Cabinet. At the same time, a new generation is taking over leadership in the party, as well as in the Storting, the Cabinet, and LO – a change that is affecting the general style of decision making (Bergens Arbeiderblad (Bergen), December 27, 1978; Dagbladet (Oslo), December 23, 1978).

Prime Minister Nordli is quoted as saying, "If you cannot get the ones you love, you have to love the ones you get." For the prime ministers of the nonsocialist coalition governments in the 1960s and 1970s this was even more true. They had to work with ministers unilaterally selected by each of the participating parties. Borten learned about changes in his Cabinet through the media.

The lack of prime ministerial control of the recruitment process is also illustrated by the remarkable stability in the four first years of the Borten Cabinet. The only minister who left (because of health problems) was replaced by his own party. After winning the 1969 election, representatives of the coalition parties gathered for only two and a half hours to discuss the composition of the Cabinet. A status quo may indicate that no one dared to open up new, general discussions. When the Cabinet was later reorganized the Prime Minister did not take the initiative, but observed the process from a distance (Brunvand, 1973; Lyng, 1978: 147–50; Solstad, 1969; Vassbotn, 1971: 103). Again, the process has been explained by reference to the special leadership style of the Prime Minister. Things happened in a planless way because the Prime Minister was unable to assume leadership and take initiatives, because he was too concerned with details, and because he did not clearly signal to the ministers his own preferences and intentions. Yet this explanation has to be supplemented. In a coalition in which four parties were jealously protecting their autonomy and identity, and leading Cabinet members were publicly differing on major issues, strong initiatives and leadership would probably have been unacceptable.

To summarize, the potential for prime ministerial leadership is highly dependent on his position in the party and the strength of that party, as well as on his relations to major interest groups. The prime minister's constitutional prerogatives are few, his administrative resources modest, and the power to appoint ministers lies largely with the parties.

Gerhardsen comes closest to hierarchical leadership because of his long tenure, his leadership talents, and the support he received from a majority party facing a split opposition and from LO, which also had a stable leadership[6] with whom Gerhardsen had routine contacts. There was also a fairly high consensus about economic growth as a main goal and Keynesian economics as an instrument of governance. Gerhardsen had clashes with other major actors, such as the chairman of LO (Larssen, 1973: 71–73), however, and the Labor Party never implemented some of its most ambitious plans (Bergh and Pharo, 1977: 86–87, 116–22, 484). Still, Gerharsen had a greater leadership potential than any of his successors. The problems of political capacity, understanding, and authority have not been accompanied by a major expansion of the prime minister's ability to govern. He has to work through the ministers, and the administrative apparatus in Norway favors political specialization rather than coordination by the prime minister.

Ministers: specialists or generalists?

How likely is it that the politically appointed heads will become leaders of the ministries in a world of expanding problems, where most orders are not self-executing (Neustadt, 1976: 114), and where ministers have to act upon the advice of civil servants? How likely is it that ministers will identify with their roles as ministers more than with their functions in the Cabinet (Mayntz and Scharpf, 1975: 43), and that they will promote the policies of their administrative staffs and of well-organized client groups more than party platforms?

The enlarged public agenda has been countered by a delegation of authority from the Cabinet to the individual minister, making him or her more independent. At the same time, some decisions have been moved from the ministries to other central administrative agencies or to local and regional authorities. The underlying ideology is that ministries should be the political secretariats of the ministers and that decisions covered by an adequate set of laws or rules should be delegated (Bloch, 1963: 56; Debes, 1978; NOU 1974: 18; NOU 1974: 53; Innstilling om den sentrale forvaltnings organisasjon, 1970).

While the number of ministries and of employees has changed modestly since 1945, the number of departments and divisions and the budget size have grown considerably (table 3.2). The functional differentiation is also illustrated by the fact that central administrative agencies outside the ministries have become relatively more important. In 1947 they employed 18.7 percent and in 1977, 27.7 percent of state administrative personnel (Roness, 1979: 62).

As in France, a Norwegian minister can expect civil servants to have strong loyalties toward their own institutions, tasks, and professions. Each ministry has a great potential for indoctrinating and disciplining its personnel (Lægreid and Olsen, 1978; Suleiman, 1974; also chapter 4), and for defending its territory and jurisdiction. Attempts at coordination across administrative boundaries are often viewed as unwanted intervention. The tendency toward parochial identification and local rationality is likely to be strengthened as the participatory rights (Lægreid, 1975; Sætren, 1983) of employees and their organizations increase. The same tendency is likely to result from increased rights of participation in governmental processes for organized interests in society.

The concept of pressure groups is inadequate in the Norwegian context. Organized interests, especially economic-producer groups, are integrated into the governmental process through a hearing system, and through daily, informal consultations (chapter 5). The individual ministry has become *the* most important point of contact in the political system for economic interest organizations (table 5.3). With the exception of the Norwegian Federation of Trade Unions (LO), most contacts are between administrators from both governments and interest groups. The tendency is that the higher the administrative status, the more contacts there are and the less likely it is that the contact is centered on routine matters (Gaasemyr, 1979; Lægreid and Olsen, 1978).

Table 3.3: *Contacts of elected leaders and administrators in economic producer organizations, 1976 (percentages).*

	% Having at least one contact	
	Elected leaders	Administrators
Contacts with Ministry.............................	37	84
Contacts with Storting	15	33
Individual representatives in Storting	37	54
Contacts with Authorities		
County.......................................	22	39
Local	31	48
Contacts with political parties......................	24	26
Interviews by mass media	44	65
Publications about own work in		
newspapers and journals	40	72

Note: Data are for 475 elected leaders and 536 administrators in economic producer organizations; data are drawn from the sixty-three most resourceful economic-producer organizations and a random sample of sixty-three of the remaining organizations. Questionnaires were sent to elected leaders and to administrative personnel; 72 percent responded.

Elected personnel in full-time, paid positions are counted as administrators; they belong primarily to trade union organizations. The larger and more resourceful organizations are more strongly represented in the sample of administrators than in the sample of elected leaders simply because many small organizations do not have full-time administrators. (See also Gaasemyr, 1979.)

The result is that ministers face not only an administrative apparatus with a well-developed division of labor but also agencies with routine support from strong interest groups. The tendency toward segmentation of the political-administrative system is also strengthened by the fact that contacts with research and educational institutions are highly specialized, and most of the contact between ministries and the Storting goes through a specific committee (Bratbak and Olsen, 1980; Lægreid and Olsen, 1978). Members of the Storting have traditionally shown a dualism. Though they may be concerned with the overall growth of budgets and administrative staffs, as members of committees they usually defend the ministry and institutions connected with their own committee, arguing that the Ministry of Finance has been too eager to cut budget proposals (St. forh. 1950: 1647).

Is it likely that a minister can match this kind of coalition? Is he or she likely to want to do so? Does he or she stay in the ministry long enough to do anything?

Ministers: masters or guests?

Obviously ministers are sometimes strangers in the ministries. Since they represent a fragile and transient element in the executive process (Heclo, 1977), they easily become the prisoners of and the spokesmen for projects that have been in the pipeline long before they themselves were appointed.

The Norwegian situation is a blend of visitors and veterans. Since 1945, 63 percent of the ministers have been members of only one Cabinet, 27 percent have been in two, 5 percent in three, and 5 percent have been members in more than three Cabinets. The average number of years in office is 4.1, with ministers from the Labor Party averaging 5.2 years and those in nonsocialist Cabinets 2.4 years. While 21 percent of the ministers have a tenure of less than one year, 14 percent have served one or two years, but 45 percent have served more than five years. When new Cabinets are appointed, the ministers already have an average of 1.9 years of Cabinet experience, and they serve one Cabinet an average of 2.6 years. The average minister leaves the Cabinet with four years of service and has five years of service when he or she leaves for the last time (table 3.4).

There is a difference between nonsocialist and Labor Party Cabinets, and there is also a tendency toward less experience and shorter tenure for Labor Party ministers over time. Still, these Cabinets include people who are obviously not strangers to the governmental process or the ministries. Nor are Norwegian ministers likely to stay so long in a ministry as to be totally indoctrinated in the ministerial culture.

Table 3.4: *Tenure of Norwegian ministers, May 1979.*

Cabinet	Years of service			
	Before entering specified Cabinet	Within specified Cabinet	Including specified Cabinet	Total in Cabinets
Gerhardsen, 1945–51 ..	0.9	4.4	5.0	8.1
Torp, 1951–55	4.5	2.2	5.3	7.7
Gerhardsen, 1955–63 ..	2.8	4.1	5.2	6.7
Lyng, 1963	0.0	0.1	0.1	2.6
Gerhardsen, 1963–65 ..	5.9	2.0	7.5	8.1
Borten, 1965–71	0.0	3.9	3.9	4.0
Bratteli, 1971–72	1.3	1.5	2.8	4.7
Korvald, 1972–73	0.8	0.9	1.6	1.6
Bratteli, 1973–76	1.3	2.0	3.2	4.8
Nordli, 1976–	1.7	2.8	4.1	4.1
Total average	1.9	2.6	4.0	5.0

Note: The data are for 190 ministers, except in the first column, which includes only ministers appointed when the Cabinet began its term of office.

Headey (1974: 95–96) argued that if a minister stays too long, he ceases to be a minister and becomes a sort of second permanent secretary – a creature of the department. According to Headey, three years is the maximum time a minister should spend in one department, and about the optimum too. It is unclear what criteria or data Headey uses, and it is likely that the extent of indoctrination will depend on the strength and unity of the ministry, other affiliations of a minister, such as with the party, and the external networks in which he or she operates.

In Norway three-fourths of all ministers have served in only one ministry, while only seven persons have been in three or more ministries (the prime minister's office included). There is considerable variation across ministries, however. On the one hand, 73 percent of the ministers of finance have been in another ministry, as have more than half the prime ministers and ministers of defense, commerce, justice, and foreign affairs. On the other hand, only 10 percent of the ministers of fisheries have been the head of another ministry.

Ministers with long tenure tend to be political generalists who have headed at least two ministries. The most outstanding exception is Halvard Lange who headed the Ministry of Foreign Affairs for twenty years. Ministers with long tenure also have long party careers. In my judgment, therefore, it is unlikely that length of tenure will be a major factor in forming the ministers into spokesmen of the ministry and its clients. But ministers may take that role if they are identified with a specific sector *before* they enter the ministry and if this identification is a major reason for their appointment.

Paths to the ministries

"No prime minister could have recruited his ministers so consistently from the outside as Gerhardsen and Torp, had the party faction in the Storting been a really strong element in the political game," (Stavang, 1964: 155; also Bergh and Pharo, 1977: 457). If this reasoning is accepted, experience in the Storting really has lost significance as a path to a ministry since World War II compared with any other period since the parliamentary system was introduced in 1884 (table 3.5). Less than half the ministers have held a seat in the Storting, and only 11 percent have been members for more than fifteen years.

Table 3.5: *Ministers' tenure in the Storting when first appointed to the Cabinet (percentages).*

Number of years in the Storting	Period first appointed				
	1814–84[1]	1884–1920[2]	1920–45[3]	1945–78[4]	Total
More than 15	7	11	21	11	13
11–15	11	20	12	7	13
6–10	14	16	23	11	15
1–5	23	18	12	19	18
None	44	35	32	52	42
Number of ministers	70	114	77	130	391

Note: Percentages may not add to 100 because of rounding.
[1] From the 1814 Collegium to Christian H. Schweigaard.
[2] From Johan Sverdrup to Gunnar Knudsen II.
[3] From Otto B. Halvorsen to Johan Nygaardsvold.
[4] From Einar Gerhardsen I to Odvar Nordli.

During the late 1960s and 1970s, experience in the Storting was again more important than it had been in the 1950s. At the same time, a seat in the Storting is less of a guarantee of a generalist orientation than it used to be. Parliamentary work focusses more and more on committees, and members have to specialize in order to catch up with the expanded agenda.

The role of mayor, another political generalist, has also become less important as a springboard to the Cabinet. Since 1945 the number of ministers with experience as mayor is little more than half what it was from the time the parliamentary system was introduced until World War II (table 3.6). Still, nearly two-thirds of the ministers have experience in local politics, although local politics has also become more specialized and is no guarantee of a generalist orientation.

Table 3.6: *Norwegian ministers' experience in local government, 1814–1978 (percentages).*

Participation in Local Government	Period first appointed			
	1814–84	1884–1920	1920–45	1945–78
Mayor	10	39	42	22
Representative.............	11	22	34	42
No experience	79	40	25	35
Number of ministers	70	114	77	130

Party experience may partly counteract the tendencies toward specialization. Norwegian ministers have, with few exceptions, long party memberships. This is especially true of Labor Party governments, as illustrated by the party background of the Bratteli government (table 3.7). Even when under secretaries of state and (the mostly young) political secretaries are included, a third have more than twenty-five years of party membership. Just a little fewer have held public office at the local level and 10 percent have held office at the national level for more than twenty-five years. None had less than four years of party membership. Even if party work has become more specialized, the working of a Norwegian Cabinet cannot be understood if the integration provided by the common party background is overlooked.

Table 3.7: *Party background of ministers, under secretaries of state, and political secretaries in the Bratteli government, 1975 (percentages).*

Number of years	Membership in Labor Party	Party office at local level	Party office at national level
25 or more	33	27	10
10–24	42	46	31
6–9	16	12	9
5 or less	9	15	50

Note: Data are for forty-six government leaders.

Political indicators of a specialist-generalist orientation vary across ministries, as do social indicators such as vocational background, education, and connections with interest groups. When the parliamentary system was introduced, Norway broke away from recruiting ministers largely from the higher civil servants in the ministries. From 1814 to 1884,

84 percent of the ministers had reached the top after a regular bureaucratic career. In the post-World War II period only 31 percent were higher civil servants before they became ministers; another 18 percent held various white-collar jobs in public service; 19 percent were independent owners; and 18 percent were employees in the private sector. Of the latter group (twenty-three persons) eleven came from economic-producer organizations, four from other interest groups, and six from political parties. That is, employees from the rest of the private sector are virtually unrepresented. Not one person was a blue-collar worker when called to the king's table, because workers first become trade union or Labor Party employees or members of the Storting before they are appointed ministers. Only 3 percent of the ministers had been fishermen and 8 percent farmers.

The same trend is reflected in the educational background of the ministers. From 1814 to 1884, 86 percent of the ministers held a university degree; half were trained in law, one fourth had a military education, and 7 percent were theologians. In the post-World War II period, 57 percent have had a university degree. Law is still the most common discipline (22 percent), but both military and theological education have disappeared from the ranks, while 9 percent have held degrees in economics and 7 percent in agriculture. The tendency in the Cabinet is toward increasing variation in educational background.

As should be expected from the selection processes used, the distribution of social backgrounds across ministries is far from random. In the post-World War II period the Ministry of Justice has had ten ministers, all educated in law, eight of them with jobs related to the administration of justice. Furthermore, the nine ministers who have left office all went to work in this sector. Only one of the heads of the Ministry of Fisheries has held a university degree, but nine out of ten have been connected with the fisheries either by vocation or through an interest group, although only two of the nine returned to jobs related to fisheries. Six out of twelve heads of the Ministry of Agriculture have held a university degree, and five of them were in agriculture. Eleven had vocational or interest-group affiliation with the sector, and seven out of eleven went back to jobs in agriculture. Eleven of thirteen heads of the Ministry of Industry have held a university degree, seven of them in law. Seven have been affiliated with the sector through jobs or interest groups, and four out of eleven have gone back to the same sector. The lack of specialization is most clearly seen in the Ministry of Defense. No profession dominates, and of eleven ministers only three were affiliated with the sector and no one went back to jobs in that sector.

For some ministries patterns are hard to discern because there have been few ministers, and it is difficult to establish precise criteria for counting vocations and interest group affiliations as being within a sector.

The numbers should therefore be considered as illustrative of a more general pattern. It is likely that ministers will have specialized knowledge and affiliations, but there is also great variation across ministries.

The Cabinet is no longer a college of bureaucrats, firmly anchored in their ministries through a lifelong career. Still, ministers are not alien to the values and points of view dominating the ministries they lead. Through education and experience from agencies and interest groups close to the ministries, many of them are already indoctrinated before they sit down for the first time in the minister's chair. Their links to powerful outside groups are reinforced through frequent contacts.

Organized interests and agencies in their own sector are (together with the civil servants in their own ministry) among the partners ministers say it is most important to cultivate.[7] There are of course variations. Meetings with organized interests take more time for a minister of agriculture or a minister of fisheries than for a prime minister or a minister of finance. But in general ministers agree with a committee on the organization of the central administrative apparatus: Today government can in many cases reach its clientele only through interest groups (Innstilling om den sentrale forvaltnings organisasjon, 1970: 20).

The same specialization is seen in the contacts with the Storting. All the ministers in the Bratteli Cabinet (1975) report daily or weekly contacts with "their" committee in the Storting but interact less frequently with the others. In. fact, they never interact at all with most committees.

To summarize, ministers are heads of administrative units with a great potential to mold and discipline their civil servants. The administrative division of labor is reinforced through the civil servants' specialized external contacts. The ministers' ability to counteract administrative subcultures is not severely hampered by the shortness of their tenure. Ministers are not strangers to their ministries, and they do not stay long enough to be indoctrinated into the particular culture of the ministry. More likely they already possess the same values and viewpoints, which are reinforced through specialized contacts. The chances for a specialist orientation, with ministers identifying more with their roles as ministers than with their roles as Cabinet members, have increased because ministers are less often recruited from political generalist positions such as member of the Storting and mayor.

Growing functional differentiation and increased workloads have affected recruitment patterns and made it more difficult for ministers to assume leadership and to provide coordination across administrative sectors and levels. One remedy suggested has been to provide the minister with more politically appointed helpers. Another has been to fight fire with fire by introducing new types of civil servants.

Ambivalence toward political friends

When the Gerhardsen Cabinet took office in 1945 the question of strengthening the political leadership of the ministries was immediately raised. The task of rebuilding the country was overwhelming, and the number of civil servants had increased (table 3.2). In 1947 the first seven ministries added the position of under secretary of state. Today there are one or two in each ministry. This expansion has not been met with general enthusiasm. Some higher civil servants have opposed the idea that the highest tenured civil servant, the secretary general, should be subordinated to the under secretary of state. Increasing the number of political appointees is seen as confusing the lines of authority and responsibility, reducing the continuity in the work of the ministry, and making the positions of higher civil servants less interesting (Brinch, 1975; Evang, 1974a, 1974b; Innstilling om reglementer og instrukser for departementene, 1966; NOU 1974: 18; Archives in the Ministry of Justice).

Many of the arguments of the higher civil servants have been accepted by the nonsocialist parties in opposition. In 1947 they voted against introducing the position of under secretary of state, basing their stand on a bureaucratic interpretation of the ministries formulated by the Ministry of Justice. According to this view, the role of the Cabinet is to take care of the common interests of the people, not to achieve party political goals (Innst. S. nr. 147, 1947). Thirty years later nonsocialists, again in opposition, argued that an independent civil service could counteract a too powerful political leadership (St.forh., 1976–77: 3179–94). But in the meantime two nonsocialist Cabinets had increased the number of political appointees.

The arguments of the higher civil servants and the opposition may be interpreted as a struggle for power. The greater the number of political appointees in government, the easier for the political echelons to control the nonpolitical ones. This was the idea behind the Gerhardsen initiative. And the chairman of the Committee on Administration in the Storting thirty years later repeated that more politically appointed positions would strengthen political leadership against bureaucratic power (King, 1975a: 196–97; St.forh., 1976–77: 3179–94). But many do not accept this argument.

A Cabinet committee chaired by the minister of justice in 1961 had several reservations. To some degree the chairman accepted that the under secretary was a foreign element in the ministries, while the committee argued that the role had become too administrative and not political enough. Nearly half the under secretaries held an administrative background in the ministry to which they were appointed.[8]

More generally, ministers are somewhat ambivalent about inviting

97

more political friends to the ministries.[9] Of the members of the Bratteli Cabinet (1975), only one-third thought that the political leadership needed to be strengthened, while 63 percent of the under secretaries and 92 percent of the political secretaries held this opinion. Actually the number of ministers who think that more political appointees will increase leadership problems match the number who think that problems will be reduced (table 3.8). Those who want to increase the number of political appointees do not want dramatic changes in the organization of the political leadership of the ministries.[10]

Table 3.8: *Attitude of ministers, under secretaries of state, and political secretaries toward strengthening the political leadership of the ministries (percentages).*

| Respondent | Number | Political leadership should be strengthened | More politically appointed people will | | Reorganization will help solve problems[1] |
			help solve present problems	increase problems	
Ministers	15	33	27	27	53
Under secretaries of state	19	63	42	21	37
Personal or political secretaries	12	92	67	8	50

Note: Data are based on respondents' replies to this survey question: The wish to strengthen the political leadership of the ministries has been a central question for a long time. To what degree do you think there will be a need for a further strengthening in the future?

[1] Includes splitting up ministries, decentralizing certain decisions, changing salaries or selection procedures to recruit better people, defining tasks and rules better, and allowing the under secretaries of state to meet in the Cabinet.

A main argument among ministers against inviting in more politically appointed helpers is that the lines of authority become more ambiguous. Civil servants, the Storting, and the public may be confused about who are the responsible leaders. Coordination among the leaders may be difficult. Furthermore, civil servants may not as willingly volunteer their services if the most interesting decisions are given only to the political leaders. Finally, ministers know that they are political symbols. Representatives of communities and interest organizations want to meet the minister. If they do not achieve substantive results, at least they have taken the issue to the top. Such symbolic functions cannot be taken care of by others.

Variations in attitudes reflect variations in the ways under secretaries and political secretaries function. Some under secretaries work as the minister's equal in special fields. Others are clearly subordinated to the minister. Some political secretaries function like under secretaries. Others primarily help the minister organize his agenda and correspondence.

Variations in attitudes may also reflect ministers' unequal control of the selection of under secretaries and political secretaries. Ministers in the Bratteli Cabinet (1975) got nine under secretaries and five political secretaries they themselves asked for. They got respectively eight and five assistants they did not know. Some were informed that they would get a specific person. Others were allowed to pick from a list composed by the prime minister's office and the party office.

The selection process is not very different from the one used to recruit ministers. The prime minister and the top leaders in the party and in LO are important actors, and the party organization in different regions is activated. The higher the minister's position in the party or in LO, the more likely that he or she will be allowed to pick his or her helpers. But certain criteria have to be met. Regions should be represented; so should women, vocational and educational groups, and different factions of the party.

A minister does not get helpers he or she is strongly against, but political leaders have to be able to cooperate, and ministers may accept secretaries with whom they disagree on important issues. With few exceptions, however, disagreement is not a problem. The recruiting process does indicate that if the number of political appointees is increased, more heterogeneity may be introduced and problems of coordination may arise. In such situations it may be easier to achieve leadership through tenured civil servants than through political friends. At least, a few more political friends may not be worth the price of antagonizing higher civil servants.

Do under secretaries and political secretaries relieve ministers of some of their political overload? In intrasectoral work, yes; in intersectoral coordination, the political secretaries normally play a modest role. But under secretaries play a significant role in interdepartmental work. They have weekly meetings, and frequently important issues are turned over to committees of under secretaries. For example, over a two-year period a committee of nine under secretaries, headed by the under secretary of the Ministry of Finance, had thirty-five meetings before presenting a proposal to the Cabinet for a four-year program. Another example is that decisions on commissions to be appointed by the Cabinet have to go through a committee of under secretaries (Nordli, 1978; NOU 1973: 52:26).

There are no studies of the decision-making process of these committees, but in general there is no reason to believe that they operate very differently from committees of ministers. Through social background and patterns of communication, under secretaries and political secretaries are as firmly linked to groups and agencies in their own sector as are ministers. Thus, they are equally likely to identify with the institutions and tasks for which they are responsible. Is there, then, reason to believe that coordination problems between sectors and levels are relieved by the other type of ministerial helpers introduced since World War II – the planners?

Fighting fire with fire

As in most Western European countries, postwar planning in Norway meant economic planning and was partly initiated by the Organization for Economic Cooperation and Development (OECD). The first fifteen years after the war was the great period for economists and economic theory. In Norway economic planning was located inside the ministries. "The Labor Party wanted planning, but did not know how"; the economists offered a solution (Bergh, 1977; Bergh and Pharo, 1977). The result was a new philosophy of governance, a new administrative infrastructure with planning divisions, national budgets and long-term budgets, and many positions for economists. Planning was supposed to move the minister from a passive role as the final link in a long chain of bureaucratic decision makers, and to supplement the legalistic orientation of the Rechtsstaat with a goal and future-oriented policy making.

The heyday for economic theory and economists meant a central role for the Ministry of Finance. But during the late 1960s and the 1970s aspirations of hierarchical macroeconomic planning and governance based on financial criteria have become more problematic. Economic growth is no longer a generally accepted supergoal, and it is difficult to achieve. The Cabinet's program for 1978–1981 is more a political program than a traditional economic program.

Today there are planning units in all ministries and "planning" stands for many different things. For some it signifies the future use of financial resources. For others the management of natural resources is more important, or the concern with social welfare criteria, the effects on local government, foreign relations, and so on. The coordination of various planning centers has itself become an issue.

In many ways planners are different from the traditional rule-oriented civil servants. They are younger than other civil servants in the ministries and few are trained in law. Economics is the most common training, but several other professions are represented. Planners are more active in political parties, less constrained by rules, and seldom find similarities between their own role and that of the judge, like civil servants trained in law do. Planners perceive more conflict in their work than in other fields, especially conflicts between ministries, and they are change-oriented. At the same time, planners tend to leave the ministry more often than their colleagues with other functions (Lægreid and Olsen, 1978: 116–18, 309, 320). Strong pressures, however, make planners conform to established subcultures. This conclusion, based on questionnaire data, is consistent with the picture outlined by a veteran planner:

> Planning to a great extent must deal with the relationship of one's own system to the environment. But we have also learned that in doing this, planners must never form alliances with parts of the meta-system in order to fight their own system . . .
> I learned quite a lot about the conditions under which a new agency in charge of functions rather threatening to the rest of an organization can be subject to organizational immunity, isolating the agency and making it absolutely harmless. I also learned some of the rules of the game that will permit such units not only to survive, but to interact constructively with other parts of the organization (Eide, 1978: 18).

One interpretation is that (at least in the short run) adding political friends or friendly planners will not produce miracles or change an otherwise segmented structure. What has been described as governance by ministers conceals stable, functional coalitions of organized public and private interests. Given this structure, the resources gathered around the prime minister, and the types of persons filling the major roles, how likely is the Cabinet to take leadership?

The Cabinet: united team or sprawling fence posts?

In a small country such as Norway, half a hundred political appointees may be a significant political force, *if* they can pull together, and *if* they are able to concentrate on important issues instead of being immersed in details. The two conditions seem more difficult to fulfill in coalition Cabinets, with their demands for interparty management, than in one-party Cabinets.

When Borten turned the keys to the prime minister's office over to Bratteli, he stated that the leader of the Labor Party was lucky in being backed by a united party. To lead a coalition had been a difficult task, similar to carrying sprawling fence posts. Others have emphasized the long and dreary discussions in the Cabinet conferences that too often focussed on mere details (Brunvand, 1973: 73, 89; Lyng, 1978: 92–93, 106, 107; Solstad, 1969; Sørebø, 1971; Vassbotn, 1971).

The sprawling fence posts situation is usually explained by the fact that the coalition parties jealously protect their autonomy and by the lack of leadership shown by the prime minister. However, the difference between one-party and coalition Cabinets may be one of degree rather than of essence. Parties large enough to get a majority are themselves coalitions. As we have seen, there certainly are other structural bases for cleavages than political parties; consensus cannot be assumed by any Cabinet. Prime Minister Nordli points out that there often are strained situations in any Cabinet (Nordli, 1978); others say there are "free and lively discussions".

A major task of the Cabinet is to organize decision-making procedures in order to find politically acceptable solutions that "all in all can get the most support and that cause the least disappointment and feeling of defeat" (Nordli, 1978: 12). The Cabinet is an arena where political problems are discovered, clarified, and sometimes solved. Ministers test proposals and identify the important cleavages and the intensity of internal and external conflicts. Ministers get advice or moral support. What kind of resources does the Cabinet have to match the tasks of finding politically acceptable solutions in a segmented system?

The Cabinet as a college has few and weak constitutional powers and no planning capacity or administrative infrastructure of its own. The size of the Cabinet has increased, but the idea of establishing an inner Cabinet has received little attention or support. Dividing the Cabinet into an A and a B team "is not suitable for Norway" (Bloch, 1963: 164; Nordli, 1978: 12; Solumsmoen, 1962–63; Torgersen, 1948a). There are few, though some important, Cabinet committees, but they have become less rather than more crucial over the last two decades (Bloch, 1963: 112–24; Innstilling om den sentrale forvaltnings organisasjon, 1970).

The procedures of the Cabinet have been formalized since Gerhardsen inherited a seniority system. There was then no organized preparation of Cabinet meetings, and the minister with the longest tenure would present his or her issues first. The youngest minister sometimes had to leave without a chance to present even the most urgent and important issues. The system also made it difficult to find time for general political talks (Berggrav, 1978; Bloch, 1963; Gerhardsen, 1978: 84; Interview with former Prime Minister Einar Gerhardsen; Interviews with the Bratteli government, 1975).

Today a minister lists with the prime minister's office, at least one day before a Cabinet meeting, the issues he or she wants on the agenda, and a two-page note is circulated to the other ministers. The prime minister's office prepares the agenda and provides minutes of the meetings. The streamlining of Cabinet procedures has been most significant in budgetary decisions. Priority debates before the process and the use of quotas for ministries have considerably reduced the number of budget conferences and the time spent. Ministers view these changes as improvements. Decision making is less time consuming, and they feel better informed because a two-page note is read whereas voluminous reports are not. There is less of a chance of a minister's being surprised that a decision is made while he or she is away or of being unprepared when an issue is presented in the Cabinet.

Still, the formal setting of Cabinet meetings is less consequential than informal roles, rules, and communication patterns. A Cabinet has a culture, a set of norms and viewpoints that reflect problems of capacity, understanding, and authority and that also reflect the need to balance an inevitable division of labor with the necessity to coordinate and operate as a team. There is an agenda problem: Which of hundreds of thousands of decisions made in the name of the government should a Cabinet attend to? And there is a problem of procedure: If all ministers are allocated equal speaking time, the average time per minister would be approximately one minute per decision in an average Cabinet meeting.

A ground rule is to keep decisions out of the Cabinet. If that is impossible, one or more possible solutions should be found before the issue is presented at a Cabinet meeting. Ministers are supposed to clear a decision by briefing affected parties and eventually finding a compromise.[11]

If consulting and clearing processes are ignored or a compromise is not achieved, so that dissenting views must be aired in the Cabinet, conflicts may be resolved during the meeting. More likely, however, some other course of action is followed. The responsible minister may be asked to consider the points of view presented by the opponents and to return with a new solution. The ministers in conflict may be assigned to make a new attempt to find an acceptable compromise. A problem may be sent to an interdepartmental committee of under secretaries or civil servants, or to a Cabinet committee. More likely there will be an informal group including the minister concerned, the parties in discord, and one or two leading Cabinet members. Often they will include the prime minister, the minister of finance, or Cabinet members with a high position in the party. In some cases it may be obvious that an acceptable solution cannot be found, and the decision is postponed. As one minister argued, the Cabinet, like other decision-making units, has its boiling point. It senses when it is impossible to reach an agreement.

In case of conflict, the prime minister is expected to take initiatives and to act as arbitrator. But he is also expected to be unbiased, except in budgetary matters, where the prime minister sides with the minister of finance. Ministers may have a significant impact on a decision outside their own sphere of interest, if intervention occurs only once. If it happens often, intervention is highly disliked. Ministers do not approve of others meddling in their business. A minister's position is strengthened, however, if it is supported by the party program or a decision at the national conference of the party.

For several reasons intervention in decisions not affecting one's own ministry is infrequent. Time is scarce; so is goodwill, and ministers do not want to antagonize colleagues whose help they may need soon. Furthermore, few ministers have the surplus energy to familiarize themselves with issues outside their own field so that they can have a reasoned opinion. They may write letters while the minister concerned, others directly affected, and a few generalists debate. Ministers realize that they become specialists, somewhat removed from general politics (Tor Halvorsen, Arbeiderbladet (Oslo), July 30, 1979; Jens Haugland, Aftenposten (Oslo), September 11, 1979; Interviews, Bratteli Cabinet).

The result is an informal leadership group, based partly on formal position in the Cabinet and partly on position in the party hierarchy. Communications between Cabinet meetings, often by telephone, primarily reflect functional interdependencies. When asked with whom of their colleagues they most often had contact, a majority of the ministers in the Bratteli Cabinet (1975) answered the Prime Minister, the minister of finance, and the minister of local government and labor. The ministers of commerce and shipping, of fisheries, and of defense were mentioned most seldom. But the communications network is primarily characterized by clusters of contact among three or four ministers, the functional equivalent to nonexistent formal Cabinet committees.

The Constitution requests that the Cabinet, or rather the Council of State, be concerned with important matters. To the Cabinet, importance is defined politically. The sampling of issues is only partly a function of their substantive properties. Small issues sometimes have significant political effects. And if they threaten the unity of the coalition, cause problems in the news media, or are important for important people, they are attended to by the Cabinet, whatever their substantive properties.[12]

Ministers think the Cabinet is an important policy-making unit, and without doubt some crucial decisions are made there. More often, the Cabinet approves decisions made somewhere else, or the college of ministers gives direction to or constrains decisions to be made by other units. The Cabinet is a clearinghouse for information about what is politically possible; that is, what is preferred and what is acceptable in the ministries, parties, Storting, interest groups, and other countries, and among local and regional authorities, mass media, and the people in general.

At the same time it is not difficult to discern limitations on the coordinating capacity of the Cabinet. Lack of constitutional powers, of its own administrative resources, and of time and energy clearly reduces the

Cabinet's ability to take hierarchical leadership and to counteract the tendencies toward segmentation. It now remains to be seen whether the picture of a specialized and segmented structure is supported when we move from analyzing agencies, roles, rules, and actors to studying executive processes.

THE EXECUTIVE IN ACTION

Executives have long working days; they have gone from part time to full time to overtime. But what do they do when they govern? How do executive institutions work in practice; how are decisions made; and how great is executive authority and power? There is remarkably little academic literature on these subjects, in Norway as in most countries (King, 1975a: 113). Here attention is focussed on four themes: How does a Cabinet work in times of crisis? What is the importance and what are the limits of governing on the basis of a party platform? How do the most central actors themselves perceive the distribution of influence in public policy making? And what are the major forms of coordination used in executive decision making in Norway?

Cabinet crises and the importance of routines

The Bratteli Cabinet gave permission for a detailed time study of the forty-five ministers, under secretaries of state, and political secretaries during the week of December 9–16, 1974. The political appointees agreed to give a detailed account of who they met, who took the initiative, what the purpose was, and what the results were. The office secretaries also registered incoming telephones and letters. At the end of the week, a questionnaire was administered to all the political appointees. They were also interviewed for one and a half to two and a half hours. About one-third of the participants made available their calendars for the whole year (1974). Somewhat later another study was undertaken, in which the office secretaries registered those who tried to get in touch with the political appointees without an appointment.

When permission for the study was granted, no one knew that the week would be a special one, and that the Cabinet would have to face a major crisis in the Storting. The Bratteli Cabinet wanted to buy 25 percent of Canadian stock in an aluminum company, in order to achieve a 75 percent majority. Approximately two weeks before the debate it became clear that there was no majority for this proposal in the Storting. The Labor Party had no stable support from any other party. Together with sixteen left-wing socialists the Labor Party had 78 out of 155 votes. But the leftist socialists would not vote for the proposal. They wanted to buy all foreign stock in the aluminum industry within a few years. The nonsocialists found the transaction too costly and the terms not good enough for Norwegian interests.

When the debate started at 10 A.M. Friday, December 13, Bratteli made it clear that the Cabinet would resign if a majority voted against the proposals. When the Storting took a break at 3 P.M. a crisis seemed unavoidable. Speakers from all the major parties said they did not want a crisis, but a majority would not vote for the Cabinet's proposal.

When the meeting started at 6 P.M. the Center Party – to the surprise of Bratteli, as well as of other participants and observers – declared that they would provide subsidiary support to the Cabinet's proposal if their own proposal were defeated. A fundamentally new situation had come into existence (St.forh. 1974–75: 2135). When a vote was taken at 9:45 P.M., a majority of 86 to 69 voted for the Cabinet's proposal.

The crisis was averted through a unilateral decision in the Center Party, not through negotiations. In the Storting several speakers regretted that the opportunity for consultation had not been used.[13] The Prime Minister said that the decision had been comprehensive, important, and difficult for the Cabinet, but not for a moment had it occurred to him that it could produce a crisis (St.forh. 1974–75: 2118).

The feeling of a very special week was spread by the mass media. A close look at the behavior of ministers, under secretaries, and political secretaries gives a somewhat different picture, illustrating the importance of the political division of labor and of routines even in times of crisis.

For the Prime Minister and for the minister of industry the week was unusual because so much time was devoted to a single decision. The procedures and networks used, however, were standard. The Prime Minister and the minister of industry were in contact with each other and with the party faction in the Storting, with the party faction in the Committee on Industry, and with the chairmen of the party faction in the Storting and of the responsible committee. Furthermore, the issue was discussed in the party directorate. The under secretaries at the Prime Minister's office took an active part in the process. There were frequent contacts with the LO unions affected. The potential crisis was discussed in two Cabinet meetings.

The activity within these networks was hectic. The Prime Minister took political leadership, accompanied by the minister of industry. Both also had other things to do. The minister of industry at 6:50 A.M. the day before the debate had to comment on the radio on plans for developing new power plants. The Prime Minister took part in a TV program on torture. Most of their time, however, was focussed on the crisis.

The situation was quite different for the other ministers, the under secretaries, and the political secretaries. Most of their time was organized around commitments in their own sectors. Ministers took part in Cabinet conferences where the crisis was discussed, but the minister of finance was the only Cabinet member who joined the Prime Minister and the minister of industry in the debate in the Storting, where he talked about his specialty, the tax aspects of the deal. Other ministers and political appointees tried to attend the informal discussions in the Storting that week, but mostly they did not have the time.

Ministers were away in London, Brussels, Frankfurt, and Stockholm. The minister of fisheries spent most of the week with his Russian counterpart traveling in the western part of Norway. The minister of local government and labor was troubled by the threat of a strike. And the minister of agriculture used more time on issues such as the use of horsewhips at race tracks, the castrating of horses, sheep disease, the use of barbed wire, and policies on the future provision of food, than upon the crisis. In general, ministers and their political helpers were concerned, but their behavior was mostly directed by routine. For some, the crisis also receded into the background because of family events.

Of the forty-five political appointees, 3 percent described the week as quite normal, 27 percent as somewhat normal, 16 percent said both normal and abnormal, 35 percent said somewhat special, and 19 percent held the opinion that the week had been very special. About two-thirds of those who found the week abnormal mentioned the crisis. For some respondents private reasons – such as the birth of a child, the return of a spouse, or a car accident – were more important than the crisis. Others judged the week special because they had been away. More than half of those who mentioned the crisis also gave other reasons. Despite the fact that calendars were filled with appointments, only half a dozen meetings were canceled or postponed. These were all intraministerial meetings or meetings with political appointees in other ministries. In one case a meeting with a Danish under secretary of state was postponed, but because of problems in Denmark. The possibility that the Cabinet would resign caused only four deviations from the planned schedules, which seems a remarkably small number, even for a more normal period than the week studied.

The use of time is highly contextual. Substantial variation in attention stems from other demands on the participants' time rather than from the decision in focus (March and Olsen, 1976). Ministers are busy people. They meet with busy people, and routines provide viable solutions to a relatively complicated problem of coordinating time. This simple mechanism works because most of the duties and responsibilities of the ministers are sector-oriented, and ministers are solidly anchored in their sectors. The use of time in times of crisis is consistent with the view of a specialized and segmented structure. An alternative interpretation is that the ministers execute specialized programs in the party platform. The specialization may be part of a hierarchical structure, but the coordination takes place in party organs, not in the Cabinet.

Limits of governing through party platforms

Norwegian parties have few full-time positions at the national level,[14] and the influence of the party apparatus on the daily work of the Cabinet tends to be limited. It is the party faction in the Storting that arrives at a decision on unexpected issues (Gerhardsen, 1978: 10). A party's major impact is through its platform, and a great deal of energy is spent building one.

The introduction of published political score cards has made platforms more realistic, but parties share a dilemma with legislatures. They may specify general principles and goals, but intentions are often distorted during the implementation. Or they may specify operational goals, rules, programs, and deadlines, only to discover that the conditions and assumptions under which the platform was written have changed. The increasing complexity of modern welfare states makes it increasingly difficult to write a set of substantive rules that covers future conditions. Leadership assumes a fine balance between consistency over time, on the one hand, and, on the other, the ability to correct the course to allow for variations in the social, political, economic, or natural environment.

Students of politics have been most interested in the fact that legislatures and parties are often unable to specify operational substantive goals or rules; they specify only the framework for future decision making, and civil servants and organized interests fill in these frameworks. Members of the Bratteli government faced many difficulties because the party program was too specific.

During the Borten period the Labor Party was out of power for the first time in thirty years, with the exception of the four-week Lyng intermezzo. This caused hectic activity within the party. New programs were developed, in many cases with specified deadlines. Several future ministers, under secretaries, and political secretaries took part in the process. Later they had to tackle some problems that illustrate the limitations of governing through a well-specified party program. One minister commented:

> We [sometimes] run like a steam roller, independent of what is taking place around us. We implement policies that people have never been interested in and policies they have lost interest in. We are criticized for things we expected would give political credit. At the same time we are unable to react when new opportunities and problems come along because there is no surplus energy.

Others used different words, but many agreed that the platform had been too detailed. It had been too specific about what should be done, how it should be done, and when it should be done. The result was a lack of flexibility. "The party program should provide the Cabinet with working material and be a compass. Now it has become a straightjacket", another minister complained. "There is never adequate research behind each part of the platform. New aspects are discovered as the ministry starts working on an issue, but there is little we can do. We are afraid of not keeping our promises and of losing our trustworthiness."

Basically there was agreement that the party could never go back to winning an election on one single issue or one single slogan. But it was also agreed that in the future the program has to be less specific, taking the form of a manifesto and formulating principles without specifying the solution of a problem.

My interpretation of these experiences is that a party may take a stand on sample issues and have a crucial impact on the Cabinet's handling of these issues. But a party cannot specify substantive, conditional rules in enough fields to make the Cabinet an executive committee of the party. Specifically, that will not be possible when a Cabinet is supported by a minority party, which has to discover the politically possible through interaction with many other organized interests. The need to take other organized interests into consideration is clearly reflected in the perceptions of influence held by major participants in governmental processes.

The limits of hierarchy

A majority of the Norwegian people believe that the members of the Cabinet and the Storting are the most powerful participants in public policy-making processes (Aftenposten (Oslo), March 3, 1979). Those who participate directly in government perceive politically elected and appointed leaders as having a less heroic role.

Rokkan (1966: 106–7) argued that votes count in the choice of who will govern, but that other factors decide the actual policies pursued by the authorities. He maintained that the bargaining and consultation processes between government and organized labor, business, farm, and fishery interests have come to affect the lives of the rank and file more than the formal elections. The Cabinet, he wrote, has increasingly had to take on the role of mediator between conflicting interests.

I agree with Rokkan in many respects. But my interpretation suggests that civil servants are important participants, and that most of the bargaining and consultation between government and organized interests takes place at the ministerial, not the Cabinet, level. There are many bargaining tables and many policy-making arenas.

Table 3.9: *Perceptions of civil servants of the importance of agencies and groups in initiative, choice, and feedback processes in the respondents' own field.*

Agency or Group	Percentage of respondents ranking each authority or group as very or somewhat important		
	Initiative	Choice	Feedback
Own ministry...........................	69	96	69
Own national administrative agencies outside ministry........................	18	48	40
Own regional or local agencies	16	46	49
Other ministries and their subordinated agencies	17	59	38
Governmental boards and committees	15	46	27
Court system	1	0	11
Storting...............................	12	68	34
Cabinet...............................	16	75	30
Opposition parties	1	16	10
Regional and local authorities..............	7	33	28
Economic-producer interests	13	49	35
Other interest organizations	4	16	13
Citizens' initiatives	1	3	6
Mass media	3	18	33
Research and educational institutions	7	24	28
Firms, companies	5	13	14
Single persons representing themselves or their families......................	5	8	9
International governmental organizations....	9	15	16
Other countries	5	11	11
Total number of responses.................	768	764	757

Note: The questions asked for each process were:

Initiative: «When it comes to taking initiatives to new programs/policies in your work-field, how often are initiatives coming from each of the following authorities and groups?»

Choice: «Could you in general say how important the following authorities and groups are when important choices are made in your field? More specifically, will you indicate how important each of the following authorities/groups are?»

Feedback: «How do you keep yourself informed about the practical results of various programs/policies, that is, how important are each of the following authorities and groups when it comes to such information?»

For each question the respondents had five alternatives, ranging from very often or very important to very seldom or very unimportant.

Civil servants in the ministries differentiate among three kinds of influence: taking initiatives in their own field, making formal choices, and affecting interpretations of how programs and policies are working in practice. In all three respects their own ministry is perceived as important

110

by a majority of the respondents (table 3.9). The constitutional powers of the Storting and the Cabinet are viewed as influential in the formal choice process, but less significant in the feedback phase, and few civil servants think the constitutional powers are important when it comes to taking initiatives. In contrast to the significance attributed to the constitutional powers, economic – producer interests are thought to be important in all three phases, whereas the mass media are viewed as essentially reactive, interpreting new programs but not taking many initiatives.

This response pattern supports the notion of a specialized system more than the idea of a hierarchical system based on a parliamentary chain of command and responsibility. That specialization is most developed in the initiative phases, an important observation because most participants believe it is necessary to get into policy-making processes at an early stage in order to affect the end result.

The perceptions of the civil servants by and large coincide with those of another key group of participants, elected leaders and administrators in the economic organizations. They, too, view civil servants as important participants, and they view the ministries as highly influential in policy-making processes. What then are the perceptions of ministers, under secretaries, and political secretaries?

The ministers and their politically appointed helpers do not feel impotent, but they are aware of the limits of their powers. Time and energy is the constraint mentioned most often. Ministers know that they are responsible for thousands of decisions which they do not take part in or hear about. They know the limitations on their capabilities for taking initiatives. Ministers even perceive their roles as somewhat more reactive than under secretaries and political secretaries perceive theirs. Their descriptions of an ordinary working day are similar to those given by other organizational leaders. They have to respond to a steady stream of initiatives from others, to deadlines, and to the pressure of the moment. They act on options mostly framed by others (Cohen and March, 1974; Cyert and March, 1963; Glenn, 1975; Headey, 1974; Neustadt, 1976: 34, 223–24).

Ministers know that they need the cooperation of the civil servants, and that they need to release the energy potential of their administrative apparatus. The problem is not that civil servants obstruct ministerial effort but that they do not volunteer their initiatives and services. Ministers know that life becomes complicated when civil servants do not respond to the same signal given in different situations but demand specific orders in each case. At the same time, ministers know that civil servants need ministers who will sponsor their projects. If the minister is not willing to fight for them, success is very unlikely. Ministers are also aware that they are constrained by powerful, organized interests, by other administrative agencies and professions, and by properties of the economic system and of cultural traditions. Despite all these constraints, most ministers do not feel a gap between their influence and their responsibility.

One interpretation may be that ministers do not view civil servants and organized interest groups as opponents. Both politicians and civil servants perceive little conflict between politically appointed personnel and civil servants. In cases of confrontation ministers are likely to win (Lægreid and Olsen, 1978: 247). But most of the time there is no need for confrontations, and ministers know that they cannot afford to win many confrontations. Similarly, ministers and representatives of organized interests most of the time do not perceive each other as opponents. It is more likely that a minister will represent "his" interest groups to the rest of the Cabinet or to the minister of finance (Norbom, 1971).

Finally, ministers perceive their under secretaries and in some cases also their political secretaries as influential. While they are not eager to get more political appointees, they do not view the influence of their secretaries as problematic. Only in one case was there a confontation between a minister and an under secretary, with the result that the secretary had to leave.

Of the under secretaries, 84 percent view themselves as influential, compared with 33 percent of the political secretaries. Both groups describe their jobs in terms of interesting experiences rather than in terms of influence. Significant phrases are: "We know each other pretty well" and "I know how far I can go". In my interpretation these phrases are a key to the more general processes through which the politically acceptable is discovered or defined in Norway.

Anticipated reaction and "sounding out"

Styles of collective decision making vary from the formal aggregation of preferences explicitly expressed by a vote, through the synthesizing of preferences which are expressed only indirectly through social interaction, to autonomous adjustment where actors keep an eye on each other, anticipate possible actions and reactions, and take them into consideration when they make decisions. In a small and fairly transparent political system such as the Norwegian one, it is not surprising that anticipated reaction (Friedrich, 1937) is a major form of coordination. Implicit criteria filter out most alternatives. Only a small number are left for explicit consideration. A majority of ministers, under secretaries, and political secretaries report that in most cases they have a fairly clear picture of what is acceptable and how others will react. While under secretaries report surprises more often than the other appointees, they are usually surprised because of the strength of the reactions or because the debate is focussed on a specific detail in the proposal. The less time for consulting, the more often things turn out differently than executive leaders had expected. On the average it is easier to predict the reaction of others than the long-term substantive effects of new programs and policies.

Civil servants agree. Less than 10 percent of all the civil servants in the ministries report that it is very or somewhat difficult to know the goals and intentions of political leaders in their ministry; to know which decisions to present to the minister; to know which issues will attract a public debate and which positions different groups will take in such a debate; or to predict the effects of new programs. More people (20 percent) say it is very or somewhat difficult to be sure what the substantive effects really have been (Bratbak and Olsen, 1980).

The difference between the Norwegian and an international decision-making system is commented on by a director general in one of the ministries (Eide, 1978: 16): "I discovered that my mastery of Norwegian research policy consisted of knowing exactly what reactions to expect from professor X and doctor Y, from institution A and agency B. In an international context such experience was without value, as nobody knew the individuals or agencies involved." If actors do not know what is politically possible, they know how to find out. They use a lot of energy to find acceptable solutions through careful discussions, adjustments, and negotiations, as a foreigner has observed (Eckstein, 1966: 159). A lot of work and willingness to compromise is needed in order to pull a decision to shore. A prime minister indicated that before presenting a proposal to the Storting, he has to have a reasonable feeling about what can be accepted (Nordli, 1978: 19). And an under secretary argued that if there were more consultation than there is today, nothing would ever be done.

A major commandment in executive policy making is: Do not announce a position; do not commit yourself at an early stage. Instead a sounding out process is used (Olsen, 1972; Thompson and McEwan, 1958). Participants in the first phase try to reveal the direction of their thinking and preferences and attempt to move the final outcome toward the most highly valued end result, but they avoid specific indications of preferences and beliefs. They retain counterarguments and some degree of ambiguity, contradiction, or openness in their statements. The final outcome is a result of more and more participants accepting a certain solution as the best, while other choices fade away. The support for the chosen solution may vary from enthusiasm to abstention from obstruction. If it is difficult to establish unanimity, the participants avoid clear, stable, and joint arenas for the decision-making process. The choice is moved from joint meetings to discussions in smaller groups.

The process is quite different from planning procedures that first establish operational goals and then search for the best way to achieve them. Goals are formed as a part of the decision-making process and in close interaction with the development of alternatives and with the registration of political support.

Ministers describe Cabinet decision making as a process in which "agreement crystallizes" or "we talk ourselves into agreement". First, the responsible minister gives an orientation, then the others cautiously feel their way in order to register the different standpoints and divisions (Berggrav, 1978: 6–7; Bloch, 1963: 74; Solstad, 1969: 155). The prime minister may draw a conclusion, most often that an alternative is acceptable. He may argue that the decision has to be cleared with the party faction in the Storting, a committee, or the party directorate; or the responsible or affected minister may be asked to take a new look (Berggrav, 1978:4).

Thus, the prime minister frequently intervenes in the procedure. In case of conflict his word is important, but even then he tries to have the responsible minister announce the agreement (Bloch, 1963: 24; Interview, Bratteli Cabinet). The same type of "talking ourselves into agreement" is used with the rest of the governing environment. Before positions are announced and become a matter of prestige, the Storting, the party faction, the responsible committee, or a representative from a district particularly affected will be informed and consulted. So will important, affected interest groups. One result is that the formal aspects of the decision-making processes, such as voting procedures, become less interesting.

Sounding out and consultation are certainly not the only forms of interaction and coordination in executive decision making in Norway, but they are important and not well understood. Some substantive benefits may be lost as a result of compromises, and sounding out is a time-consuming process. Using a large amount of time on a single choice means relinquishing time from other activities and decisions. Executive leaders also lose the ability to act quickly and to adapt to a rapidly changing environment. Why, then, does a potential majority sometimes not establish a minimum winning coalition, but instead uses a great deal of energy to establish general acceptance?

A decision process is not only a means of choosing between substantive alternatives and of economizing on time and energy, but also a legitimizing procedure. Sounding out is used when executive leaders are afraid of pyrrhic triumphs. It is used when the negative effects of the losses of legitimacy, loyalty, cohesion, friendship, and trust are more important than the potential benefits of substantive programs and time saved. It may also be used to express and develop goodwill and trust.

Sounding out will be most common in systems in which resources and sanctions are spread out among the participants. The smaller the decision-making system, and the more closely knit the decision makers are, the more likely that sounding out will be important. That is often the case in policy-making processes within a segment and a sector. The less certain the substantive effects of new programs, the more important it is to avoid uncertainty through negotiated environments.

MONTESQUIEU REVISITED

The Norwegian case suggests that when the executives' environment is dominated by a complex network of interdependent and interpenetrated formal organizations, we need supplements to models that assume monolithic (hierarchical) or anarchic (open) structures. In an anarchic or unsegmented structure any participant can take part in any choice. Executive leadership changes continuously, as an informal, shifting aggregation of key individuals or as a shifting network of issues or coalitions. Issue or candidate enthusiasts take control (Campbell and Szablowski, 1979; Heclo, 1978: 375, King, 1975a; 375: March and Olsen, 1976; Neustadt, 1969). An unsegmented, highly situational leadership is based on weakly developed political institutions and division of labor. There are many sources of authority and power, changing goals, and shifting cleavages and coalitions. Planning is weak, and almost any opportunity for choice may become a garbage can that gathers participants, problems, and solutions (Cohen et al., 1972; March and Olsen, 1976). Leaders are those who are interested in choices and have the time and energy to spend. Choices are defined by the problems and solutions activated at the time. Unsegmented structures complicate political calculations and decrease predictability. Those charged with formal governmental leadership are under considerable strain and may come to play a ceremonial role loosely linked with substantive policy making.

In a monolithic or hierarchical structure policy makers and choices are arranged in a stable hierarchy so that important choices must be made by important policy makers and important policy makers can participate in any choice. In such a structure the prime minister is the superstar; alternatively, the Cabinet or some external unit (the legislature, party, or interest group) operates as the apex of the hierarchy. Standard answers to problems of capacity, understanding, and authority are to expand the prime minister's office or some other central agency and to introduce more politically appointed personnel as well as more analytical staff. An inner Cabinet or a hierarchical committee structure is developed. Command or confrontation are the major forms of coordination.

Today, executives are more often in a bargaining situation both within the governmental apparatus and with organized interests in society, and the main tendency is toward specialization. The major response to the problems of capacity, understanding, and authority has been a political-administrative division of labor. And administrative sectorization has increased because the various ministries, departments, and divisions have developed specialized external patterns of contacts and support. The result is a segmented structure with stable, nonhierarchical functional coalitions.

In a purely specialized or segmented structure, each executive leader is associated with a single class of choices, each class having a single group of policy makers. Leaders specialize in the choices to which they attend, and the coordination of them is relatively weak. Ministers are recruited from the relevant sectors and professions. The prime minister's office is poorly developed. There is no inner Cabinet or hierarchical system of Cabinet committees. Political staffs are developed around each minister. Sectoral planning agencies are more important than analytical staffs directly related to the prime minister's office. Expertise is sector-defined, not general. There are few attempts to coordinate goals or to provide comprehensive analytical theories. Executive leaders operate under parochial perceptions and priorities. They are spokesmen for the institutions and the tasks for which they are responsible. They are accountable to specialized constituencies rather than to the head of the government.

Specialization in an executive system may be combined with a hierarchical organization within sectors. But more often specialization arises in a negotiated environment in which a minister's independence from a single coordinating center is based on support from organized interests in his own sector. Executive leaders avoid uncertainty and negotiate authority through a series of tacit understandings and contracts with organized groups in society as well as with civil servants. Such functional coalitions may encompass all levels from local to international. Consultation and anticipated reactions are more important forms of coordination than command. The role differentiation between politically appointed leaders and civil servants and between public and private groups is blurred.

The main tendency in Norway is toward specialization and segmentation. Still, there are counterforces. The surge in citizens' initiatives in the last part of the 1960s and the early 1970s introduced elements of unsegmented leadership. But generally their immediate impact on central processes of governance seems modest (table 3.9).

A more significant counterforce has been attempts at hierarchical coordination and leadership by political parties, by the Cabinet, and by the Ministry of Finance. The elements of hierarchy and central planning were probably strongest during the 1950s. Since then the Labor Party has lost its majority in the Storting and has probably become more heterogeneous and less centralized. There is no longer any obvious party leader, and a change of generations is taking place among the top leaders. Economic growth is no longer a generally accepted goal, there

116

are fewer slack resources, and the adequacy of economic theories and economic planning is questioned. Organized interests have become integrated into government, but they have preferred participation at the ministerial – not the Cabinet – level. Civil servants have obtained increased participatory rights, and usually they defend specific institutions and parochial interests.

The tendency toward specialization and segmentation and the tendency toward consensus and anticipated reactions partly counteract each other. The system is probably more segmented in its behavior patterns than in the substantive premises that enter into policy-making processes. The two tendencies may also be related to features of Norway affecting the generalizability of this study.

Norway is a small country where political actors often know each other personally. In the post-World War II period the country has changed from being comparatively poor to comparatively rich. Until recently this process has provided a fair amount of slack resources. Class cooperation in the service of economic growth has been more prevalent than class conflict. Political, economic, and cultural life is highly dependent on the trends in other countries, primarily Western societies. At the same time, egalitarianism is emphasized, and differences between people and the open use of power are much disliked (Bergh and Pharo, 1977; Torgersen, 1968).

It may be that a homogeneous, unsegmented society is a condition for a segmented state. The fewer the major cleavages, the easier it is to accept a division of labor that allows those most interested to make the decisions. At the same time, the smaller and more homogeneous the society, the easier it is to develop a consensual policy-making style and to use anticipated reaction as a major form of coordination. The more efficiently coordination through anticipated reactions works, the easier it is to exploit the benefits of specialization and segmentation.

It remains to be seen how closely the consensual, specialized style is related to a slack resource situation, nationally as well as internationally, and whether it will work only as long as policy making is incremental and focussed on distributing new resources. One guess is that when slack is reduced, Norway's well-organized and "responsible" parties and organized interest groups will make it more likely that a segmented system will move more toward hierarchy than toward anarchy – at least in the short run.

It may also be that a segmented system is related to the substance of major policies. The more selective the benefits and the constraints of public policies, the more likely that intensive minorities will demand special attention or participation. The idea of one center of authority and power, and one chain of accountability, is related to the making of general policies that have an impact on society as a whole (Egeberg,

117

1981; Schattschneider, 1935; Wolin, 1960). Thus, if the government reduces the use of selective incentives and constraints, as it did in Norway in 1979, it may make hierarchical decision making more likely.

It is most likely, however, that major aspects of the segmented state will survive through pragmatic adaptations to local problems. The metaphor of a segmented state is thus an alternative to the classical, Montesquieu-inspired interpretation of Western democracies. Montesquieu's suggestion was to separate legislative, executive, and judicial powers. In the segmented state, powers are also separated, but contacts and cleavages do not follow the institutions Montesquieu trusted. Instead they cut across these institutions. The government is separated into functional, nonhierarchical coalitions, a fact reflected in executive institutions, their personnel, and their operation.

Notes

* This chapter is a slightly revised version of an article which first appeared in Richard Rose and Ezra Suleiman (eds.), Presidents and Prime Ministers (Washington, D.C.: American Enterprise Institute, 1980). The chapter has benefited from the advice, comments, and help from several friends and colleagues. I want to thank Richard Rose and Ezra Suleiman, and the other participants in the Ross Priory Conference on Organizing Political Leadership, and Berit Bratbak, Morten Egeberg, Per Lægreid, James G. March, Paul G. Roness, Harald Sætren, Reidun Tvedt, and Mariann Vågenes for their help and support.

[1] Prime Minister Nordli resigned in February 1979 due to health problems and a difficult political situation. Norway, then, got its first female prime minister, Gro Harlem Brundtland (Labor); who was replaced by Kåre Willoch (Conservatives) in October, after the general election. There have also been some changes in the ministries (Roness, 1981), and in recruitment patterns (Bratbak, 1981a). These modifications do not, however, change the main conclusions drawn in this chapter.

[2] The argument here is based on interviews with all the ministers, under secretaries of state, and political secretaries of the Bratteli government (1975). During the fall of 1978 the five former prime ministers still alive were invited to Bergen to give lectures on their experiences. All accepted, and they also commented on Cabinet work in more informal talks. Later they were interviewed – some for several hours, others more briefly. The Minister of the Law of the Seas, Jens Evensen, had a special mission and was not head of a ministry; he was excluded from this study, and so was his under secretary of state.

[3] Other persons may be called in, especially in budget matters. The Borten Cabinet introduced a new routine in 1970 whereby under secretaries of state met regularly as alternates in the absence of their ministers. This practice was not continued by the Korvald Cabinet or the Labor Party Cabinets (NOU 1974: 18: 16).

[4] The coordinating committee meets for one hour every Monday. Since 1965 these meetings are alternately led by the party chairman and the chairman of LO. The meetings are advisory only. A division of labor and of responsibilities is recognized, and the party, LO, and the prime minister are all on guard against violations of their autonomy (according to an interview with Trygve Bratteli, who has been a member of the committee since 1945).

[5] Prime ministers disagree among themselves about the administrative adequacy of the prime minister's office. For instance, Bratteli finds the present capacity adequate, while

Korvald would like to strengthen the politically appointed staff, but not the group of tenured civil servants. Korvald would also like to have an under secretary of state who could follow the budgetary procedures in the Ministry of Finance and eventually in other ministries (interviews).

[6] Einar Gerhardsen, Trygve Bratteli, Konrad Nordahl (chairman of LO), Haakon Lie (secretary general of the party), and Halvard Lange (minister of foreign affairs) were all members of the party directorate from 1946 to 1965. The stability of the leadership, along with the fact that the party in most of the period had a majority in the Storting, provoked the comment that the Cabinet had become an executive committee of the party and that Norway had become a one-party state (Seip, 1963; Tingsten, 1966).

[7] This section is based primarily on interviews with ministers in the Bratteli Cabinet (1975) and upon data about their use of time.

[8] "Tilråding fra utvalget til å drøfte statssekretærordningen", 1961. In addition, a leading member of the Labor Party and the president of the Storting were members of a committee that defined the role of the under secretary in a fairly restricted way. The committee wanted further to constrain the activities of the political secretary so that he should be merely assistant to the minister, not a second under secretary (NOU 1974: 18).

[9] This description is based on interviews with, and questionnaires to the Bratteli government (1975). The same trend is found in NOU 1974: 18: 59–64, where ministers and under secretaries from various governments comment on their experiences with, or as, under secretaries. Among the prime ministers interviewed by the author, one stated that he was happy each time a minister did not want an under secretary. Another prime minister argued that there should never be more than one under secretary in a ministry, and that political secretaries should be appointed only if there were a definite need and the right person could be found.

[10] One minister, however, claimed that the political organization around the minister is quite amateurish. And a former minister of finance has argued that the leadership in the major ministries is very weakly developed (Norbom, 1971: 36).

[11] Again, the description is based primarily on interviews with the Bratteli Cabinet (1975), but it is generally consistent with the points of view presented by others (Berggrav, 1978; Bloch, 1963: 25–26, 85, 88–89; Innstilling om den sentrale forvaltnings organisasjon, 1970: 45; Korvald, 1978; Larssen, 1973: 141; Lyng, 1973, 1978; Nygaardsvold, 1947: 227).

[12] A former minister of finance has complained about the unnecessary amount of detail in discussions in both the Cabinet and the Storting. Other ministers sometimes demand that he decide on such issues as the allocation of office space (Norbom, 1971).

[13] Especially former Prime Minister Korvald (Stortingsforhandlinger 1974–1975: 2115–2116). One week before the debate took place the Prime Minister had informed the faction leaders of the Center Party and the Christian People's Party about the decision to resign (Stortingsforhandlinger: 2152). The leader of the Labor Party faction in the Committee on Industry had talked with two of the leaders of the leftist socialists, but one of them regretted that the Prime Minister had not made contact (Stortingsforhandlinger 1974–1975: 2143, 2152). Although there had been consultations between the leftist socialists and parts of the Labor Party faction, the pattern of consultation has to be seen in the light of their competition for the votes of the workers, as well as the competition between factions within each party. The incident is described by one of the participants (Gustavsen, 1979).

[14] The Labor Party reports nine full-time employees, two of them elected, at the national level. In addition, there are nine in the youth organization, one in the women's secretariat, and forty full-time positions in the party's educational organization. The other parties have fewer employees, except the Conservatives who report 125 full-time positions, regional offices included, plus twelve positions in the youth, women's, and educational organizations (Moren et al., 1976).

4

TOP CIVIL SERVANTS – KEY PLAYERS ON DIFFERENT TEAMS*

TOP CIVIL SERVANTS AS LEADERS OF ORGANIZATIONS

Max Weber considered bureaucratization the most significant feature of the modern western state, and he predicted a continuing spread of bureaucratic administration. Fully developed, that would mean an office hierarchy, with the means of administration concentrated in the hands of one master – a social structure very hard to destroy (Gerth and Mills, 1970: 221, 228, 232).

There are, however, many interpretations of how a modern administrative apparatus works. Some locate power to the political institutions, assuming that top civil servants are responsible to and totally subordinated to Parliament or the Cabinet. Others emphasize social power, viewing civil servants (as well as elected politicians) as the instruments of a ruling class, powerful organized interest groups, the mass media, or of impersonal technological, economic, demographic, or cultural forces. For smaller countries especially, such forces are often located outside national boundaries.

An alternative emphasizes bureaucratic immunity from political and social intervention. If power is located in the administrative apparatus itself, top civil servants may act as a unitary elite, as leaders of petty kingdoms with considerable autonomy, or as rivals in permanent conflicts over administrative territory and jurisdiction. Power may also disseminate to the lower ranks of the hierarchies. Top civil servants, like elected politicians, may be overwhelmed by the expanding public agenda; and depend on their subordinates' willingness to cooperate. The more comprehensive and complex the public agenda, the more expertise, information and real decision making power accrue to the lower echelons of the central administration, or to local and regional units that implement central decisions.

We believe each of these perspectives captures some aspect of the public policy making process and of the role of top civil servants. Their perceptions, attitudes, behavior and influence emerge from rather complex intra- and interorganizational processes which cannot be adequately captured by concepts of total autonomy or subordination.

Today, top civil servants are leaders of formal organizations operating in an environment primarily populated by other organizations. We are interested in how their thinking and behavior are influenced by the organizations they head, by the environment they face, and by their social background. Furthermore, we consider how these factors affect their ability to form and give direction to their organizations and to society. We need to understand which resources top civil servants have of their own, as well as the extent to which they are backed by a nesting of reserve sources of authority and power (Stinchcombe, 1968: 158–160).

By "top civil servants" we mean the top administrative positions in the ministries: Secretary General, Director General, and Assistant Director General. In 1978 these amounted to 126 persons (table 4.1). Together with Deputy Directors General and Heads of Division (492 persons) they constitute the "administrators". The term "civil servants" also includes executive officers in the ministries (grade 19–25). Civil servants outside the ministries are only included under certain circumstances. The same applies to the political leadership of the ministries.

Table 4.1: *Central government employees by service group and salary grade. Full time employees 1978.*

Salary grade	Ministries	Other central administrative agencies	Other civil service	Universities and the like	Governmental enterprises	Defense	Health services	Total
1–14	590	2 817	12 541	3 516	39 327	11 652	4 358	74 801
15–18	431	1 702	9 385	2 490	12 519	4 609	1 524	32 660
19–25	1 102	3 600	8 205	4 241	3 790	6 579	1 308	28 825
26–30	492	844	795	1 118	354	468	396	4 967
31–35	126	79	169	19	22	42	63	520
Total	2 741	9 042	31 095	11 884	56 012	23 350	7 649	141 773

Source: Wage and employment statistics for central government employees. Central Bureau of Statistics, Oslo. NOS B 32.

While we observe some tendencies which are inconsistent with Weber's prediction of a universal bureaucratization, he provided a framework for studying actual administrative development. Particularly useful is his treatment of how the thinking, behavior, and influence of civil servants is affected by *the organization of careers, expertise and authority.*

First, we consider the degree to which careers of civil servants – recruitment, promotion, and departures – are controlled from within the administrative apparatus or by groups or forces in the political or social system. Secondly, we analyze the extent to which top civil servants monopolize expertise and information, whether secrecy is an available resource, and which factors affect their beliefs and attitudes. Finally, we analyze the role of authority. To what extent is everyday-life of top civil servants governed by an impersonal and legitimate order of authority – shared understandings of the rights to command and the duty to obey? Or, does the concept of interest coalitions better portray how top civil servants relate to each other, to their subordinates, to politicians, clients, and to other social groups?

To provide a perspective for this discussion, we give a brief account of the roots of the present system.

THE ROOTS: A CIVIL SERVANTS' STATE PAR EXCELLENCE

The events in 1814, when the Danish-Norwegian union was dissolved, a new Norwegian state was founded, and a Swedish-Norwegian union established, all in a matter of months, remind us how a small nation is subject to events beyond its control – in this case the defeat of Napoleon. At the same time they illustrate the robustness of an administrative system in the face of external turbulence. The civil service continued to function – bolstered by its deep roots in the Danish-Norwegian absolute monarchy. Norway was a typical civil servants' state for two hundred years – from 1680 to 1880, probably more so than any other state in Europe. The historian Sverre Steen (1958: 168), aptly describes this by stating that prior to 1814, the civil servants governed the country in the name of the King. After 1814 the same men governed in the name of the people (also Benum, 1979; Maurseth, 1979; Seip, 1974; Sejersted, 1979).

The position of Norwegian civil servants during the first half of the 18th century is typified by their irremovability and protected careers, their professional qualities, their unity and the absence of competing political and socio-economic elites.

The king and his court were far away in Stockholm. There was little or no nobility. The bourgeoisie was weakly developed. Norway was primarily a nation of small-holders. In other words, the social elites that dominated most other countries in Europe did not challenge the hegemony of civil servants in Norway. Potential rivals also lacked adequate political organization. Organized political activity and campaigning was prohibited by law in 1828. There were few interest organizations, and the prevailing ideology was that special interests were disqualified from participation in public policy-making.

The Cabinet was generally an integrated part of a civil service career (table 4.2), and the civil servants dominated the Storting (parliament). The Constitution of 1814 was their creation, and they wrote into it extensive protection for the civil service. The risk of losing office was slight indeed. The recruitment process was virtually closed, and civil servants developed a life style quite different from that of the nation they governed. They were closely knit by a common Danish-European culture; by a common higher education – primarily in law; by the Latin language; by a considerable professional self confidence; and by extensive intermarriage. Their ideology came close to what Weber later labelled an ideal bureaucracy operating under legal-rational authority. The main task of civil servants was seen as the implementation of enacted rules – to find the proper solution and to guard the public interest, unhampered by arbitrary outside pressure. The role model was the objective and impartial judge, and their primary loyalty was towards an impersonal system of laws.

Table 4.2: *Ministers, 1814–1978, by occupational background and time periods. Percentages.*

	1814–1884	1884–1920	1920–1945	1945–1978	Total
Occupational background:					
(Public) administrators	84	58	31	31	48
Other public employees	1	11	16	18	12
Private employees	0	1	7	18	4
Business/liberal professions	13	21	27	19	20
Farmers.....................	1	9	18	8	9
Manual workers, fishermen, others......................	0	0	1	6	3
Numbers	(70)	(114)	(77)	(129)	(390)

Source: The Norwegian Social Science Data Services.

The political environment has since changed considerably. There has been a general tendency towards political mobilization and reduced political illiteracy, as well as cycles of dispersion and concentration of political power. In periods of power concentration, political authorities gather initiative and responsibility in their own hands. They emphasize that the role of civil servants is to be reliable instruments for the exercise of political power. In periods of power dispersion, initiative and responsibility are spread. Civil servants are encouraged to be active and independent (Jacobsen, 1964, also 1966).[1] Such cycles are related to the level of political conflict in society. In periods of little conflict the administrative apparatus routinely handles problems in a predictable and

– for the governing coalition – acceptable way. Imbalances between administrative routines and the demands/interests of leading political and social groups, tend to set off demands for political power concentration. Then the criteria for recruiting to the civil service are discussed. The definition of expertise and the relevance of various types of knowledge are debated, and attempts are made to reallocate formal authority.

The interplay between political mobilization and the growth of the public sector has a long history. From the 1840's new services, new professions, new agencies, and new clientele relations were introduced – often in conflict with the established bureaucratic tradition. Thus, the increased number of civil servants and the growing indispensability of their services did not automatically increase their power. The main tendency was towards a more heterogeneous civil service – an administrative apparatus where internal conflicts could occur. And they did. Conflicts between "bureaucrats" or generalists – trained in law and located in the ministries, and specialists trained in various disciplines and often located in new agencies outside the ministries, illustrate the classical conflict between the needs for hierarchical coordination and technical sector expertise.

The traditional rule-orientation was challenged by an increased interest in the consequences of administrative intervention. More often than before expertise and information were located at the lower levels of the hierarchy. Top civil servants had difficulties comprehending and controlling the activities of their subordinates. Rules of competence and authority became more vague and open. In sum, an expanding public agenda moved real decision making downward in the administrative hierarchy (Benum, 1979; Debes, 1961).

This expansion took place alongside demands for participation in public policy making from groups that discovered that the state could be used for material or professional development. As subjects became citizens, the old bureaucratic rule that any group with a special interest in a decision is disqualified, was challenged. Gradually it was replaced by the idea that democracy would benefit from the participation of those affected by public policies (Olsen, 1978).

The result is that the administrative apparatus consists of layers of agencies established to deal with problems in terms of specific values, goals, and technologies. The original intentions are reflected in the recruitment patterns, in the definitions of expertise, and in the distribution of authority, which are often institutionalized and internalized. A consequence is a reduced ability to learn and adapt. It is difficult to transform an agency even when situations change and the consequences of established routines are quite different from what was intended or expected. It is even harder to dissolve an agency, and it is nearly impossible to discontinue functions and services. In Norway the standard procedure has been to move tasks and offices around (Roness, 1979). Professions, political and social groups who have occupied a niche are difficult to drive out.

Consequently the analysis of the impact of intra- and inter-organizational networks on the thinking and behavior of top civil servants should be supplemented by an archeological perspective. Structures, procedures, and rules are formed by their "time of birth" and specific historical context (Stinchcombe, 1965; Østerud, 1979).

After World War II there was a restoration of the civil service to considerable prestige and influence, and a willingness to spread authority, initiative and responsibility (Highley et al., 1975; Jacobsen, 1968). This trend rested on a fairly widespread political consensus; the country had to be rebuilt, and it could best be achieved through economic growth and class cooperation. Organized interests, and especially the economic-producer groups, became integrated in governmental policy making (chapter 5). At the same time there were new aspirations for planning and governance (Bergh and Pharo, 1977; Bull, 1979; Haugen, 1979). These aspirations originated from the Labor Party, out of office for only seven years between 1935 and 1981, and from the economics profession. Planning agencies were set up in the ministries, and the economists emerged as the new generalists of the civil service. "We could not get enough of them," a former prime minister, minister of finance and chairman of the Labor Party once said (Bratteli, 1979).

Political consensus and cooperation contributed to a steady economic growth and to slack resources. Throughout the "confident 60's" (Bull 1979), responses to new problems often involved establishing new institutions. Lately the growth has leveled off – in spite of oil money from the North Sea. Labor Party majority governments have been succeeded by minority or coalition Cabinets. The merits of economic growth are questioned, and the confidence in economic theory and macro planning as the major instrument of governance is reduced. More organized interests demand participation, and a rising level of education increases the political capabilities of the average citizen. We want to indicate the bearings of these changes on the functioning of higher civil servants by going into more detail about the organization of careers, expertise, and authority.

ORGANIZATION OF CAREERS

Theories of bureaucracy describe promotions as a major mechanism of motivation and control. The disciplining effect will be the most effective if: employees see their lives as organized into a life-long career – a succession of promotions; superiors have promotions to allocate; subordinates want to be promoted; there is a close connection between promotion and previous performance; and subordinates are aware of such connections (Stinchcombe, 1974: ch. 5). If objective criteria of merit exist, the appointing authorities will be bookkeepers of necessity. If there are no such set standards, we need to know who defines merit and who judges individual merit. These theories are highly relevant because the careers of higher civil servants in Norway deviate little from those in the Weberian ideal bureaucracy.

A dominant norm is recruitment based on merit – traditionally university achievement. Except for the diplomatic corps, the civil service does not provide special education or examinations. Only 6 percent of the administrators in the ministries have no university degree. For top civil servants a degree is required (with a few exceptions) by law.[2] Training in law has dominated: in 1884 95 percent of administrators held a law degree, the figure for 1914 was 67 percent, and 52 percent for 1976. 21 percent of ministry administrators hold a degree in economics. The rest is trained in agriculture, philology, science, social science, medicine, or they have military training. Thus, while the lawyers is still the largest group, the trend is towards professional differentiation. This tendency is even stronger in the central agencies outside the ministries. Here engineers dominate, with 41 percent of those with a university degree. The role of jurists is proportionally reduced.

A result of the close ties between recruitment and university degrees is a civil service highly unrepresentative of the population as a whole. The pattern is well known – an overrepresentation of males born in the geographical center and in higher social strata.[3] Yet, the emphasis on merit has not produced a civil service like the one Weber expected – detached anonymous bureaucrats isolated from political life. On the average, civil servants engage more in political parties, interest organizations, and other activities than does the population. Can such civil servants be disciplined through career control? If so, by whom?

Potential for discipline

Norwegian ministers have a great *potential* for discipline through promotions. The main pattern is recruitment of young people to the bottom of the hierarchy, of which a majority expects to pursue a career within the ministry. Of the top civil servants (1976), 44 percent had been recruited before the age of 30. Only 8 percent were 46 years or older, and the average recruitment age was 32 years. 61 percent started at the junior executive level. Among the top civil servants who resigned in the period 1970–74, 81 percent had been employed in the ministries for more than 20 years.

The organizational form of the ministries, in terms of the number of positions at various hierarchical levels, is also pertinent to the career potential w.r.t. internal promotions. Inter-ministerial mobility is low. In the period 1970–74 only 7 percent of the civil servants moved from one ministry to another. However, such moves seem more common among administrators. 55 percent of the top civil servants appointed in this period were recruited from their own ministry, while 24 percent came from other ministries, among which the Ministry of Finance is an important supplier. The rest came from central government agencies outside the ministries or other civil services. Horizontal (outside) recruitment to top positions is rather rare, and usually occur from proximate state institutions. 90 percent of the civil servants in the ministries have lived in the capital for most of their occupational career. In general, the mobility between the public and the private sector is insignificant. The interaction between top civil servants and organized interests in society has not resulted in personnel mobility and cooptation.[4] Civil servants do not want to move, or outside job offers are few (table 4.3).

Table 4.3: *Indicators of the potential for disciplination and socialization in the ministries.*

(a) Number of executive officers/heads of division	2.2
(b) Number of heads of division and deputy directors/secretaries general and directors general	3.7
(c) Top civil servants recruited from outside (1970–74)	11 percent
(d) Average service as administrators (for those who left the ministries 1970–74)	8 years
(e) Average no. of years till retirement for top civil servants	12 »
(f) Plan/wish to leave the ministries:	
– top civil servants	6 percent
– other administrators	21 »
– executives	30 »
(g) Job offers from outside last year:	
– top civil servants	21 »
– other administrators	25 »
– executives	25 »
(h) Job offers received *and* plan/wish to leave:	
– top civil servants	2 »
– other administrators	8 »
– executives	10 »
(i) Average time of service, civil servants	13 years
(j) Percentage of civil servants with 10 years or more of service	49 percent
(k) Average time between promotions (1970–74)	4 years
(l) Number of veterans/newcomers 1970–74	6
(m) Replacement of new personnel (personnel recruited 1970–74) who left within three years in percentage of average intake of personnel during a three year period	47 percent

The result is that civil servants realistically perceive their career opportunities as better inside than outside the ministries, and better in the public than in the private sector. In the ministries civil servants are frequently rewarded, and the system of stepwise promotions makes the road to the top long and time consuming. Hence people occupy top positions for fairly short periods of time, a fact that further increases the disciplining potential.

The potential for discipline is high. It is used to reward insiders. But do civil servants want to be promoted? The folklore is that promotions are less attractive than before because leaders are subjected to more constraints and stress. So far, however, there is little data supporting this argument, and we assume that promotions still are attractive. Do civil servants then see any connection between performance and promotion? Who or what controls the process of promotions?

Recruitment is based on written applications and interviews. The formal procedure is that administrators are appointed by the Cabinet after nomination by the minister, who is advised by the top civil servants. Executives are appointed by the minister after nomination by a board where the employees have two representatives (an arrangement that has been in operation since World War II). Decisions may be appealed to the Storting. This happens very seldom and almost never with any success. The Storting has defined its role as controlling the adherence to formal rules (Lægreid, 1980).

This reflects a tradition of decentralized control over recruitment, which the ministries have fought fiercely to retain since 1814 (Maurseth, 1979: 241–243, 397). For a long time, only low level positions were publicly advertised, and public announcement of top positions was written into the rules as late as 1953. Yet the trend has been towards open competition for more positions.

At all levels disagreement is focussed on the question of external or internal recruitment. Initial recruitment is based primarily on university exams. At the executive level promotions primarily follow internal seniority. At higher levels, job performance is important, together with the superiors' knowledge of and evaluation of personal style, i.e. ability to cooperate, loyalty, and decisiveness. There is a tendency to take political affiliations into account when choosing between several well qualified candidates. Party politics does not disqualify for top positions, and some key positions have been occupied by active members of the governing party (Lægreid, 1980). Party background cannot, however, compensate for lack of formal education and administrative experience, and the Labor Party has not used its long period in power to fill the ministries with party members. Even today the Labor Party is stronger in the population than in the ministries (Lægreid and Olsen, 1978).[5] This is partly due to the fact that the employment authorities' choice of applicants for departmental positions is very limited.

The participants in the recruitment process report that the immediate superior has considerable influence. Division heads are the most important when hiring executives, and directors general are central in the appointments of division heads and deputy directors general. The influence of the political leadership is primarily related to top level appointments. Still, ministers seldom deviate from the nominations by top civil servants, and outsiders rarely have any influence, despite frequent demands for a part in the process (Lægreid, 1980; Tønnesson, 1965).

In sum, the recruitment process takes place within a framework of strong norms based on the merit principle, as traditionally defined by the ministries themselves, and disallowing political promotions and intervention by special interests. These norms make arbitrary intervention by political leaders or organized interests illegitimate, and violations are very likely to result in criticism from the opposition in the Storting and from the mass media.

Attempts to change the system have met with little success. Some top positions outside the ministries have been made non-tenured, but almost all incumbents have stayed as long as they wanted.

Likewise, efforts to weaken the constitutional protection of top civil servants, so that discharges would not require legal proceedings, have all failed (Eckhoff, 1976; Lægreid and Olsen, 1978). The same has been true for challenges to other rights and for efforts to change the recruitment pattern in general.

The 1945 joint program of all political parties explicitly stated as a high priority goal that the civil service should recruit more from the private sector, and also that the mobility between local and central agencies and between various sectors of the state be increased. As with many other attempts to change the recruitment patterns, these statements have had few effects. The changes that have occurred have been related to the establishment of new agencies and new functions. The most important has been the gradual weakening of the hegemony of people trained in law, and the inflow of economists and other professions, especially to the planning units. Changes in the social composition of the civil service have been influenced more by changed recruitment to higher education than by changes in the recruitment policies of the ministries.

During the past few years the political demands for a more representative civil service in terms of social class, sex, geography, education and vocational experience, have grown stronger. So far, the demand for more women in the civil service has received the most attention, but it is still too early to infer a general change in recruitment practices.

If theories of bureaucratic motivation are correct, the disciplining potential of the Norwegian system should be considerable, but difficult to manipulate. The effect would be greatest for newcomers, least so for top civil servants approaching retirement and with pension rights secured. The thinking and behavior of senior civil servants might be better

129

understood as a product of socialization than of the disciplining effects of expected promotions. While the Weberian theory focusses on behavioral control, and a separation of personal beliefs, values, and bureaucratic behavior, a theory of socialization must focus on attitude formation and the internalization of the prevailing values in a ministry.

Potential for socialization

Theories of bureaucratic socialization are less developed than theories of discipline, but it seems likely· that Norwegian ministries have a strong potential for socialization as well as for disciplination. The average time of service is long. Even in periods of growth, the ratio of veterans to newcomers has been fairly high, and the average tenure considerable. There is an ejection effect. Nearly half of the appointees leave before they have served three years.[6] While there are many reasons for this, those who leave are not representative of those who stay. Both in terms of attitudes and behavior they deviate in various ways. In the long run this process will generate a more homogenous civil service.[7]

The more important the socialization process, the more important it is to understand how ministerial ethics and conception of events diffuse and are internalized. The more important the disciplination processes, the more important it is to understand how civil servants evaluate costs and benefits of behavioral alternatives. Presently we only conclude that Norwegian top civil servants reach the top after going through several filters of both socialization and disciplination.

We draw three conclusions. *First,* in spite of extensive changes in the environment, civil servants have been able to retain their historical rights, written into the 1814 constitution. This protection against arbitrary intervention from politicians and organized interests, provide a basis of autonomy for the civil service.

Secondly, a result of the present system is that the behavior of top civil servants is fairly predictable. They are unlikely to introduce measures that deviate strongly from established ministerial norms. Consequently, they are likely to be predictable coalition partners, and those who share their values and beliefs may be willing to grant considerable autonomy to the civil servants.

Thirdly, a decentralized recruiting procedure with strong mechanisms of socialization and disciplination should produce a heterogeneous civil service in terms of knowledge, attitudes, and "models of the world".

ORGANIZATION OF KNOWLEDGE AND BELIEFS

Bureaucracy essentially means domination through knowledge. Those who want to control a bureaucracy need both authority and knowledge. The autonomy of the bureaucracy increases with a monopolization of technical knowledge gained through formal education and training, and of practical knowledge growing out of experience in the service (Weber, 1968: 228). The bureaucratic influence also increases with the ability to keep secret their intentions and knowledge.

Monopoly on knowledge?

For Weber the only challenge to the bureaucrats' monopoly on expert knowledge came from private economic interests, which are superior to the bureaucracy in matters of business (Gerth and Mills, 1970: 235). Today the situation is different. The expanding public agenda – with more interventions in the everyday life of citizens and a variety of services – has broadened the competence base of the bureaucracy. This is reflected in the number of professions attracted to the ministries. At the same time, organized interests have also strengthened their base of competence. They have established own bureaucracies of a size and professional level that match those of the ministries (Moren et al., 1976). Institutions of research and higher education also have relevant expertise, and they are increasingly involved in public policy making. The same is true for the mass media, for private firms, and even citizens' initiatives sometimes mobilize expertise of considerable magnitude (Olsen and Sætren, 1980a). For most professions, less than 1 percent of the graduates are employed in the ministries. Hence there is always a potential for "counter expertise". Furthermore, Norwegian bureaucrats are frequently confronted with international expertise, from other countries as well as international organizations.

Civil servants in Norway have extensive education, long training, and considerable expertise. But they do not have a monopoly on knowledge. They are comparatively stronger in terms of practical knowledge gained from experience in the service. Long careers, most often within one sector, give specialized knowledge, but seldom a monopoly. Nearly half of the civil servants in the ministries report that they depend on knowledge and expertise from the outside (Bratbak and Olsen, 1980; Innstilling om den sentrale forvaltnings organisasjon, 1970).

The configurations of expertise vary across policy fields. In certain sectors ministerial staffs are well developed, in other sectors not. The same is true for external groups. Also, in some issue areas (e.g. morals, abortion) expertise is less relevant than in others (e.g. economics, healthcare). The importance of expertise as a power base depends on the unity of various expert groups – the degree to which they fight or cooperate. It also depends on the degree to which civil servants are able to keep their knowledge secret.

Secrecy

In 1848 the Cabinet refused to increase the openness of the administrative process because it would make the process slow and more expensive, and because the bureaucracy more often would have to defend and explain its decisions. This argument was based on the view that the role of the bureaucracy was to implement laws and rules given by the Storting without intervention from the outside. "Publicity would reduce the independence which a correct procedure demands" (Lorentzen, 1978: 7).

This view has frequently been challenged, and an important chapter of Norwegian administrative history is the struggle between ministry jurists and the mass media about what constitutes a reasonable level of openness. Still, the media have focussed more on the parliamentary arena than on the administrative process. It was not until 1970 that Norway got a law on publicity in administrative affairs, giving the public better access to the administrative process. The Storting stated that while there would have to be exceptions to the general rule on publicity, these should be restricted to a minimum.

Empirical research also indicates that civil servants more often than before give information on their own initiative; that information is provided earlier in the process; and that civil servants refuse less frequently to give information to the media (Lorentzen, 1978: 124–126). Still the media behavior of the civil servants in the ministries differs from that of other elites. It is generally characterized by a willingness to give information when approached by the media, but a reluctance to take the initiative (Bratbak and Olsen, 1980).

The demand for public information is reflected in a recent wave of criticism against "the bureaucracy" for being inhuman, inefficient, overcentralized, high handed, and arrogant (Kjellberg et al., 1980; St. meld. nr. 75, 1976–77: 84), and a demand for less use of the classified-stamp – especially in military and foreign affairs.[8] The perceived need to provide such information is illustrated by a surge of public relations positions and agencies in the ministries, and in an increasing number of ombudsmen. A much less frequent political strategy has been leakages from the civil service.

In sum, the use of secrecy is still a relevant aspect of the political-administrative process, but its importance seems less than assumed by the Weberian theory of bureaucracy. Civil servants in Norway have been better able to protect and control their careers than to keep their monopoly on expertise and information, and to keep their knowledge secret. They have also been less able to maintain *unity*.

Bureaucratic unity – and some sources of differentiation

What are the normative views of top civil servants? How do they perceive the world and their work? What do they agree/disagree about and which factors form their models of the world?

The ideal Weberian bureaucrat is rational, objective, and disciplined, and such norms are still strong in Norwegian ministries. Civil servants emphasize their professional authority and independence. They claim they will forward a proposal they think is professionally right even if they know that their superiors are against it. They say that official channels of authority and information should be followed, and they are strongly opposed to leakages to the public. There are norms of moderation of political participation. Civil servants should participate in political processes, but they should avoid job related issues. The higher the respondents' position, the more restrictive the view on political participation.[9]

Among civil servants there is a high level of satisfaction with the way the administrative apparatus operates. Civil servants perceive themselves as initiators, but their orientation is definitely incrementalistic (chapter 3). Their attitudes are illustrated by their response to how major problems in their own field should be dealt with. Very few want major changes in political, economic or social relations in Norway or abroad, and they rely heavily on solving problems by means of more information and better knowledge. Few believe that problems can be solved by reducing the level of governmental intervention and transferring decisions to the private sector (table 4.4). Civil servants are also satisfied with the present structure of participation and representation in administrative decision making. They seldom want to include new groups, and when they do want changes, it is to increase the participation of organized interests already present. Likewise they are satisfied with the way various interests – especially organized groups – are treated by the administration.

The main tendencies are clear, but there are variations in perceptions, attitudes, and values. Typically, these variations can be explained by role-related factors like formal position, type of function, institutional belonging, external networks of contact, and profession. As should be expected from the strong potential of socialization and disciplining in the ministries, the social biography – with the exception of educational background (but including party affiliation) is of little or moderate importance in explaining variations in the civil servants' models of the world.[10]

The defense of traditional bureaucratic values and the level of satisfaction is strongest among those most integrated in the ministries, i.e. with high positions and long tenure, and those who belong to traditional ministerial professions and who have traditional functions. Conversely, those of lower position and short tenure give less support to bureaucratic values. They are less satisfied, and they are more change oriented. The same is true for those who belong to professions that are either new or small in the ministries, and for those who work with comparatively new functions like planning and public relations. This general pattern can be illustrated by an analysis of the civil servants' perceptions of their own roles.

Table 4.4: *Perceptions of problem solving instruments among civil servants (percentages).*

Instruments:	Top civil servants	Other administrators	Executives	Total
More information and knowledge	93	84	78	82
Strengthening the public apparatus (more money, people)	66	51	47	51
Reorganization of the administrative apparatus.....................	46	36	30	34
Strengthening international cooperation	45	28	31	31
Extensive changes in political, economic and social relations in Norway	11	10	13	12
Extensive changes in international political, economic and social relations.......................	13	11	13	12
Transferring tasks to the private sector	6	4	4	4
Number of respondents	(80)	(285)	(396)	(761)
Number of non-respondents	(2)	(7)	(14)	(23)

Note: Data based on the respondents' replies to the following survey question: «When considering the most important problems in your own field, how do you judge the following instruments for confronting these problems?» (Respondents were given the list above).

Role perceptions

In the Norwegian bureaucratic culture the role of civil servant has traditionally been compared to that of judge (Innstilling fra Komitéen til å utrede spørsmålet om mer betryggende former i den offentlige forvaltning, 1958). This conception is still strong. More than half of the top civil servants and 37 percent of all the civil servants in the ministries see a resemblance between their own job and the role of a judge (table 4.5). This similarity is linked to the fact that a ministry is the highest bureaucratic authority – the top of a hierarchical chain of command and appeal. Traditionally a ministry has also been the highest professional authority, and this function is reflected by the fact that 40 percent find similarities between their own job and the role of a scientist. Interestingly, this sense of expertise varies little between hierarchical levels.

The role conceptions of the civil servants reflect a shift from organizational forms based on hierarchical command and professional expertise to forms relying on bargaining and persuasion. "Negotiator"/ "mediator" is the role mentioned most often, and negotiations and persuasion is an aspect of the job of nearly all top civil servants, and of 40 percent of the executives (table 4.5). Likewise, more top civil servants find a resemblance with the role of company manager than with the role of judge.

The element of bargaining and persuasion does not make top civil servants see similarities between their own job and the role of party politician or representative of an interest group. The distance to party politicians is emphasized the most. And only "accountant" is ranked below the "representative of an interest organization".

Table 4.5: *Role perceptions of civil servants in the ministries (percentages).*

Role as:	Top civil servants	Other administrators	Executives	Total
Judge	54	44	30	37
Scientist	44	43	36	40
Negotiator/mediator	89	65	40	54
Company manager	81	51	15	35
Accountant	5	10	15	12
Party politician	9	7	5	6
Representative of interest organization	26	13	13	14
Number of respondents	(80)	(286)	(390)	(756)
Number of non-respondents	(2)	(6)	(20)	(28)

Note: Data are based on the respondents' replies to the following survey question: «A list of occupations is presented below. We would like to know – for each of them – if they, in your opinion, have anything in common with your present position?»

Resemblance between one's own job and the role of a judge is related to training in law and to functions which traditionally have been occupied by jurists – the preparation and implementation of laws and rules. At the same time, this view is related to contacts with persons who only represent themselves or their nearest family, rather than with representatives of organized interests or institutions (table 4.6). When civil servants confront organized interests which can forcefully back up their views, it is often not enough to find the appropriate rule or the right professional solution. It becomes necessary to balance various views and interests and to find compromises.

Table 4.6: *Perceived resemblance between own position and the role of a judge; by the civil servants' education, function and contact with individuals*[a] *(percentages).*

3. Education	Not trained in law				Trained in law			
2. Main function	All others[b]		Making laws/ rules, or single decisions		All others		Making laws/ rules, or single decisions	
1. Contact with individuals	Seldom/ never	Often	Seldom/ never	Often	Seldom/ never	Often	Seldom/ never	Often
Percentage who sees resemblance with the role of the judge	13	20	27	53	61	76	79	80
Number of respondents	(209)	(75)	(55)	(30)	(57)	(42)	(66)	(81)

E^1: 12 percent, E^2: 16 percent, E^3: 46 percent.

Note: [a] Individuals here refer to people who represent only themselves or their nearest family, and not an organized interest or an institution.
  [b] The list of «other functions» is found in table 4.7.

The same tendency can be seen in the analysis of the role as negotiator/ mediator. This resemblance is mentioned most often by top civil servants, those in contact with economic-producer organizations, those whose major function is coordination, and those who work in the two ministries with the most contacts with other countries – the ministry of Foreign Affairs and the ministry of Commerce. There is also a weak tendency related to the respondent's sex – females see a resemblance with the negotiator/mediator less often than men, even when we control for all other factors.

Two major reasons exist for finding resemblance between one's own job and the roles most strongly repudiated, party politician and interest group representative. One is having a position that ties the civil servant into a network of contacts with various political institutions at the national level. The other is related to the civil servants' own political activity. This factor matters most to young people in executive positions with job offers from outside and not committed to a life long career in the ministry.

Also, people trained in law generally find fewer similarities with these roles than others.

The roles of higher civil servants are complex, but the analysis illustrates a simple point. While social background is important in determining who is recruited to the ministries, it has little effect on values, attitudes, and perceptions. In Norway, unlike some other countries (Mayntz, 1981; Putnam, 1973), there does not seem to be a generation gap in the civil servants' view of the world. Age is not an important factor, and has little explanatory power when controlling for other characteristics. On the other hand, tasks, professional background, position, institutional connection, and the task environment, are important sources of *differentiation*. Norwegian civil servants are not likely to agree on which values, beliefs, and clients to defend. They have more in common in terms of philosophy of governance – a definite incrementalistic style.

The analysis is also consistent with an "archeological perspective". The defense of bureaucratic values is strongest in the profession, the task groups, and the institutions established during the 19th century. People trained in law usually adhere to bureaucratic norms. The same is true for those whose work primarily is rule implementation, i.e. the application of rules to individual cases. Their opposites are those who primarily have planning functions. The institutional stronghold of bureaucratic values is the Ministry of Justice, while the Ministry of the Environment (established in 1972) more frequently deviates from bureaucratic norms. Finally, bureaucratic values and beliefs flourish where there is a clear difference in power between civil servants and their clients. The more densely populated a ministry's environment is by organized interests, the less likely traditional bureaucratic values are to thrive. We will now show that the same is true for bureaucratic authority and processes of coordination.

ORGANIZATION OF AUTHORITY AND INTERESTS

The idea of a legal-rational authority and a shared understanding of a normative order is useful to gain insights into how top civil servants relate to each other, to subordinates, politicians, clients and others. But we also have to take account of the constellation of material and ideal interests within which they act, bargaining relations and coalitions formed. Recent empirical studies describe the administrative apparatus as a conglomerate of semi-feudal, loosely allied organizations with a substantial life of their own. Agencies are acting on the basis of different perspectives, information, and resources. They compete for influence, resources, and prestige. They defend their domains and jurisdictions and enlist allies. Their rivalries are major obstacles to coordination and joint policy making – attempts at coordination are often seen as unwanted intervention (Allison, 1971; Mayntz and Scharpf, 1975; Peabody and Rourke, 1965; Suleiman, 1974).

What, then, do Norwegian civil servants actually do, how and with whom do they interact? The largest group is still those performing a classical bureaucratic function – the application of rules to individual cases that affect a single person, firm or institution, or a limited group of such entities.[11] The second largest is engaged in planning. While coordination is an important task for top civil servants, rule application is central even at the top. Likewise, junior civil servants fairly often engage in planning, They are not restricted to routine activities (table 4.7).

Table 4.7: *Main functions of the civil servants (percentages).*

Main functions:	Top civil servants	Other administrators	Executives	Total
Personnel administration	15	13	11	12
Budgetting	1	8	6	6
Preparing laws/rules	10	13	8	10
Planning	18	22	19	20
Rule application (Single decisions)	21	25	31	28
Control	1	3	8	5
Coordination	27	6	6	8
Public relations/information	0	5	6	5
Other	7	5	6	6
Number of respondents	(73)	(265)	(384)	(722)
Number of non-respondents	(9)	(27)	(26)	(62)

Note: Data are based on the respondents' replies to the following questions. First: «Approximately how much of your working time did you spend last year on each of the functions listed below?» (The list was presented.) Then: «Into which of the categories mentioned would most of your work fall?» The table presents responses to the last question.

There are, however, differences in work style. The proportion spending most of their time at their desks decreases from 46 percent of the executives to 6 percent of top civil servants. Along the same line, 45 percent of the top civil servants, compared to 9 percent of the executives, spend most of their time in meetings. The pattern reflects a stepwise decision making procedure, as assumed by theories of bureaucracy, but the process does not end with a decision by a single top civil servant. Instead, the result of the bureaucratic stepwise procedure is presented in meetings, where a decision is (sometimes) taken.

Two thirds of the civil servants in the ministries report to have participated in intra- or interministerial task forces in the last year. Among top civil servants ¾ have participated. The share is smallest among those with typically "bureaucratic" functions – rule application or control. Top civil servants are even more active on committees and boards where organized interests also participate. 88 percent of the top civil servants report membership of at least one such committee, compared to 40 percent among executives. Such activity may counteract the tendencies towards specialization. Committee members, however, are often more concerned with promoting the interests of their own institutions than with cross-sectorial evaluation. Committee work may thus result in a "negative" coordination, where members are better at defending their institutions against external influence than at promoting their own ideas and premises (Mayntz and Scharpf, 1975).

In general, the bureaucrats have extensive patterns of contacts. The closest connections exist between divisions in a ministry (table 4.8). There is more extensive contacts with other administrative organs than with the political leadership. As regards organized interests, there are well developed relationships with economic organizations. Civil servants have three times as much contact with these as with other types of organizations; as much as with municipal authorities. It should be noted that contacts with the Storting are few, and even less so with citizens' initiatives.

There need not, however, be a singular relation between contact frequency and importance. Some groups may be taken account of by anticipated reaction. Top civil servants may, for instance, keep informed about Storting debates without direct contacts (Mayntz, 1980).

Top civil servants take care of a traditional leadership function – transactions with the environment and especially with the decision making centers (table 4.8). But with an expanding public agenda, transactions with the environment are spreading down the hierarchy. At the same time, most top civil servants meet with their ministers daily, alone or in small groups. They report that they are quite able to anticipate which issues the ministers will be interested in, and what solutions they prefer. Ministers agree with this evaluation (chapter 3; Bratbak and Olsen, 1980: 109). Relations between top civil servants and ministers are most of the time characterized by trust and cooperation.

Contact patterns are *specialized*, i.e. civil servants usually interact with *one* committee in the Storting, a small number of administrative agencies, interest groups in their own sector etc. Variations in contacts are even greater than variations in attitudes and beliefs related to the top civil servant's formal position, profession, function, and institutional belonging. Such variations are connected weakly, or not at all, to the social background – including party affiliation – of the individual civil servant.

Table 4.8: *The contact patterns of civil servants (percentages of weekly contact with various groups or institutions).*

Weekly contact with:	Top civil servants	Other administrators	Executives	Total	Number not responding
Storting and its organs	4	2	1	2	5
Individual members of the Storting	13	2	1	2	13
Minister, undersecretary in own ministry	80	44	9	30	7
Other departments in own ministry	94	78	68	74	12
Central agencies under the ministry	66	40	38	42	100
Local, regional agencies under the ministry	36	44	39	41	69
Other ministries	57	47	33	41	0
Local, regional agencies under other ministries	10	8	7	8	54
Local and regional authorities	15	20	16	17	47
International agencies, other countries	22	13	8	11	2
Economic-producer organizations	35	22	11	18	24
Other organized interests	9	8	4	6	42
Citizens' initiatives	0	–	1	1	17
Individuals acting on behalf of themselves or nearest family . . .	25	25	18	21	16

Note: The high number of non-respondents for central agencies and local/regional agencies under own ministry reflects that some ministries have few such agencies. Non-respondents are otherwise likely not to have contacts, so that the actual percentages with contacts are lower than indicated.

–: less than .5%.

As a result, the role of top civil servants as bureaucrats is more important than their political role. Forceful ministry norms differentiate between administrative work and political activity. The majority of civil servants do not favor political engagement in own field. Those with central ministerial positions are the most willing to restrict political activity. Also, the Constitution states that civil servants in the ministries may not be elected to the Storting. Civil servants are not, however, excluded from political activity. More than ⅓ of top civil servants hold or have held party office, and 14% have been nominated for election, primarily for local elections (table 4.9).

Civil servants also hold jobs in the political leadership of the ministries. Much of the political staff has public service experience. One third of the

Cabinet ministers have been public administrators (table 4.2), as have more than half of the undersecretaries. Many, however, do not come from central government.

Table 4.9: *Political activity among civil servants in the ministries (percentages).*

Activity:	Top civil servants	Other administrators	Executives	Total
Party representative (present)	13	13	9	11
Party representative (former)	23	10	12	13
Nominated for public election (former)......................	14	18	12	14
Number of respondents.............	(80)	(288)	(40Ⅰ)	(770)
Number of non-respondents.........	(1)	(4)	(9)	(14)

Ministers are largely dependent on the civil service for assistance and support, and such cooperation is normally smooth. The relations between civil servants and their political leadership are perceived as very peaceful. Generally, civil servants are inclined to see harmony in their own field (Lægreid and Olsen, 1978: 151–161). Those who report disagreements most often mention conflicts between the ministry and its clients, usually related to disagreements among groups of clients.

To some degree external contacts are a source of conflicts. Civil servants do not perceive Norwegian society as totally homogeneous. Their views of the level of conflict and of major cleavages coincide with those of other elites and the population in general; focussing on economic organization and allocation, regional conflicts and conflicts related to meritocracy.

The views of the civil servants deviate little from other descriptions of elite interaction in Norway (Highley et al., 1975). The major tendency has been cooperation and a mutually satisfactory division of labor, rather than conflicts and jurisdictional strife. Policy making has been characterized by attempts to have one's views accepted as premises for decision-making and to achieve as broad acceptance as possible. This is reflected in the coordination process. Internal as well as external transactions differ from those assumed by standard theories of bureaucracy.

Only ⅓ of the civil servants say their daily activities are determined by rules or established procedure. The proportion varies only moderately across hierarchical levels. While people lower in the hierarchy are less programmed than assumed by theories of bureaucracy, top civil servants

141

are constrained by rules, codes, and agreements reached through interaction with representatives of other organized interests. Still, programming through rules is primarily related to classical bureaucratic functions like control, accounting, rule application on single decisions; to a low level of conflict in the work field; and to contact with the ministry's own regional and local agencies.

The use of another classical bureaucratic means of control, direct corrections – for example, superiors making substantive changes in the recommendations by their subordinates – is even less common. Only 10 percent say it happens regularly, and generally these respondents have a low degree of integration in the ministries.[12]

Moderate use of hierarchical control like rules and direct corrections would be expected in organizations with a high potential for socialization and disciplination. Our data also indicate that socialization may be more important than disciplination. Only 7 percent of the civil servants report that they often have to prepare or to implement decisions with which they personally disagree. Such tensions between behavior and preferences are primarily related to conflicts with the minister, and to plans for leaving the ministry.

The response pattern also indicates that civil servants do not see ministerial policies as products of external pressure or constraints. They are able to retain their autonomy, and also relatively successful in getting their proposals accepted by external groups. They perceive the most success in their dealings with constitutional bodies and the least with groups directly affected by policies and public opinion.

More than ⅔ of the civil servants feel that their ministry has succeeded well in having its views accepted in the Storting, the Cabinet, or the implementing agencies, while 50% have the same view of success with public opinion. Top civil servants consider the penetration force of their divisions with all groups greater than do other administrators and executives.

The perceived success does not reflect a bureaucratic power monopoly. Other groups also report satisfaction with the processes. In a study of employees of economic-producer organizations, only 10 percent state that their organization has been unsuccessful in having its view accepted by public authorities. 6 percent say there is little consistency between what the organization proposed and what public authorities have done, and 15 percent claim that members of their organization have benefited less than the average citizen. A similar study of elected officials in economic-producer organizations show the same pattern (respectively 15, 13 and 22 percent). And in a national survey only 9 percent of the population say that public policies run contrary to their organizations. 14

percent say people in their community have received less benefits from society than average, and the respondents are generally satisfied with the distribution of influence in Norway (NOU 1982: 3).

The level of acceptance may be related to the fact that Norway is a small and fairly homogeneous country, as well as to the policy making institutions. As more and more discretion has been transferred to the ministries, organized interests have tried to influence that discretion. During the last decades the bureaucratic demand for "distance" from affected groups has been replaced by a norm of participation by such groups in policy making processes. The main participants in this channel are top civil servants, representatives of organized interests, and experts from institutions of research and higher learning. Elected politicians participate only rarely (chapter 5; Christensen and Egeberg, 1979; Egeberg, 1981; Kvavik, 1976; Rokkan, 1966).

As a result the borderline between the private and the public sector has become less clear, and hierarchical command based on formal authority or expertise has become less prevalent as a form of coordination.

Internally in a ministry the relevance of hierarchical authority and command is reduced because of strong socializing mechanisms. Such coordination is harder because the professional qualifications of subordinates often match those of their superiors; and because stronger interest organizations among civil servants and increased employee participation is weakening the hierarchy and changing leadership roles. Employee consciousness has increased, and participation rights are expanding from issues related to wages and working conditions to administrative systems (NOU 1974: 60; St. meld. nr. 28, 1976–77).

Hierarchical authority is restricted in transactions between ministries and sectors because the division of labor has become more complicated with more decisions affecting several ministries, because ministries have different types of expertise and because each may enlist external support. Furthermore, there are obvious constraints on the hierarchical authority of elected leaders in terms of capacity and insights, and because civil servants have other political references and external sources of support. Ministers cannot (always) claim hierarchical authority over well organized clients with well trained staffs and with political and economic clout.

If the top civil servants' interaction with subordinates, each other, elected politicians and organized interests is not promoted by hierarchical authority, what coalitions are formed? When are civil servants attractive coalition partners?

Civil servants have useful resources. They have protected careers, expertise, and practical information, and their number as well as their material resources have increased. Their predictability as coalition partners is high, but their unity has decreased. They have also been better able to protect their rights than their external political positions. Civil servants are still overrepresented in the Storting, the Cabinet, in local and regional elected assemblies, and in political parties, but they do not dominate. Their social status is high, but not exceptional. The difference in salary between top civil servants and new recruits has declined. In 1819 the difference was 6:1 – today it is 2.1:1. Top civil servants make approximately 80 percent of the salaries for comparable positions in the private sector.

In sum, civil servants should be interesting coalition partners, and the traditional view of a bureaucracy united against the politicians is not very accurate. Virtually no battles follow such lines. Less explored is a potential coalition between the two major groups in the corporate channel – full time employees in the ministries and in economic-producer organizations. Do groups of experts act as a united bloc, or do they constitute counter-expertise and adversaries?

We do not believe in a conspiracy view of bureaucratic influence, where bureaucrats agree on policies and then sell the result to their "masters" in the ministries and the interest organizations. Neither are politicians and elected leaders in organizations so powerless, nor bureaucrats so united. The two groups of bureaucrats have different careers with little exchange of personnel. Their socialization and their incentives deviate sharply. There are also divergences in attitude toward future cooperation between ministries and organized interests. ⅔ of the civil servants do not want expanded cooperation, while ⅔ of both bureaucrats and elected leaders in economic producer organizations are in favor.[13] Moreover, each group of bureaucrats are themselves in many ways heterogeneous and represent opposing views.

Consequently we are also skeptical to the concept of a united elite – a grand coalition of politicians, civil servants, and organized interests (at least partly) in opposition to ordinary people (Bull, 1979). The idea of an intimate collaboration of the elites – a Society for Mutual Benefits based on a tacit treaty, implicit bargaining, and expressed in self restraints captures only part of reality (Neustadt, 1969). Norwegian policy making takes place within a normative order emphasizing incrementalism and compromise, and the political system has been segmented into specialized coalitions of politicians, civil servants, organized interests, experts from institutions of research and higher learning. Internal disagreement may occur (and the members may hold different opinions on the value of expanded cooperation), but they share a basic perspective. Conflicts usually evolve between segments, or between a segment and institutions trying to coordinate across segments and sectors (chapter 3; Egeberg, Olsen and Sætren, 1978).

The actual coalitions depend on the organization and resources of public agencies and affected groups, as well as on the level of attention from politicians, parties, mass media, and public opinion. The more politicized the decision becomes, the more the influence of civil servants is likely to be reduced. In the few confrontations between politicians and civil servants since 1945, the latter have been defeated (Bergh and Pharo, 1977). In major conflicts, such as the struggle over Norwegian membership in the European Economic Community, the influence of civil servants was inversely related to the level of conflict (Gleditsch and Hellevik, 1977; Gleditsch et al., 1974). Also, when politicized issues, like free abortion, is promoted by the governing party, the influence of civil servants is insignificant.

The power of civil servants thus depends on the issues, the decision making arenas, and the level of conflict. This would imply that compromise may not be a "bureaucratic mentality" (Mannheim, 1949), but a rational strategy.

The capacity for focussing on issues is much less for the Storting and the public than for the administrative apparatus and for organized interests. Since the Storting and the public focus on a very small set of issues at a time, issues and conflicts compete for attention. Selection depends on the degree of conflict between the agencies and groups participating in the first phase of the process. Intervention and politization is least likely when a compromise is reached in this phase (Grimsbo, 1973; Lægreid and Olsen, 1978). If a task force is split into several factions, a conflict is likely to become socialized in Schattschneider's (1960) term. The issue may become a "garbage can" for new participants, problems and solutions (March and Olsen, 1976), resulting in less predictability and reduced influence for the groups which dominated the first phase of the policy process.

BEYOND WEBER

Our interpretation is that top civil servants in Norway are key participants in public policy making processes. They are not acquiescing instruments for arbitrary intervention by elected political leaders or social groups. Nor have they usurped all power and created a "dictatorship of the bureaucrats" (Weber, 1924: 46). Rather, top civil servants act within institutionalized networks of organized public and private interests. The ways in which influence is achieved and exercised depend upon these intra- and interorganizational networks and the coalitions built within them. Their views are formed by the tasks they are responsible for, by the institutions and the professions to which they belong, and by the parts of the environment they interact with. Thus top civil servants seldom act as a unitary group. They share a policy making style, but they differ in terms

145

of the causes, values, and social groups they defend. They play on different teams, and when conflicts arise they take sides in predictable ways.

Yet, policy-making is characterized more by compromise than by confrontation. Analysis, anticipated reaction, persuasion, and bargaining are more frequent than force, commands, and rules.

The influence of top civil servants is primarily based upon (a) life long careers protected against arbitrary intervention by politicians or organized interests, and (b) support from stable coalition partners. Top civil servants are attractive coalition partners because they bring expertise, information and energy, and because they are predictable. However, since their basic orientation is incrementalistic, they are more attractive for conservatives and moderates than for groups that want radical changes in established programs or procedures. We view the use of secrecy, control over political positions (Cabinet, Storting or in local government), formal bureaucratic authority, and bureaucratic unity as less important.

The role of civil servants will be weakened if issues become more politized, and if there is less agreement on who should be considered experts.[14] The future power of civil servants depends even more on their ability to defend their most important strongholds – the merit principle and the autonomy of protected careers.

Notes

* This chapter is a revised version of a paper which was written together with Per Lægreid, and presented at a conference on "The Role of Higher Civil Servants in Central Government", Madrid, Spain, December, 1980. We want to thank the participants in the Madrid Conference, and Morten Egeberg, Dick Elmore, Donald Matthews, Reidun Tvedt, and Mariann Vågenes for their help and advice.

[1] Jacobsen uses the terms political contraction and detraction for power concentration and dispersion respectively.

[2] The results of this study are reported in more detail in Lægreid and Olsen (1978). The data are based mostly on a survey administered to ministry employees, from executive officers to top civil servants. Since then, there has been recruited more women to the ranks of top civil servants.

[3] Only 10 percent of the administrators in the ministries are women; one third grew up in the capital (Oslo), and 40 percent were born in a family where the main breadwinner was a university graduate or self-employed (Lægreid and Olsen, 1978).

[4] The oil sector is an exception. Here, the movement of personnel from state agencies to oil companies has become so high that it is perceived as a problem by political authorities (Forh. i St., 1980: 2836–2837). A result has been special salaries for civil servants employed in the oil sector.

[5] The survey to the civil servants did not ask directly for party affiliation. The conclusion is based on information about whether they have been active in parties, and which union they belong to.

[6] They do leave – they are not fired.

[7] In Norway there is a low correlation between various aspects of the social biography of a civil servant (e.g. class, sex, geographic background, education, practical experience, party membership, activity in interest organizations etc.). If a high correlation produces a more unambiguous pre-bureaucratic socialization, Norwegian civil servants are not "pre-socialized" and may therefore be more receptive to socialization in the ministry (Lægreid and Olsen, 1978).

[8] In this area, the level of openness is clearly lower in Norway than in the United States. Information that is "secret" in Norway may be found in Congressional documents and then used in the political debate in Norway. A public committee considering this issue has recommended relaxing the rules (NOU 1980: 51).

[9] Here we rely on Lægreid and Olsen (1978).

[10] This analysis includes the occupation and education of the breadwinner of the family in which the respondent grew up; whether the breadwinner was publicly or privately employed; the region and the municipality where the respondent grew up; sex; age; level and type of education; language used; vocational experience; career expectations; party affiliation; union membership; membership in other interest groups; and participation in citizens' initiatives.

[11] The respondents were given a list of activities. They were first asked how much time they spent on each activity. Then they were asked which was their major activity. The two questions give approximately the same results. The boundaries between the various activities are, of course, somewhat obscured. Lawmaking and planning may for example, involve some coordination. Nevertheless, significant variations are captured by such grouping.

[12] Primarily people just recruited; people who perceive conflicts with the political leadership in the ministry; who plan to leave the ministry; and who have participated in citizens' initiatives, an activity which is contrary to ministerial norms.

[13] Those who already have representation are the most in favor of expansion. Representatives of smaller and less resourceful organizations are more negative, probably because they do not expect to be included. Among civil servants those least integrated in the ministries are most likely to favor more organizational participation.

[14] This will be true as long as politicians are able to make choices. If they are not, the position of the civil servants may be strengthened. We may have a situation where politicians talk and civil servants run the system.

5

THE DILEMMAS OF
ORGANIZATIONAL INTEGRATION
IN GOVERNMENT*

Students of political systems have long been interested in the relations between governments and organized interests in societies. This interest has focussed on two elementary questions: What aspects of organized societies are, or should be, controlled by governments? How are, or should be, governments themselves controlled by organized interests? These concerns are central to the development of democratic institutions. Contemporary Western societies provide several parallel systems of policy making, coordination, and participation. The numbers of institutional forms intended to accommodate aspirations for participation by organized interests as well as governmental control have multiplied. The results are rather intricate networks of relations.

This chapter considers one way organized interests relate to governments. Some factors are examined that affect the likelihood that organizations become integrated into governments – that their representatives occupy formal roles as governmental policy makers. How is such integrated participation determined? How may organized interests affect their environments through integrated participation in public power structures? Is integrated participation attractive for all organizations, or is it a mode of participation that attracts only certain types of organizations? For certain types of issues? Under specific conditions?

The frame of reference is contemporary Western societies characterized by freedom of association and organizational self-governance. Groups are allowed to organize, but they are not forced to do so. Participation in governments is not mandatory. Integrated organizational participation signifies that organizations have formal rights to influence governmental decisions through routine participation in policy-making bodies. They meet representatives of government and of other organized interests within a context of specified rights of participation; and they deal with a specified class of issues guided by rules and routines for problem solving and conflict resolution. Participation is an action by organizations, not by individual people who happen to be members of organizations. Organizations are assumed to control the selection of their representatives. Integrated participation takes many forms. The most frequent example is participation in the networks of governmental committees, commissions, councils, and boards that initiate, design, advise and decide upon, implement and administer governmental policies.

Since World War II, there have been important changes in the macro political systems of Western societies. The patterns of power, responsibility, and accountability have modified in significant ways, and sheer numbers of votes have lost value as political resources. These modifications are closely related to changes in the relations between governments and organized interests. One central feature has been an extensive and complicated interpenetration of governmental agencies and organized interests.

The idea of integrated organizational participation in governments is an old one. Its advocates argue that participation by organized interests is a better method of aggregating interests than counting votes in territorial elections. It is also sometimes suggested that integrated organizational participation would remedy many ills of modern societies (Schmitter, 1974, 1977). But such ideas have had modest impacts upon students of organizations.

Maybe integrated organizational participation in governments tends to be overlooked because it works through myriads of committees and boards rather than national councils and legislatures; because integrated participation has pejorative overtones of corporatism that make people use names like clientele participation, citizens' representation, or organizational consultation; and because most students of organizations are located in the United States where integrated organizational participation appears to be most weakly developed and reported.

Early, functionalist theories suggested that organizations influence governments, or should do so, indirectly through the territorial elections. Political parties were the most important organized interests in the representative structure, linking organizations and individual people to the governmental policy-making bodies. Organizations articulated demands; parties aggregated and integrated them (Almond, 1958). Key (1961) viewed standing alliances between large organizations and political parties as normal, or even inescapable, in political systems with competing parties. Although empirical research has shown that organizations seek direct access to all centers of public power – such as the legislatures, the executive branches, and the courts –, the dominant theories still treat organizations as standing outside governments. They compete for access to, give information to, make claims on, and put pressure upon governmental policy makers. They provide links between citizens and governments, through political parties or directly. But they are not integrated into the governmental machinery. The interest has been variations in the governmental targets of organized interests, more than variations in the forms of coordination between governments and organized interests.

This functionalist perspective, developed on the basis of American experience, has been challenged by Europeans and by Americans studying European countries (Beer, 1958; Buksti and Johansen, 1978; Christensen and Egeberg, 1979; Eckstein, 1960; Egeberg, 1981; Elvander, 1972, 1974; Heisler, 1974; Johansen and Kristensen, 1978; Kvavik, 1970, 1976; LaPalombara, 1964; Lehmbruch, 1974, 1977; Moren, 1968, 1974; Peterson, 1977; Schmitter, 1974, 1977; Wheeler, 1975). The fluctuating, ad hoc relationships emphasized by Bentley (1967) and his followers, have been replaced by the idea of stable, intimate relationships, a symbiosis of governmental authority and organized interests. An organization succeeds in becoming accepted by a governmental agency as the primary expression and representative of a given interest; the organization, in turn, views the governmental agency as the primary partner or point of reference (LaPalombara, 1964). Public officials give organizations influence over governmental policies; organizations supply information, political support, and control over their members.

These empirical observations challenge the assumptions and predictions of the functionalist theories, but they have not produced any coherent, alternative theories. The literature does not delineate alternative forms of coordination between governments and organized interests that fit common observations, and it does not explain the conditions for different forms of coordination.

Three forms of coordination are familiar. Firstly, the organic theories suggest that coordination occurs through common, shared goals. Secondly, hierarchical commands foster coordination as highlighted by theories of jurisprudence and democratic theories which assume omnipotent legislatures with monopolies of coercive power. Finally, the interest-group theories emphasize coordination through interplays among competing organizations, with governments refereeing the battles, recording and ratifying victories, surrenders, and compromises.

These forms are undoubtedly important. They collectively indicate that forms of coordination reflect either formal separation or formal merger.

Some alternative concepts are quasi corporatism (Beer, 1958), corporate pluralism (Rokkan, 1966), societal corporatism (Schmitter, 1974), the co-optive polity (Heisler, 1974), and liberal corporatism (Lehmbruch, 1974, 1977). These emphasize the mutual interdependence and interpenetration of the public and private sectors. Governments continue to intervene in new domains. At the same time, the vast networks of organized interests make it unrealistic to base governance authority only on majorities of votes (Rokkan, 1966). Governments and organized interests are both partners (Self and Storing, 1962) and competitors for power (Schattschneider, 1960).

Insight into the conditions for, and effects of, alternative forms of

150

coordination is vital for understanding how contemporary Western democracies work or do not work. The task is enormous – the aspirations modest.

This chapter attempts to do two things: (a) to summarize the empirical studies on integrated organizational participation in government, and (b) to identify the main theoretical themes that can be inferred from those studies and from organization theory. The two efforts are in some respects antithetical. The empirical studies are characterized by attention to long lists of loosely defined and moderately connected variables, so being empirical produces a theoretical morass. The available theories are simple and static, so being theoretical violates the contextual richness of the empirical observations.

There is presently no really satisfactory resolution of this complication; the approach used here is a simple compromise. First, some theoretical themes are discussed, then a general framework is described within which to consider integrated participation. The framework assumes that an organized interest chooses, in some sense, whether to participate after evaluating the consequences, for the goals of the organization, of integrated participation in comparison with alternative forms of coordination. This framework is used to examine the empirical studies, focussing upon features of (a) the societal contexts, (b) the organizations, and (c) the policy topics. Finally, the framework is used to extract more theoretical themes from the literature and to generate predictions about the use of integrated participation in government.

BASIC IDEAS ABOUT PARTICIPATION

Why do some organizations participate, others not? A popular answer has been a simple one: organizations do not participate because they are not allowed to do so. The idea is prevalent of power struggles over rights of participation and representation, as well as over access to governmental policy makers. Political systems are portrayed as normally preventing some organized interests from participating fully. Organizations not participating in governmental policy making are absent because they are excluded. One research task is to identify those excluding, and another task is to identify those excluded – the politically poor and the politically deviant, as defined by the governing coalition (Gamson, 1968). This struggle-for-access perspective illuminates some important phenomena: much of political activity in Western societies goes into struggles over rights of participation and representation. The perspective is consistent with the idea that organizations seek access to all centers of public power (Truman, 1951), and it is consistent with the idea that establishing close ties to specific governmental agencies makes effective use of organizational resources (Beer, 1958; Eckstein, 1960; Kvavik, 1970, 1976; McConnell, 1966; Strange, 1972). Routinized access to governmental policy making is said to be so valuable that other channels become unnecessary. Organizations are seen as wanting to influence policies directly without having to act indirectly through electoral systems (Riedel, 1972). Overt, public campaigns are replaced by informal, unostentatious contacts between organizational leaders and public officials (Eckstein, 1960). Grass-roots lobbies become infrequent and their successes dubious (Finer, 1958).

There is no question that organizations are sometimes excluded from participation, either by political forces or by bureaucratic preferences (Brown, 1972; Kaufman, 1969; Moren, 1958; Schattschneider, 1960). But to tell the story exclusively in such terms would be to ignore a somewhat contradictory perspective: the reluctant organization pursued by public officials eager to elicit organizational involvement in governmental policy making.

Many organizations are ambivalent or negative towards integrated participation in governmental policy making. The labor movement has again and again debated the proper balance between accepting a formal role in governmental policy making and remaining an organization of protest, of independent criticism, and of potential revolution (Daly, 1969; Graham, 1967; Paynter, 1970). Many organizations of students, blacks, and poor people have faced the same issue. Even very resourceful organizations sometimes refuse to participate, or they threaten to leave governmental committees and boards, as will be shown later in this chapter.

Integrated participation may be viewed as an inexpensive form of public administration (Moren, 1974), or a technique to increase governmental control and legitimacy more than organizational influence (Bates, 1970). Integrated participation may threaten central values like freedom of association and organizational self-government (Kornhauser, 1959; Tocqueville, 1945). Manipulative co-optation describes situations where integrated participation blocks, rather than advances the expressions of demands from organizations (Etzioni, 1964). Participation may prevent action upon problems, distract attention, and waste time; decisions may really be made outside the bodies with formal decision-making power; or decision-making bodies may be controlled by stable coalitions (Auerbach, 1969; Blankenship and Elling, 1962; Helfgot, 1974; Peterson, 1970; Strange, 1972; Wolman, 1972). Public agencies may co-opt organizational participants in order to legitimate the agencies and their policies, to avoid criticism, and to share responsibility. Thus, formal participation should not be accepted as an indicator of influence.

The costs of participation have been emphasized especially for revolutionary and reform organizations. Sorel (1950), as well as most

Marxists, emphasized the importance of struggle as a device for keeping up class identity and loyalty. Integration into governments should be avoided because it tranquilizes and saps revolutionary spirit. The Michels-Weber interpretation of social movements and reform organizations assumes that increased interaction with established organizations and governmental agencies produces conservatism, displacement of goals, and organizational oligarchy (Lowi, 1971). Demerath and Thiessen (1966), and Zald and Ash (1966) have challenged this interpretation, arguing that there are a variety of other transformation processes, including organizational disappearances, factional splits, and increased rather than decreased radicalism.

Thus there are reasons why public officials sometimes want organizations to participate, whereas the organizations resist. These reasons counterbalance the view that participation is attractive. However, the perspectives are not exhaustive which assert that governmental agencies struggle with organized interests over access or over autonomy. It is possible that both governmental agencies and organized interests want organizational participation in government, that neither of them do, or that either or both may themselves be complicated collections of disparate interests.

Governmental agencies and organized interests may both benefit from integrated organizational participation, so integration and symbiosis are prevalent. But integration may create functional segments that become largely autonomous structures of power. They generate their own logic. They insulate themselves from control by voters, parties, legislatures, or the judiciary; from competition among organizations; from regulation by buraucratic hierarchies; from control by rank-and-file members of the organizations; as well as from influence by public opinion in general (Allison, 1971; Egeberg et al., 1978; Ehrmann, 1971; Lowi, 1969; McConnell, 1966; Mayntz and Scharpf, 1975). As a result, integration may generate costs that have to be paid by future generations, by unorganized or weakly organized interests, or by the losing coalitions in competitions between integrated structures. Some costs of integration may have to be carried by ordinary members of the organizations. Organizational leaders may join public officials in mutually satisfying coalitions that are antithetical both to their governments and to their organizations.

An overall implication is that integrated participation cannot be understood in terms of the conflict or cooperation between two unitary actors – governmental agencies and organized interests. Governmental agencies and organized interests are seldom homogeneous units, and it is necessary to attend to their internal processes, as well as to the interrelationships between different governmental agencies and between different organized interests. Perhaps as a consequence, no general theory has been proposed. Indeed, it seems unlikely that a theory can reconcile the claim that integrated participation is the best way to represent societal interests in governmental policy making, and the most effective use of organizational resources, with the claim that it undermines freedom of association, organizational self-government, control by members, unorganized interests, individual liberty, and democracy, as well as the vigor of reform and revolutionary movements.

No such grand synthesis is attempted here.

CHOOSING AMONG FORMS OF COORDINATION

Integrated participation, like all forms of coordination, mobilizes certain biases. Coordination affects the likelihood that different issues and conflicts will be resolved or suppressed, that they will be dealt with inside or outside of political systems (Schattschneider, 1960). Each form of coordination constrains, channels, and provides incentives for various organizational behaviors. Thus different organizations are more or less likely to use each form of coordination for different policies, in different political and organizational contexts (Barth, 1966; Thompson and Tuden, 1959). The understanding of corporate representation in contemporary Western societies can be enhanced by specifying the biases which integrated organizational participation mobilizes and by testing predictions about the conditions under which integrated participation takes place.

The processes by which political systems come to use integrated participation are subtle and often complicated. They combine experience, social and political traditions, contagion, coercion, bargaining, and accidents. To understand these processes fully is beyond this chapter, so the focus is upon how an individual organization comes to participate in government. Such participation is viewed as reflecting choice. The assumption is that an organization – through choices, learning, and natural selection – over time allocates its resources in a rational way, calculating marginal benefits and costs from alternative modes of participation. However, this assumption is less an assertion about reality than a starting place for developing theory. Alternatives, costs, and benefits afford a convenient framework around which to distribute empirical studies and theories. Rationality is only a starting point because the limitations of rationality as an explanation for organizational behavior are well known. Coordination is frequently unreflective and implicit rather than purposeful and explicit. Uncertainty and ambiguity, internal goal conflicts, cognitive limits on information processing, and self-fulfilling prophecies are all present. Rational explanations verge on tautologies.

154

The apostasy is even greater. To interpret participation solely as a result of organizational choices is to be overly voluntaristic and to neglect the well documented fact that some organizations are excluded from participation. Governments should not be reduced to arenas for competing organizational interests (Nedelmann and Meier, 1977). Governmental agencies have interests and resources of their own and affect patterns of participation. J. G. Christensen (1978), Fivelsdal (1978), Heisler (1974), Jarlov et al. (1976), LaPalombara (1964), and Ruin (1974) discussed the choices facing governmental representatives. This chapter takes as given that integrated participation tends to include only representatives of those organized interests from which cooperation is necessary for implementing governmental policies, not representatives from all of the organized interests affected by policies. Interdependence between governmental agencies and organizations is a necessary, but not sufficient, condition for participation. If an organization does not affect governmental performance in significant ways, it will be excluded from participation. If governmental activities do not affect an organization, it will take no interest in participation. The analysis is confined to situations where neither governments nor organizations can unilaterally avoid or eliminate their interdependence.

Alternative forms of coordination

To talk of integrated participation as a choice presumes that there are alternative forms of coordination. Coordination can be achieved (a) by specifying rules of procedure, (b) by specifying substantive rules, (c) by ad hoc interactions, and (d) by autonomous adjustments.

First, an organization may prefer to participate in specifying procedural rules for exchanges and behaviors, without specifying the substance of exchanges and behaviors. Rules of procedure regulate the channels in which participants, choice opportunities, problems, and solutions flow together in political systems (Cohen et al., 1972; March and Olsen, 1976). Rules of procedure specify decision structures, which define the rights of participation. What kinds of decision makers can be present? Rules of procedure also specify access structures, which define the kinds of issues, problems, and solutions that should be accepted as relevant. What should be taken as given? What should be taken as problematic? Finally, rules of procedure specify decision-making styles, which define the ways issues should be dealt with. How should problems be solved and conflicts resolved? What should be the terms of exchange among the participants? The importance of coordination through procedural rules is illustrated by the large number of governmental boards, committees, and councils with organizational representation in many countries.

Second, an organization may prefer to participate in setting substantive rules – laws, contracts, or standards – which specify directly the substance of exchanges and behaviors. Coordination through substantive rules is a basic activity of every government, and a major theme in studies of organized interests (Eldersveld, 1958; Truman, 1951). But the increasing complexity of modern welfare states make it increasingly difficult for legislators to specify substantive rules. One consequence has been a tendency towards policy without law; the requirement of standards has been replaced by the requirement of participation (Lowi, 1969).

Third, an organization may prefer ad hoc interaction with governmental agencies. An organization initiates particularized contacts with public officials; it acts alone and determines the substance, the targets, the timing, and the methods of contact. Such participation reflects an interest in a specific decision or event – not a general political engagement (Truman, 1951). Governmental agencies and organizations interact in ad hoc and highly irregular fashions – a contrast to the routine patterns created by procedural rules or substantive rules.

Fourth, an organization may prefer autonomous adjustment. The organization keeps an eye on governmental agencies, anticipates their possible actions, but has no direct contacts with governmental agencies. An organization may influence governmental policies simply by being present in the environment (Holtzman, 1966). Because organization theory has focussed upon coordination through joint decision making, it has not exploited some well known concepts describing alternative forms of coordination: anticipated reaction (Friedrich, 1937), autonomous individual adjustment (Lindblom, 1965, 1977), and tacit communication, where joint strategies are so obvious that organizations use them without explicit communication (Schelling, 1960).

Governmental agencies frequently operate as representatives of organized interests. The more indispensable the resources controlled by an organization, the more likely it is to be routinely attended to. Socieconomic leverage, the ability to halt or harm society (Finer, 1973; Rokkan, 1966) as well as the ability to protest and criticize (Eckhoff and Jakobsen, 1960; Kovak, 1972) have important effects on public officials. Thus, political and economic resources can evoke effects when they are not used. But an organization may also use, or threaten to use, its resources to affect governmental policies, without having any direct contact with or integrating with, policy-making bodies on a more permanent basis. There are situations of direct action and confrontation where even a well established organization takes matters into its own hands, and violates traditional norms of negotiation and compromise. For example, in a study of Danish farm organizations, Laux (1968) found that these well integrated organizations under special circumstances used production stoppage and extralegal measures in an attempt to press the government to accede to their demands. Likewise, in 1975, Danish fishermen blocked several harbors (Buksti and Johansen, 1978).

156

Distinctions between interactive and autonomous forms, between ad hoc and routinized forms, and between substantive rules and rules of procedure, roughly outline the range of alternative forms of coordination between interdependent organized interests and governments. There are important variations within this range. The diverse forms of coordination make it possible to see integrated participation as one possible choice among many, an alternative that an individual organization can choose more or less voluntarily.

COSTS AND BENEFITS OF INTEGRATED PARTICIPATION

Choice among forms of coordination presumes some assessment of the alternatives in terms of organizational goals. For example, an organization may assess how alternative forms of coordination affect its administrative procedures, internal conflicts, and the distributions of power, activity, competence, and resources among its members. But substantive outcomes of desciscions are not the only costs and benefits allocated in decision processes. There are major costs and benefits associated with the processes themselves. Decision making provides a context in which participants, and onlookers as well, construct and communicate theories about themselves and seek reinforcement for their beliefs. Status is allocated and acknowledged. Goodwill, trust, and antagonisms are collected and earned. New conceptions are developed of truth, justice, right, what is possible, identity and purpose, individual and collective interests – or old conceptions are maintained. Glory and blame are distributed. Training takes place, and competence is acquired and acknowledged. New role relationships are developed. People may divide into different factions. There are exits from some organizations, new recruits to others. Time and energy are spent (March and Olsen, 1976).

The language of costs and benefits can deceive by implying that decisions yield short lists of relatively clear outcomes. Actual decisions produce relatively long lists of ambiguous outcomes. Costs and benefits cannot be measured accurately enough to permit precise calculations of net returns. Nor is it realistic to compare one kind of cost or benefit with another. Different costs and benefits fall upon different scales which cannot be compared, if only because the costs and benefits affect different people. Thus, this chapter only uses the terms costs and benefits metaphorically to indicate that aspects of policies, organizations, and contexts make an organization more or less receptive to integrated participation.

The benefits of integrated participation can include influence over policy, cartelization, efficiency, and legitimacy. Participation provides opportunities to influence governmental policies. Integration enables organizations and governmental agencies to coordinate their activities and to exchange information. Access to information may bring technical expertise that facilitates efficiency. Participation confers public recognition on an organization and gives the organization a share in policy successes.

The costs of integrated participation can include responsibilities and losses of freedom, purity, and control by members. By accepting a position in an integrated structure, an organization and its leaders become associated with the actions of this structure. The organization has to share the blame for policy failures, because it cannot credibly claim innocence. Participation sometimes compromises an orgnization's ideological purity. Integration reduces an organization's freedom to act, and so constrains the organization's responsiveness to its members' wishes. A participating organization usually has to give the people who represent it some rights to control the organization's actions.

These benefits and costs are neither mutually exclusive nor exhaustive, but they characterize the differences among forms of coordination. They affect an organization's spontaneity, its certainty, its willingness to compromise, its ideological identity, its social status, its acceptance of responsibility of governmental policies, its role differentiation, its responsiveness to members' wishes, and its internal conflicts of interests. These effects pose dilemmas for an organization, because benefits seem to be inextricably bound together with costs.

Spontaneity versus certainty

An organization can usually trade off certainty to get flexibility. Integrated participation allows less spontaneity and uncertainty than do ad hoc interaction or autonomous adjustment, but it allows more spontaneity and uncertainty than do substantive rules.

An organization can avoid having to anticipate environmental actions by arranging negotiated environments (March and Simon, 1958), or by buffering environmental influences (Thompson, 1967). Uncertainty and risk, as well as conflict and competition, can be reduced by creating stable relationships with environmental actors. The standard answers to uncertainty include plans, contracts, laws, rules, norms, consultations, recruiting and co-optation, representation, and joint ventures (Starbuck, 1976).

Negotiating and standardizing environmental relationships bring the benefits of division of labor, expertise, and mass production. Also, the time perspective of decision making lengthens, making exchanges over time more likely (Cyert and March, 1963; March and Simon, 1958;

Starbuck, 1965, 1976; Thompson, 1967; Weber 1968; Wilson, 1973). Participation in a well defined interorganizational structure offers security and protection because the reciprocal acceptance of organizational domains – a distinct area of competence, a clearly demarcated and exclusively served clientele and membership, or undisputed jurisdiction over a function, service, goal, or cause – reduces rivalry to an exceptional thing (Levine and White, 1961; Thompson, 1967; Wilson, 1973).

The increased capabilities of problem solving and conflict resolving are, however, accompanied by rigidity. A negotiated environment is difficult to change; contracts, laws, and agreements cannot be altered unilaterally. When agreements are frozen into an interorganizational structure, changes are even more difficult. A negotiated environment reduces opportunities for exploiting sudden, favorable situations. A creditor organization does not act today in exchange for a future obligation unless it has confidence that the debtor organization will fulfill its obligation in the future, so the debtor organization must accept some system for enforcing performance or compensating nonperformance (Litwak and Hylton, 1962; Thompson, 1974; Weber, 1968).

Thus a dilemma arises. An organization wants to avoid uncertainty, but it also wants to keep its flexibility and maneuverability. It wants to demonstrate its ability to reduce uncertainty for other organizations in order to have the others reciprocate (Thompson, 1967). An important source of power is the ability to force other organizations into determinate patterns of behavior, while keeping itself unpredictable. This sets the stage for making other organizations pay for goodwill (Crozier, 1964, 1974). An organization may find it advantageous to treat the rules of the game as subject to change, improving its position by inviting in new participants, new issues, or by moving decisions to new arenas (Coleman, 1957; March and Olsen, 1976; Schattschneider, 1960). As illustrated by Laux (1968), established institutional forms are sometimes challenged even though such a challenge produces conflict and uncertainty. Since it is often difficult to appraise the relative power of organizations before a conflict has settled the issue, there will be periods when an organization wants to demonstrate and test power capabilities (Castles, 1969; Finer, 1973). Also, organizational representatives sometimes use real or imagined external uncertainty or hostility to mobilize internal energy, increase organizational cohesion, or defeat internal opposition (Coser, 1956). But an established organization is typically more interested in exploiting acquired advantages and the profits accruing from the status quo than in adjusting to new circumstances, grasping new opportunities, or innovating (Crozier, 1974).

159

Compromises versus ideological identity

An organization can usually influence public policies and obtain benefits through compromises with other organizations if it is willing to pollute its ideological identity. Kvavik (1976) interviewed organizational representatives on Norwegian governmental committees; he reported that 87 percent felt that the success of a committee depended upon the participants' willingness to compromise. Integrated participation demands more compromises and allows less organizational uniqueness than do ad hoc coordination or autonomous adjustment. Where governmental-organizational relations are coordinated through substantive rules, an organization's propensity to compromise or to express its identity depends upon the degree to which the organization participated in formulating the rules.

An organization has to obtain resources from its environment to survive (Pfeffer and Salancik, 1978; Starbuck, 1965). A distinct ideological identity can be an incentive for recruiting members and make it easier to acquire resources (Wilson, 1973). Loss of ideological purity – and the concomitant demands, uncompromised goals, simple slogans, and strong symbols – may diminish the resources obtained, intraorganizational cohesion, and political consciousness. However, in public policy making, acquiring resources and emphasizing ideological identity seldom reinforce each other. Influence and policy benefits hang together with compromises, pragmatism, and loss of ideological identity.

Integrated participation implies enduring coalitions between interdependent governmental agencies and organized interests. In political systems with freedom of association and organizational self-government, and thus exit possibilities (Hirschman, 1970), an organization is prone to compromise and to share benefits rather than to seek clear-cut victories, because it wants other participants to stay within the system. An organization's style is to seek integration and coordination of different demands through exchanges of information and influence, rather than to articulate unilateral demands. Concessions are given; goodwill, friendship, and trust are viewed as assets for future compromises, not to be overtaxed in a single decision (Adams, 1976; Heisler, 1974; Kvavik, 1976; March and Olsen, 1976; Moren, 1974).

Thus integrated participation may prevent an organization from expressing disappointment, discontent, anger, or protest. Participation may make it necessary for an organization to moderate, suppress, or camouflage its identity (Blankenship and Elling, 1962; Wolman, 1972); or participation may constrain ways an organization expresses disagreement with public policies (Peterson, 1977). How is it possible to reconcile the wish to express an ideological identity related to the goals and values around which an organization is created, with the need to compromise in order to influence the choices of other organizations and public agencies?

160

The Swedish organizational leaders interviewed by Peterson (1977) acknowledged the dilemma, but they judged the influence, policy benefits, and resources achieved through policy compromises to be more valuable than the identities lost. The Norwegian decision to stay outside the European Common Market illustrates a situation where the costs of compromise became too high to allow established forms of integrated participation to work; and where well established organizations chose to express ideological identities (Gleditsch and Hellevik, 1973; Valen, 1973).

Recognition versus freedom from responsibility

All forms of coordination are mechanisms for legitimizing participants, procedures, and policies. For an organization, there is usually a trade-off between the benefit of being recognized as a participant and the cost of accepting responsibility for policies and the ways they are made. Integrated participation offers more recognition and demands more responsibility than do ad hoc coordination or autonomous adjustment. It also offers and demands more than does coordination based on substantive rules if the organization has not explicitly participated in formulating those rules.

Participation in governmental policy making sometimes is a very visible sign of status: the participants are accepted as legitimate representatives of causes, groups, and organizational domains. The reputation and legitimacy of an organization may be enhanced. Its appeal to prospective members may increase (Brown, 1972; Gamson, 1975; Kvavik, 1976; Ruin, 1974). Thus, an organization may affect its public image through participation and establish itself as important, legitimate, responsible, and willing to cooperate. Integrated participation may also be viewed as ceremonial behavior that reduces external inspection and intervention, and that increases the survival prospects of an organization (Meyer and Rowan, 1977).

Accepting the role as policy maker and becoming identified with policies and political institutions may, however, bring blame as well as glory. Public policies may be ineffective, as when unemployment and inflation continue to grow in spite of governmental interventions; or they may be unpopular, as when incomes are not allowed to rise or taxes are increased.

Effective representatives versus control by members

Forms of coordination vary in their implications for organizational control. An organization can usually obtain benefits from delegating transactions with its environment to representatives at the cost of responsiveness

161

to control by members. Because an organization has to give its representatives discretion at the expense of control by members, integrated organizational participation gives representatives more discretionary power than does coordination based on substantive rules. The more an organization has learned about environmental variations and has established rules covering those variations, the less discretion it has to cede to its representatives (Arrow, 1974; Thompson, 1967). Ad hoc coordination and autonomous adjustment permit various mixes of discretion by representatives and control by members.

By giving its representatives the right to deal with the environment on its behalf, an organization accelerates its reactions and gains in ability to exploit opportunities. Democratic processes are costly in time and energy; often they move too slowly to exploit favorable situations, or to meet external deadlines. The external efficiency of an organization increases when its representatives are given relatively free hands – when they are trustees more than delegates – because small modifications of agreements can alter the benefits dramatically. However, an organization's representatives may strengthen their bargaining positions by having, or claiming to have, their hands tied if the opponents have degrees of freedom (Adams, 1976; Walton and McKersie, 1965).

Frequently, participation is related to complex issues demanding representatives with specialized knowledge, professional expertise, as well as considerable time and energy. Peterson (1977) reported that the universal pattern in Sweden was that representatives were expected to keep their organizations informed and consult with them on major issues, but that direct instructions on how to act were hardly ever given. Generally, an organization relied on the judgment of its representatives.

The result is intraorganizational role differentiation, especially when an organization participates over a wide range of issues (Buksti and Johansen, 1978; T. Christensen, 1978; Moren, 1974). By creating specialized positions for its representatives, an organization may profit from the accumulated technical competence of its representatives and increase its effectiveness in interorganizational bargaining.

A dilemma arises because greater discretion for representatives increases the chance that representatives become co-opted by environmental actors and that goal displacement takes place. Members are deprived of direct experiences with the realities facing an organization. They stay passive. They do not develop competence in politics and problem solving – skills necessary to influence and control representatives. Since members cannot judge directly external possibilities and constraints, their levels of aspiration will depend upon a variety of political and organizational processes (March and Olsen, 1976; Walton and McKersie, 1965).

The need for external efficiency reduces the feasibility of one device for control by members: replacing unacceptable representatives. External efficiency demands experience and expertise in interorganizational affairs, making costly a rapid turnover of those representing an organization. External efficiency also depends upon reciprocal interorganizational trust, and trust develops through repeated personal contacts over extended periods of time (Windmuller, 1969). Low turnover has a multiplier effect – competence causes activity causes competence (Weiner, 1976), and thus power differentials grow wider. How can discretion for representatives be combined with control by members? How can representatives be controlled and held responsible by the represented? How can members keep their representatives from becoming tyrants and still allow them the flexibility to negotiate effectively (Dahl and Lindblom, 1953)?

The need for intraorganizational bargaining, the intraorganizational distribution of power and how this distribution is affected by interorganizational relations have often been assumed away. In the interest-group literature, an organization has either been defined as a consensus system (Herring, 1929), or control by members has been viewed as impossible. Michels' (1949) argument – quoted more often than tested – is that organization itself makes the mandatees dominate the mandators. Exceptions are viewed as just anomalies (Lipset et al., 1956). An alternative is to view an organization as a coalition and to assume that members' control may depend upon such things as their expertise, status, involvement, and free time compared to those of their representatives. Members of an organization may themselves be powerful organizations unwilling to delegate discretion. Furthermore, an organizational representative may not want discretion and may not want to reduce control by members.

Integrated participation has different consequences for an organization as a whole than for its representatives as individual members. Typically the benefits of integrated participation for representatives have been emphasized (Bates, 1970), but delegating discretion to representatives produces dilemmas for representatives as well as for those represented. Representatives are members of two systems: they represent their organization outward to an interorganizational structure, and they also represent the interorganizational structure inward to their organization. Better than other members of their organization, they know the preferences, expectations, and beliefs of other organizations and governmental agencies. To succeed, representatives have to be sensitive to those preferences, expectations, and beliefs – risking potential claims from within their organization that they are too sensitive to them (Adams, 1976; Thompson, 1962, 1967; Walton and McKersie, 1965; Wilson, 1973).

Representatives are caught between internal and external forces. If an organization does not participate in governmental policy making, its nonparticipation may be the result of a situation where members or leaders refuse to give the necessary discretion to representatives, and where the latter lack the power to get their will through. But nonparticipation may also occur because representatives do not want discretion: they do not want to carry the costs of insisting that their organization should fulfill commitments, that earlier commitments should be accepted as constraints, or that a sudden, favorable situation should not be exploited. Rather than accepting compromises and facing the charge that they sold out and did not get as much as possible, representatives may display their loyalty to organizational norms and ideology by making utopian demands. They may find it too costly to be the ones who deal with competitors or enemies and so implicitly recognize them as legitimate representatives of groups or causes.

Some predictions

The costs, benefits, and dilemmas of integrated participation give bases for predicting some variations in such participation. Specifically, integrated participation should flourish: (a) where many organizations value predictability and certainty, (b) where many organizations are willing to make commitments, (c) where few organizations value spontaneity and flexibility, (d) where compromises can be beneficial, (e) where few organizations strive to protect their ideological identities, (f) where many organizations seek recognition as the legitimate representatives of causes, groups, and organizational domains, (g) where many organizations are willing to accept responsibility for governmental policies, (h) where many organizations readily delegate discretion to their representatives, or (i) where few organizations value high involvement and control by members.

Such characteristics imply that organizations are satisfied with the status quo. They take as fixed premises the other organization's properties and the current methods of policy making. They accept current conceptions of justice and legitimacy, and they believe the theories that different participants hold about themselves and about society in general. They do not propose major changes in the way people group themselves or in their organizational identities. Neither do they attempt to change established policy making. This is what Mill (1951), in his critique of the utilitarians, called the business side of politics – a concern for substantive benefits and a lack of interest in ideological identity and change.

This analysis suggests why organizations are unlikely to make major changes in their environments through integrated participation in government. It also provides a framework within which to interpret the empirical studies of participation.

CHARACTERISTICS OF THE DATA

The literature on interest groups has an impressive volume. Yet, studies of integrated participation constitute a small, but growing, fraction of this writing.

In a review of the literature on American interest groups, Eldersveld (1958) put the studies into three categories: (a) studies of a single interest group, (b) studies of interest groups operating in single arenas, especially the legislative arena, over short times, (c) studies of interest groups concerned with particular laws or policy conflicts.

Eldersveld did not give much attention to organizational participation in government. He did suggest that the power positions of organized interests form an ordering – with penetration into formal policy-making bodies on the top, and with rejection by the power structure and agitation and resistance on the bottom –, but he also concluded that organized interests and governmental institutions had merged into interorganizational structures which had not yet been institutionalized.

Since Eldersveld (1958) wrote, it has become clear that this institutionalization exists in many political systems. Private, voluntary organized groups have de facto authority to participate in governmental policy making. The literature on integrated organizational participation has been growing, but it has retained the major characteristics observed by Eldersveld. Studies of single organizations, single issues, or single decision-making arenas have dominated (Chapman, 1973; Komarovsky, 1975). Most often, the contexts of the studies have not been made explicit or have not been discussed. The studies identify long lists of explanatory variables that do not divide into obvious categories. Attention has focussed upon which organized interests participate, yet there is little direct information about the processes through which participation is achieved, about the control organizations have over who represents them, and about what organizations expect to achieve through participation. Little is known about how the governmental boards and committees make policies or about the effects of those decisions. However, Schmitter's (1974) analysis of corporatism as a distinctive, modern system of interest representation, and the conceptual specifications he suggested, generated a large number of working papers and international conferences. There has been some convergence in research interests and in conceptualizations, but still speculations dominate over empirical observations, and studies of the anatomy of the system of interest representation dominate over studies of its actual working.

Integrated organizational participation is probably best documented in the Scandinavian countries. Data archives have been built that describe the national population of organized interests – their relations to each other as well as to political institutions and to organizations in other countries – more completely than has been done for any other countries (Buksti and Johansen, 1978; Christensen and Egeberg, 1979; Egeberg, 1981; Hallenstvedt and Hoven, 1974; Hallenstvedt et al., 1976; Jarlov et al., 1976; Johansen and Kristensen, 1978; Kvavik, 1976; Meijer, 1969; Moren, 1968, 1974; Moren et al., 1976).

Countries are difficult to compare because variations reported may reflect real differences in the phenomena or variations in the data. Interactions may be formal or informal. Participation may involve fact finding and inquiry, advising, decision making, or implementation of policies. Arrangements may be temporary or permanent. Interorganizational structures may span nations, regions, or local areas. Participating organizations may be selected by the governmental agencies or by the organizations themselves (Egeberg, 1981). Likewise it is problematic what should be considered an organization. These variations also make it desirable to concentrate attention upon a few general tendencies, rather than the details of specific studies. Such tendencies can be discerned.

The empirical evidence about integrated participation is reviewed in three clusters. The next section examines the influences of various societal contexts. Two ensuing sections consider the influences of organizational characteristics and policy content.

INFLUENCES OF SOCIETAL CONTEXTS

In some societies more than others

A starting point is the variations across political systems: integrated participation occurs more frequently in the Scandinavian countries than in Great Britain, and much more frequently than in the United States.

In the Scandinavian countries, organizations have legitimate and institutionalized rights to participate in all phases of governmental policy making as representatives of specific interests. Routinely, representatives appointed by the organizations meet public bureaucrats, experts from universities and research institutions, and – somewhat fewer – party politicians and legislators in hundreds of committees and boards. In Norway there are around 1000 governmental committees, the majority permanent ones at the national level. Organizations are represented in approximately 40 percent of these committees, by around 2,000 representatives (Hallenstvedt and Hoven, 1974; Kvavik, 1970, 1976; Moren, 1968, 1974; Moren et al., 1976). Johansen and Kristensen (1978) reported a similar pattern in Denmark. In 1975 there were 668 committees; organizations were represented in 55 percent, by 1,607 representatives. Integrated participation in Sweden is well documented (Elvander, 1966, 1972, 1974; Heckscher, 1946; Meijer, 1969; Peterson, 1977; Ruin, 1974; Wheeler, 1975), but it is difficult to compare the Swedish statistics with the Norwegian and Danish ones because of differences in the administrative systems. Swedish organizations appointed 22 percent of 1,989 commissioners serving on 519 governmental committees of inquiry from 1961 to 1967 (Meijer, 1969). But more important, organized interests have achieved a comprehensive representation on the governing boards of the semi-independent governmental agencies below the cabinet level – ämbetsverken. Hadenius (1978) reported that organizations were represented on 71 percent of these agencies and appointed one-third of their members in 1976. In comparison, Ruin (1974) found organizations represented in 64 percent of the boards in 1964, and 28 percent in 1946.

British organizations, like their Scandinavian counterparts, have legitimate and institutionalized rights to participate. In Britain, 500–600 advisory committees are attached to the governmental agencies at the national level (Ehrmann, 1971; Finer, 1973; Wootton, 1970), but it is unclear how many of these include representatives appointed by organizations. The number of representatives that specific organizations have in governmental committees – to be discussed later in this chapter – indicates a level of participation in Britain somewhat below that in Scandinavian countries. Moreover, the tendency is that participation in Britain more than in the Scandinavian countries concentrates upon information exchanges and inquiries, and that participation less often includes policy formation and implementation (Beer, 1958, 1965; Chapman, 1973; Eckstein, 1960; Kimber and Richardson, 1974; Shonfield, 1965).

American agencies, too, are enmeshed in advisory committees. In 1976 there were 1,159 such committees, with near 60-million-dollar budgets, attached to agencies of the federal government. The Department of Health, Education, and Welfare alone had 349 advisory committees (United States, President, 1977). However, Nadel and Rourke (1975) observed that the majority of the committees did not include organizational representatives. They did not indicate the exact size of organizational representation. In the United States, organized interests are frequently represented, but the practice is to recruit individual people who may be said to have special qualities, experience, or expertise, rather than formal representatives of organizations. Indeed, the overt American practice is explicitly to exclude such representatives. For instance, the Defense Production Act of 1950 required that nonmembers as well as members of organizations should be represented. The Federal Advisory Committee Act of 1972 emphasized that the advice and recommendations given by an advisory committee should be a result of the committee's independent judgment – it was not to be inappropriately influenced by the appointing authority or by any special interest. A result is that advisors are recruited directly from the business community, and especially from the large corporations (McConnell, 1966; Wootton, 1970). Organized groups have succeeded in establishing or capturing specific governmental agencies so

167

that some regulatory agencies, for example, act as instruments for the regulated interests; or governmental authority is delegated to organized interests (Bernstein, 1955; Kohlmeier, 1969; Leiserson, 1942; Lowi, 1969; McConnell, 1966). But such clientele arrangements tend to be bilateral relationships between a governmental agency and an organized interest more than an institutionalized decision-making system including representatives from several governmental agencies and organized interests. They illustrate the power of specific industries and groups, more than the power of organizations.

A main difference is that clientele relationships and organizational representation in governmental policy making are perceived to be less legitimate in the United States than in Britain and the Scandinavian countries (Lowi, 1969; McConnell, 1966; Salisbury, 1975; Shonfield, 1965). In the·Scandinavian countries the dominant view is that integrated organizational participation in all phases of policy making is promoting a democratic development (Olsen, 1978). In the United States the Federal Advisory Committee Act of 1972 emphasized that the function of advisory committees should be advisory only. The Congress found that the need for many existing committees had not been adequately reviewed and that the number of committees should be kept to the minimum necessary. The result has been a decreasing number of committees. During 1976, 180 new committees were established, while 287 committees merged, expired, or were abolished (United States, President, 1977). In the 1978 State of the Union Message. President Carter proposed to abolish about 500 federal advisory committees as a part of a crusade against bureaucracy and as a means for promoting democracy. Furthermore, organizations are not viewed as legitimate spokesmen for their sectors (Wilson, 1978). Rather, organized groups have been perceived as a problem of popular government ever since James Madison formulated his view upon factions at the time of the ratification of the Constitution (Mulhollan, 1977). In accordance with this tradition, Lowi (1969) and McConnell (1966) have stressed the fundamental contradiction between a representative system based on democratic elections and one based on organized interests, and they have expressed the suspicion that organized interests would tyrannize the majority.

Differences across political systems have especially been related to variations in governmental intervention and to variations in the political role of the trade unions. Specifically, Scandinavian and British unions have been more able to mobilize workers, they have more ideological unity, and they have achieved political power through symbioses with social democratic or socialist parties (Heisler, 1974; Lehmbruch, 1974, 1977; Panitch, 1977; Schmitter, 1974; Wilson, 1978). These relationships will be discussed, but first: there are also variations within each system over time.

168

In some situations more than others

Participation prevails in crises more than in ordinary circumstances. During wars, depressions, or other national crises, as well as during crises in specific sectors of society, integrated organizational participation becomes more frequent. Crises emphasize the mutual interdependencies between organizations and governments, crises increase the symbolic costs of refusing to participate, and crises produce more governmental intervention and regulation, so that organizations become more motivated to participate than in normal times.

This observation generalizes across political systems. Even in the United States, substantial numbers of committees have included organizational representatives in times of crisis. But such arrangements have not become permanent. One network of advisory committees, established through the Voluntary Agreements Act in 1947, was in effect for a year and a half and then lapsed; the committees that survived were mainly those with narrowly technical domains, such as manufacturing standards. The Korean war produced a new interest in cooperation between government and organized interests; but in 1951, the labor unions walked out of the Wage Stabilization Board, and subsequently, labor representatives walked out of the boards of other agencies. In 1956, the U.S. Congress said there were 5,000–6,000 advisory committees, but it is unclear exactly how many included organizational representatives (McConnell, 1966).

In the Scandinavian countries, World War I produced an unprecedented amount of formal cooperation between public officials and organized interests; many of these committees and boards disappeared over the following years. The period following World War II brought a new wave of committees and boards, with the difference being that most of them have not disappeared. But since the mid 1950s, when postwar reconstruction was drawing to an end, there has been a leveling off in the numbers of governmental committees with organizational representatives (Heckscher, 1946; Johansen and Kristensen, 1978; Moren, 1958, 1974; Wheeler, 1975). In Norway this leveling off is clearest for temporary committees of inquiry, where even the Norwegian Federation of Trade Unions reduced its participation nine percent between 1951 and 1966 (Solvang, 1972). Similar trends have occurred in Sweden (Meijer, 1969): new committees of inquiry have recruited more public officials and fewer organizational representatives. The large labor-market organizations had only two-thirds as many representatives in the 1960s as they had in the 1940s and 1950s. An interpretation is that Swedish politics entered a period of decelerated political reform. Following a decade, stretching from the end of World War II to the mid 1950s when a large number of new programs were introduced, the next decade was characterized by the technical and administrative elaborations of previous legislation rather than the initiation of radically new programs (Meijer, 1969). A generalization of this interpretation says that crises and active-reform periods are naturally followed by periods of consolidation and diminished policy making.

It is debatable whether crises increase the benefits of participation more than they increase the costs of non-participation. National crises introduce more regulations and restrictions. Since there are many unpopular decisions, organizations might be less willing to share the responsibility and possible criticism following from participation. Yet, national crises create feelings of common purpose that increase the benefits and reduce the costs of participation. It becomes costly to express unwillingness to cooperate when national survival is threatened. Interorganizational as well as intraorganizational conflicts are suppressed when cooperation has clear payoffs in terms of planes, ships, or guns produced (McConnell, 1966). When internal opposition softens, representatives feel less threatened, and thus they become more willing to compromise. The costs rise of stressing organizational uniqueness and identity, of challenging representational rights of others and the legitimacy of the established policy-making structure, or of demanding control by members.

The effects of crises upon symbolic costs and benefits are dramatized by the observation that participation also increases in societal sectors which are relatively unaffected by the crises. Moren (1958, 1974), studying governmental-organizational cooperation in Norway between 1914 and 1921, observed that although organized interests often were reluctant to accept the combination of increased governmental intervention and increased participation, participation rose in sectors with no immediate relationships to the war. Moren's interpretation was that a crisis has a spillover effect, creating a general climate of cooperation. An alternative interpretation may be derived from theories of diffusion and imitation: a form of coordination may spread across sectors if an innovating sector has high status, even if the various sectors face different conditions. There is a tendency to imitate choices rather than rules for choosing (Starbuck, 1976).

INFLUENCES OF ORGANIZATIONAL CHARACTERISTICS

Economic-producer interests

Economic-producer interests, especially large, powerful employers' associations and labor unions, together with the organizations in agriculture and the associations of various professions, dominate the structures of integrated participation. The phenomenon appears in all contemporary Western societies and influences most of the literature cited in this chapter.

Typically, organizations show a three-tier pattern: first, operational units with individual persons as members, exemplified by a local labor union or an employers' association; second, organizations of organizations, like a national labor union or a national employers' association; and third, peak organizations, like the American Federation of Labor and Congress of Industrial Organizations and the National Association of Manufacturers, the Trades Union Congress, and the Confederation of British Industries, and the Norwegian Federation of Trade Unions and the Norwegian Confederation of Industries (Wootton, 1970). Peak organizations are the most important participants in governmental policy making. However, it is not always easy to say when a person participates on behalf of a national labor union or an employers' association, and when that person participates on behalf of a peak organization (Johansen and Kristensen, 1978). In Britain for instance, the Trades Union Congress was represented on some 60 committees at the end of the 1950s, with the Confederation of British Industries not far behind (Beer, 1958; Finer, 1958). In 1972, the Trades Union Congress reported 117 memberships, and the Confederation of British Industries 130 memberships, in governmental committees (Kimber and Richardson, 1974). Counting governmental committees at the local level as well as the national one, Moren et al. (1972) reported that the Norwegian Federation of Trade Unions, together with its component unions, was represented in 172 committees in 1964. The Norwegian Confederation of Industries participated in approximately 100 committees, and five of the major organizations of employers were together represented in 256 committees. In all the Scandinavian countries the pattern is a few peak organizations with many representations together with many, smaller organizations with only one, or a few, representations (Buksti and Johansen, 1978; Johansen and Kristensen, 1978; Moren, 1974; Peterson, 1977).

Table 5.1: *Committee representations in Norway, 1970–1971.*

Employees, labor unions	785
Employers, business	776
Agriculture, fisheries	136
Social, humanitarian	93
Scientific and cultural interests	40
Engineering and technological interests	30
Youth and leisure interests	27
Religious interests	6

The contrast between the economic-producer interests and promotional interests – religious, humanitarian, and the like – can be illustrated by some Norwegian statistics. Table 5.1, taken from Moren (1974), gives the distribution of 1893 committee representations among some major types of organizations. Johansen and Kristensen (1978) used a somewhat different classification of organizations, but found a similar pattern in Denmark.

The representation in table 5.1 denotes individuals participating; one organization may have more than one representative in a committee. Five organizations had more than 50 representatives, eighteen more than 20 representatives. Consistently these have been economic-producer interests (Moren et al., 1972). Under the Ministry of Social Welfare, economic-producer interests had 78 percent of the representations. Even under the Ministry of Church and Education, economic-producer interests held 90 percent of the organizational representations, while religious interests had one percent, and scientific and cultural interests six percent.

Large labor-market organizations have increased their integrated participation more than any other type of organization. These increases have matched changes in the goals and intraorganizational structures of labor-market organizations.

The social peace between employers and employees in many countries during the 1930s signified important changes in the ideological positions of the labor unions, changes often related to the weakening or defeat of the Communists and the strengthening of the Social Democrats, in the unions as well as in national elections. Important tendencies were de-emphasis of the class-struggle ideology, faith in reform through the political system, and support for the idea that poverty could best be conquered through production and efficiency. The unions accepted formal participation – at first in purely advisory boards, then increasingly in committees with formal policy-making functions (Solvang, 1972). Organizational unity in the labor movement, lack of a large Communist faction, and close cooperation between unions and a Social Democratic or a Socialist party promoted integrated participation (Johansen and Kristensen, 1978; Lehmbruch, 1974, 1977; Panitch, 1977; Schmitter, 1974). On the employers' side, there was a growing acceptance of the unions as legitimate representatives for the employees. Important beliefs were modified concerning laissez-faire in economic systems and owners' unilateral control of work inside plants: the employers took interest in the benefits that could be achieved through cooperation and collective bargaining, as well as through using governmental authority. While both employers' associations and labor unions still emphasized their freedom, and especially that wages should be determined without state intervention, both parties showed a taste for modifying market conditions through governmental policies.

Reduced polarization, reciprocal acceptance, emphasis upon incremental action through the political system, and agreement upon the

172

desirability of increased production have been accompanied by shifts in resources and by modifications of intraorganizational structures.

The social peace since the 1930s has put less pressure on strike funds and has nourished affluence. Both labor unions and employers' associations have had large, stable memberships, and both have concentrated their power in managerial groups, attempting to maintain members' support by means of increasing numbers of services (Eldersveld, 1958). The unions have lost much of their character as protest movements – including mass mobilization and enthusiasm.

Eckstein (1960) pointed to general tendencies in both British voluntary associations and the British government to delegate inordinately wide discretion to leaders and representatives, and to ratify decisions taken by leaders almost as a matter of form. Headey (1970) compared labor unions in thirteen Western societies and concluded differently. His centralization index took into account: (a) whether national confederations were empowered to intervene in collective bargaining; (b) whether confederations had power to control strikes, refuse permission for strikes, and to withhold strike funds; (c) the size of staffs at confederations' headquarters for every 100,000 members; and (d) the finances of the confederations. Both unions in the United States and Britain scored low on centralization compared to their counterparts in the Scandinavian countries. Swedish and Norwegian unions scored somewhat higher than the Danish.

In a detailed study of the Norwegian Federation of Trade Unions, Solvang (1972) showed that even though the central leadership was defeated in 1934 because it had cooperated with government and with the employers' association on matters which should have been internal union affairs, there has subsequently been very little criticism of the union's participation in governmental committees. When the issue has been raised, it has been to ask for more participation rather than less. However, the left-wing oppositions in some unions and the problems of enforcing discipline – as illustrated by wildcat strikes – could make participation in government a topic of internal conflict.

The broad trends in the development of economic-producer interests have been similar in the United States to Britain and Scandinavia, but there have been differences, and these differences contribute to an understanding of why integrated participation has been less prevalent in the United States. Besides traditional cultural differences like a stronger emphasis upon economic action, voluntarism, and laissez-faire, the United States distributes power differently among various organizations. Specifically, the peak organizations in the United States have achieved less power than their counterparts in Britain and especially in Scandinavia. The giant, multinational corporations deal with governments directly, rather than through trade associations (McConnell, 1966; Wilson,

1973; Wootton, 1970). Individual unions have maintained their autonomy from the national federation of unions. Indeed, some major unions
do not even belong to the national federation.

Compared to other organized interests, economic-producer groups are
powerful. They have economic leverage. They have administrative staffs
and technical expertise that increase governmental problem-solving
capacity. They have status that legitimizes policies. These properties
make integrated participation more likely. In all these respects, however,
American organizations tend to lack authority to act on behalf of whole
sectors or groups. Members, and potential members, are not willing to
delegate the authority necessary for integrated participation. Also,
differences in labor-union centralization between Britain and the
Scandinavian countries (Headey, 1970) may make integrated participation more permanent and more directly related to policy formation in the
Scandinavian countries than in Britain.

Variations in propensities to participate

The following all make integrated participation more likely: pragmatism,
incrementalism, acceptance of the status quo, control by leaders,
bureaucratization, professionalization of leadership, de-emphasis of activities by members, stable memberships, and of course, a lack of opposition to participation. Consequently, integrated participation appeals to
organizations which are relatively centralized, with full-time, elected
leaders and staffs of professionals or experts. These organizations have
stable memberships of people who are not very active. Integrated participation also attracts peak organizations rather than organizations of
individuals. These have significant socioeconomic leverage, affluent
treasuries, and strong bureaucratic staffs. Their actual members include
high proportions of their potential members. But peak organizations are
heterogeneous, and heterogeneity sometimes makes it difficult to act in
ways acceptable to members (Truman, 1951). In their studies of policy
making about tariffs, Bauer et al. (1963) observed that their heterogeneity prevents big firms and trade associations from taking stands even
on issues of central concern to themselves. The more an organization
represents the business community as a whole, the more unlikely it is to
commit itself on a general issue such as foreign-trade policy. Inability to
define a common interest produces passivity. LaPalombara (1964)
observed the same in Italy: heterogeneous peak organizations are less
able to act effectively toward government than are smaller, more
homogeneous organizations with narrow interests. Thus peak organizations do not necessarily express opinion on issues where substantive
stakes are high.

Peak organizations may find informal participation easier than formal participation. They have little to gain in terms of status and recognition through formalization. At the same time, formal participation in an institutionalized policy-making system may involve a loss of agenda control: other participants may demand that an organization take a stand even if the issue creates destructive intraorganizational conflicts. Formal participation also tends to force an organization to maintain a consistent position on different issues. Informal participation, on the other hand, offers possibilities for avoiding intraorganizational conflicts through postponing issues, through noninvolvement, or through series of contradictory responses. Heterogeneity and internal conflicts are less likely to impede formal participation if membership in an organization is extremely valuable. Where membership has high value, where membership is obligatory, where there are no alternative organizations to go to, or where creating new, competing organizations is very difficult – under any of these conditions a governing coalition may accept integrated participation in spite of internal opposition. Thus, peak organizations with national membership monopolies or with high values for their members may participate formally in spite of their heterogeneity.

Integrated participation is used by organizations which seek to protect vested interests more than by organizations which seek to promote specific causes or values (Finer, 1958). The organizations most active as participants are based on their members' occupations and on their roles as producers more than their roles as consumers (Beer, 1965). Furthermore, the participating organizations are concerned with material benefits more than with solidarity and expressive benefits (Clark and Wilson, 1961; Wilson, 1973). Generally, they have accepted the established political and economic order as a point of departure for incremental reform.

Economic-producer interests are more likely to participate than are consumer interests merely because there are no strong organizations representing consumers. In situations where interests without organizations, or with weak organizations, are given representational rights, difficulties frequently arise – as illustrated by the problems of many community-action agencies in American cities established through the Economic Opportunity Act (Peterson, 1970; Wolman, 1972). At least in Western societies, people put their roles as producers ahead of their roles as consumers. Producer organizations sometimes achieve the right to represent consumer interests (Stø, 1978).

Economic-producer interests are also more likely to participate than are the organized interests which promote causes or values. Two possible explanations for this difference are: (a) that promotional organizations lack power and cannot get access, and (b) that promotional organizations lack motivation to participate because their domains are less regulated by governments. The latter explanation neglects the mutual reinforcements between governmental regulation and integrated participation: they arise together because each nourishes the other. Although regulation causes integrated participation, it is equally true that integrated participation causes regulation. The former explanation, however, is also inadequate. The struggle for access does not alone explain, for instance, why Norwegian religious organizations participate so little, in spite of their resources, a state church, and a national Ministry of Church and Education.

In the absence of empirical studies it is possible only to suggest a few points of view that supplement the explanations of access to power and of variations in governmental regulation. For one thing, promotional organizations often have as their raisons d'être that governmental agencies or other organizations do not handle certain causes or values properly, so members and resources are mobilized by portraying the organizations as unique. Making compromises undermines their uniqueness. Other promotional organizations base their raisons d'être upon the claim that governments cannot legitimately influence certain causes or values. Religious organizations are an obvious example: they dare not compromise in matters considered sacred and above human judgment. Wilson (1961) argued that protest movements become prisoners of their pasts: by emphasizing the moral or sacrosanct qualities of their goals during periods of mobilization, they severely limit their possibilities for compromise and bargaining later.

Furthermore, expressive and solidary rewards, the pleasure of participation in itself, are more important for the ordinary members of promotional organizations than for the ordinary members of economic-producer organizations. Thus, the members of promotional organizations resist delegating discretion to representatives, and emphasize members' activity – as illustrated by the women's liberation movement (Freeman, 1975).

INFLUENCES OF POLICY TOPICS

Types of policies

Different policies elicit different types of participants and generate different patterns of interaction (Dahl, 1961; Eckstein, 1960; Lowi, 1964, 1972). Peterson (1971) argued that students of British politics, like Beer and Eckstein, concluded that direct contact with the bureaucracy is most effective, and that other channels may safely be ignored, because they concentrated upon pluralist issues. Pluralist issues focus upon technical details in domains where consensus is fairly high because social statuses are not at stake. On the basis of studies of educational reform in Great Britain, Peterson concluded that close contact with the administrative bureaucracy may be most effective for pluralist issues, but that organized interests have to influence parties and elections in order to affect issues such as the basic organization of the school system. These are status issues with broad consequences for the statuses of social classes, and consensus is low.

In all countries, integrated participation is used primarily as a form of coordination in economic policy making (Schmitter, 1977). However, economic policy making raises diverse issues: economic growth, productivity and efficiency, income, employment, welfare, conditions in labor markets, credit and monetary policies, imports and exports, vocational training and education, and the licensing of professionals. Within this variety, a pattern can be observed: integrated participation is used more often for specific, limited issues than for broad, general issues.

Although it has been easy to establish integrated participation around well defined matters, often a pragmatic and technical nature, issues of a general, ideological nature have been dealt with in settings more temporary than permanent. Some Norwegian examples illustrate this pattern.

In spite of a general acceptance of integrated participation in Norwegian policy making, the major economic organizations have several times resisted governmental attempts to institutionalize participation in general economic policy making. In 1946, fifteen major employers' associations agreed, several of them reluctantly, to send representatives to a Board for Economic Coordination. This board was to make policies concerning postwar reconstruction, regulation of prices, unemployment, the currency, wages, consumption, and rationing. Only a year later, as it became obvious that the Board's activity involved important principles concerning the structure of the economy, and as the participating organizations were publicly criticized for the policies adopted, the justification for the Board was challenged by the employers' associations. Being a minority, they felt themselves to be hostages of the government. A series of confrontations and crises followed, and in 1952 the employers' associations announced their withdrawal. Two years later the Board was formally dissolved. The employers' associations wanted to interact with government within a less institutionalized framework. Forms of cooperation should be decided for each issue. After several new initiatives from the government, the employers' associations agreed to participate in a board on wages and subsidies and a board on general economic policy. The first was explicitly labeled The Contact Committee to signal that its purpose was solely to enable opposing interests to get in touch with each other. The agreements to participate on the other board came after some hesitation, on the conditions that the board should have a free position vis-à-vis the government and that there should be free exchanges of opinions and information, with no written statements (Bergh and Pharo, 1977; Kvavik, 1976; Moren, 1958, 1974).

In 1975 a new attempt to institutionalize integrated participation was stopped. The issues were prices and wages, and this time the Federation of Trade Unions refused to participate whereas the employers' associations were willing. The labor unions agreed that a bargaining structure like the one suggested, involving the major organizations and public officials, should be used for one year to set wages and salaries for all major groups in an attempt to reduce inflation. But the unions refused to institutionalize such a structure, and they claimed their freedom to reconsider the structures to be used from year to year. This position, taken by the Social Democratic leaders of the labor unions, was probably influenced by a temporary strengthening of the left-wing opposition, attacking the proposed structure in terms of traditional ideologies about unions' autonomy and the right to fight for better working conditions. The 1976 experience with a centrally negotiated incomes policy also cooled governmental enthusiasm. Government had to pay a high price for its participation – a bill that had to be honored by oil still below the North Sea (Schwerin, 1980).

The reluctance to accept integrated participation permanently in the context of broad, general issues stands in contrast to Norwegians' widespread willingness to participate on committees dealing with specific, limited issues. And this pattern is not specifically Norwegian. Generally it has been difficult to establish permanent structures for integrated participation in incomes policy making – and it has been difficult to protect them from breaking down (Lehmbruch, 1974, 1977; Lijphart, 1968; Panitch, 1977). The Social Contract in Britain was not produced through a formal apparatus like the National Economic development Council, but through bilateral negotiations. Lehmbruch (1977) observed that organizations were unwilling to accept integrated participation in Ordnungspolitik – that is, policies that affect the organizational and institutional framework of the economy. Others have described the tendency to handle difficult general issues through temporary structures or through political parties and elections (Ehrmann, 1971; McConnell, 1966; Peterson, 1971; Ruin, 1974). Politization of an issue may, however, reduce an organization's influence when its members identify with different parties, as shown by Wheeler (1975) in a study of the Swedish Central Organization of Salaried Employees.

The relationship between integrated participation and issue generality is not monotone. Although organizations do not deal with broad, general issues by means of integrated participation, neither do they use integrated participation to work out specific details. Studies of committees in the Ministry of Agriculture and the ministry of Social Welfare in Norway have shown more extensive participation in structural decisions establishing general rules for future choices than in one-shot decisions (Gjedrem, 1975; Lund, 1976).

Several reasons help to explain why integrated participation is used primarily in economic policy making. Integrated participation reinforces and is reinforced by governmental regulation. People accept regulation more readily when they themselves help to determine the regulations, and those who determine regulations, promote the idea of regulation. Western societies have regulated economies, but regulation is weak and inconsistent in the noneconomic sectors. The economic sectors attract regulation because they are amenable to integrated participation. Widespread consensus has supported the ideas: (a) that societies should pursue economic goals such as wealth, productivity, and employment, (b) that societies can simultaneously attain such diverse goals as full employment, stable prices, and technological development, (c) that economic phenomena are well understood and are accurately portrayed in economists' theories, and (d) that economic variables are accurately measured by existing numerical indicators. Thus, compromises have been made between economic policies without damaging organizations' ideological identities. Since the goals can be attained simultaneously, they should be pursued simultaneously. Since accurate theories can be used as bases for decomposing general issues into specific issues, resolution of specific issues will eventually help to resolve the general issues. Accurate theories and accurate, numerical indicators imply that specific issues should be resolved by calculating trade-offs, which are technical problems rather than political ones. Although different interests quibble among one another about how economic gains should be divided, everyone can gain something and there do not have to be losers.

A prediction is that the more the participants' trust in Keynesian economics is reduced, and the stronger neo-Marxist economists become in the labor unions, and the stronger strict liberal monetarists à la Milton Friedman become in the employers' associations, the less likely that integrated participation will be used as a major form of coordination (Lehmbruch, 1977).

A policy topic's organization-sets

A policy topic is a cluster of interdependent policies, and a policy topic's organization-set is a cluster of interdependent organizations which take interest in that topic (Evan, 1966). One policy topic may have one or several organization-sets.

Organization-sets depend upon characteristics of policy topics, of course, and also upon characteristics of governments and societies. For instance, a few organizational leaders in Scandinavia and Great Britain can speak on behalf of organization-sets. Because Scandinavian and

179

British organizations are likely to cover large proportions of their potential constituencies, and because large fractions of these organizations unite into organizations of organizations, the leaders of peak organizations can legitimately claim to represent whole organization-sets. In the United States, organizations compete for the rights to represent others, and each organization covers a smaller fraction of its potential constituency. For instance, only 30 to 35 percent of American farmers are members of producer organizations. There are several competing organizations, and they disagree fundamentally on issues like the role of government. Some, like the American Farm Bureau Federation, have urged government to get out of agriculture. In Britain, between 70 and 85 percent of the farmers have joined the National Farmers' Union; and in the Scandinavian countries, 85 to 100 percent of the farmers are members of producer organizations. There is a well developed division of labor, and although Norwegian farmers have split into two organizations, and Danish farmers into three organizations according to the sizes of farms, organization-sets are small, and most of the time farmers talk with one voice (Buksti, 1974; Gjedrem, 1975; Lindblad et al., 1974; Self and Storing, 1962; Talbot and Hadwiger, 1968; Wilson, 1977).

Likewise, in the United States, the National Association of Manufacturers includes less than ten percent of all the firms, and 20 to 25 percent of the firms employing more than ten persons. The Confederation of British Industries organizes approximately 85 percent of the firms with more than ten employees. In the Scandinavian countries, percentages are even higher, and with one dominant peak organization in each country. Finally, American labor unions include little more than a quarter of the workers, and some major unions – like the Teamsters, the United Auto Workers, and the National Educational Association – do not belong to a peak organization. In Britain, approximately half of the workers are union members, and most unions belong to peak organizations. In Sweden, more than 90 percent of the blue-collar workers are affiliated with the Confederation of Swedish Trade Unions; the Central Organization of Salaried Employees organizes 75 percent of the white-collar workers; and the Swedish Confederation of Professional Associations includes 90 percent of the professionals. Danish and Norwegian white-collar workers have traditionally been less willing to join a single peak organization; from 60 to 66 percent are members of various occupational organizations. However, several mergers have occurred, reducing the heterogeneity. Danish and Norwegian blue-collar workers are affiliated with one national confederation of trade unions, but the proportions represented have been less impressive than in Sweden – 60 to 80 percent. In Norway, the tendency is that while older unions, like the metal workers', still organize close to 100 percent of their potential members, the overall percentage is going down. Including only 56 percent of the blue-collar workers in 1975, the Norwegian Federation of Trade Unions still has no rival and no challenges to its right to represent all blue-collar workers in governmental policy making (Beer, 1958; Brautaset, 1973; Elvander, 1966; Karlsen, 1977; Kvavik, 1976; Lindblad et al., 1974; Pestoff, 1977; Salisbury, 1975; Wilson, 1977).

Often membership statistics are uncertain, and it is difficult to determine who are, or should be, included in the potential constituency of an organization. Yet, the tendency is clear: economic-producer groups in the United States are organized in ways that make organization-sets larger and less representative than in Britain and Scandinavia. Partly, the differences are related to variations in socioeconomic bases: the smaller size of the Scandinavian countries and the less diversity in commodity patterns as well as sizes of companies and farms, make it easier to consolidate a sector into a single peak organization (Salisbury, 1975). Also Scandinavians generally are joiners of organizations. Whereas 53 percent of the adult population in Britain and 40 percent of the American population are nonmembers (Almond and Verba, 1963; Verba and Nie, 1972), only 21 percent of the Swedes, 30 percent of the Norwegians, and probably a similar share of the Danes, have not joined any organizations (Hallenstvedt and Rønning, 1975; Martinussen, 1977; Pestoff, 1977). Finally, differences in the ways groups are organized reflect differences in political and administrative systems.

Relevant governmental decisions are far more likely to be made centrally in the Scandinavian countries and in Britain than in the United States. For example, the National Union of Teachers in Britain – as well as its Scandinavian counterparts – must be able to bargain with the national ministry, whereas in America there are some 3,000 school boards with autonomous authority (Eckstein, 1960; Salisbury, 1975). Thus, governmental organization affects a policy topic's organization-set in two ways: indirectly, through the effects upon the ways interests in societies organize themselves; directly, through the number of governmental units that may demand participation in a policy topic. On the government side, organization-sets evidently depend upon the degree of functional specialization within a political system. Although it is difficult to find exact measures of functional specialization, the tendency is clearly that functional specialization is greater in Britain and the Scandinavian countries than in the United States.

Standard descriptions (Beer, 1958; Dexter, 1969; Eldersveld, 1958; Mulhollan, 1977; Truman, 1951) emphasize the multiple foci, overlapping competences, and fluid character of American politics. Organized interests are provided multiple access points due to the principle of separation of powers and a complicated division of labor between federal authorities, the states, and legal agencies. Also, loose and sprawling political parties at the federal level permit personal followings and power for individual representatives, low party discipline, and powerful committee chairpersons in Congress. Actually, the dominant configuration – a policy topic with a large organization-set, governmental power distributed among many, countervailing agencies and public officials, as well as organized interests in society – has to be supplemented by a quite different configuration. In some policy topics, governmental power is monopolized by single agencies; this is the configuration described in studies of some independent regulatory commissions and their symbioses with regulated interests (Bernstein, 1955; Kohlmeier, 1969; Leiserson, 1942), as well as in studies of professional associations which are given de facto control over licensing (Gilb, 1966).

By contrast, Britain and the Scandinavian countries are not federations. They emphasize the principle of parliamentarianism rather than separation of powers. Party discipline at the national level is strong. All these factors contribute to a concentration of power at the national level, but given the limited decision-making capacity of legislative assemblies, power is transferred to ministries and other administrative agencies. The result is that governmental powers related to most policy topics are likely to be concentrated within a few governmental agencies. Organizations develop specialized channels of contacts. Congruences proliferate between the intraorganizational structures of governmental agencies and those organized interests which deal with them. Governmental agencies and organizations also use the same types of specialists (Eckstein, 1960; Ehrmann, 1971; Hallenstvedt and Hoven, 1974; LaPalombara, 1964; Windmuller, 1969). Structures of integrated participation, in turn, reinforce functional differentiation between governmental agencies and reduce the chances of successful coordination across sectors (Egeberg et al., 1978).

Integrated participation is an intermediate alternative between totally dispersed power and monopoly. Integrated participation is most likely where governments as well as organized interests can be represented by a few units, where small numbers of agencies share control over governmental policies, and small numbers of organizations can realistically represent organized interests. Scandinavian studies have reported that most governmental committees and boards with organizational representatives have ten or fewer members (Meijer, 1969; Moren, 1974).

The sizes of organization-sets depend upon where organizations want to participate in government. Specifically, organizations may seek to participate in environments which are sparsely inhabited by competitors (Starbuck, 1976). Both in Sweden (Ruin, 1974) and in Norway (Moren, 1974), organizations can avoid competitors by participating with administrative agencies below the departmental level. The relation between integrated participation and organization-sets is also reflected in the observation that organizations are showing preferences for contacting governments through many specialized channels rather than through one general channel. This is consistent with the finding that organizations identify homogeneous networks of interdependence and create semi-autonomous subsystems rather than pool interdependencies in a single system (Cyert and March, 1963; Simpson and Gulley, 1962; Thompson, 1967). Finally, the relation between integrated participation and organization-sets is illustrated when organizations merge in order to achieve integrated participation, and when government makes mergers a condition for establishing structures for integrated participation (Bradley, 1965; Grand and Marsh, 1977; Heckscher, 1946; LaPalombara, 1964).

A reasonable interpretation of these observations is that integrated participation is a form of coordination which is more likely to be used in policy topics with small organization-sets, and that organizations prefer environments with small organization-sets. The benefits of coordination and cartelization disappear as the numbers of interdependent units increase. Representative bodies face a trade-off between representativeness, which calls for large numbers of participants, and decision-making efficiency, which calls for small numbers. In large organization-sets, interorganizational perceptions diffuse and generalize: the potential impacts of one organization upon another dwindle in importance, and organizations behave in terms of the general properties of the whole organization-sets (Starbuck, 1976). Ideological purity, uniqueness, and special competence have higher values in large organization-sets, but recognition and status have lower values, and the costs of responsibility are lower. Finally, large organization-sets and many external sources of uncertainty create different sources of intraorganizational power for those able to cope with the various uncertainties (Crozier, 1964). Many independent bases of intraorganizational power make the holders of such power better able to resist giving discretion to their representatives.

INTEGRATED PARTICIPATION AND AMBIGUITY

The configuration of integrated participation

The picture sketched by the empirical literature is one of highly specialized systems of organizational participation. Integrated participation is most likely in policy topics with small organization-sets, where interdependence is shared by small numbers of governmental agencies and organized interests. Thus, integrated participation prevails where societies segment into functionally autonomous sectors, especially sectors characterized by small numbers of well defined, stable interests; so that for each policy topic it is easy to specify stable rules about which organizations can participate, which problems and solutions are relevant,

183

and which rules of the game are legitimate. Specialized systems make particular policy issues relatively independent of the broader contexts within which they arise. Specialized systems prevent policies from becoming garbage cans, from becoming fortuitous result of the inter-meshing of loosely coupled processes (Cohen et al., 1972; March and Olsen, 1976).

Integrated participation has attracted economic-producer interests, especially those which are ordered into organizations of organizations and peak organizations. These economic-producer interests are generally concerned with protecting their vested interests, but their goals for integrated participation are most often immediate and specific. The organizations have hierarchical intraorganizational structures and pro-fessional managers who take care of boundary transactions; their mem-bers' activity and enthusiasm are low, and voluntarism is restricted.

The empirical findings are fairly consistent with the ideas that inte-grated participation occurs where predictability, certainty, compromises, recognition, role differentiation, and effective representation outwards offer high benefits, and where the costs are low of commitment and rigidity, of not expressing ideological purity and uniqueness, of accepting responsibility for governmental policies, and of transferring control from members to representatives. The empirical findings also suggest that organizations' choices about integrated participation reflect the ambi-guities of the choice situations. Firstly, integrated participation is more prevalent where there is little ambiguity concerning the extent and character of interdependence and power. For instance, integrated par-ticipation is most likely in policy topics which interest only a few organizations that have stable divisions of intraorganizational labor and power. Secondly, integrated participation concentrates on policy topics where organizations' interests and preference orderings are reasonably well specified, where the magnitude and character of value disagree-ments are clear, and where organizations know how much of the attain-ment of one goal they are prepared to sacrifice in order to attain other goals somewhat more fully. Finally, integrated participation focusses upon policy topics where the causal world is well understood, where decisions have predictable consequences, and where it is easy to know who has competence and expertise.

The effects of ambiguity

Focussing upon variations in ambiguity makes it possible to relate the study of integrated participation to a broader framework of theoretical ideas concerning organizational choice (Cohen et al., 1972; March and Olsen, 1976). It also suggests some predictions.

Consider the ambiguity of interdependence and power. Participative structures, specifying organizations' rights as well as relevant issues, reflect stable distributions of power. Institutionalized power is exercised most of the time without either open demonstrations of, or challenges to, power distributions, because attempts to change power distributions rationally take account of the ease of making such changes. In situations where interdependencies and power distributions are changing rapidly, there are fewer benefits from being able to predict how participating organizations will behave, and there are higher costs of rigidity and of not exploiting sudden opportunities. Consequently, organizations are less likely to participate in policy topics which are undergoing major changes, and during periods when the organizations themselves are undergoing changes in values, perspectives, priorities, or resources. Organizations remain reluctant to participate until their priorities and resources, and thus their interdependencies, become clearer.

The greater the ambiguity of interdependence and power, the more difficult it is for organizations to compromise and to accept others as the legitimate representatives of causes or groups. Rather, claims of representation are challenged, and appeals are made to wider audiences. Ideological purity and uniqueness gain value. Where the ambiguity of interdependence and power involves organizations in conflict, interorganizational coalitions have high values, and members' control over their organization is weak. Conversely, where intraorganizational interdependencies and power are ambiguous, members' control is strong, and coalitions between organizations have low values.

However, organizations are also disinclined to participate in the situations where interdependence and power are extremely clear. These situations enable organizations to deal with their interdependencies through autonomous adjustments which are guided by norms, traditions, and forecasts, and through conditional rules specifying substantive behaviors (Arrow, 1974; Thompson, 1967). An implication is that integrated participation is unusual in highly traditional and stable political systems. Integrated participation thrives where there is high stability concerning who depends upon whom, but where variations in the ways these interdependencies occur generate needs for information about deviations from predicted conditions and needs to exchange instructions about changes in behaviors; that is, where organizations coordinate by feedback (March and Simon, 1958).

Next, consider the ambiguity of interest. Participative structures assume clear criteria for what organizations should be represented. A traditional justification for participation is that particular governmental policies affect some organized interests more than they do the rest of societies. Likewise, organizations with specific and unambiguous interests are more prone to participate than are organizations with diffuse and ambiguous interests.

Specific interests make logrolling easier. Specific interests also make it easier to compare interorganizational exchanges at the margin. As a consequence, an organization can limit participation to policy topics where substantive gains are substantial at the same time as the organization's ideological purity is not threatened. Furthermore, the less complicated it is to compare interorganizational exchanges at the margin, the easier to monitor the performances of representatives, and the less costly to give them discretion. Thus, to attract participants, participative structures have to limit the responsibilities that participating organizations have to carry. There is greater willingness to give representatives discretion and less insistence upon control by members.

Lastly, consider the ambiguity of understanding. The more obscure the causal world, and the harder to see the connections between organizations' actions and their consequences, the less willing organizations are to accept participation. The costs of participation are easily observed – rigidity, losses of ideological purity, acceptance of responsibility, and losses of members' control. Such possible benefits from participation as certainty, policy compromises, and external efficiency remain ambiguous. Public recognition is the only benefit that is fairly easy to anticipate. Thus, the participating organizations will be those that struggle for recognition and legitimacy.

Specifically, ambiguity of understanding may make potential representatives unwilling to participate. Often the opposite prediction is offered. Potential representatives are assumed to be more willing to participate in ambiguous situations. They are seen as gaining power because they can interpret ambiguous situations and because they seem able to influence situations which members cannot control. Ambiguity allows the use of appropriate arguments while reaching interorganizational agreements and different arguments when explaining the agreements to their constituencies (March and Simon, 1958; Michels, 1949; Turk and Lefcowitz, 1962).

However, if members cannot evaluate their representatives' interpretations, neither can they check the alternative interpretations given by the representatives' opponents. The representatives' opponents benefit from the fact that representatives have to compromise, that they seldom get everything they want. Their opponents can attack the representatives for being ineffective as well as disloyal, and the opponents can question the benefits from participation. Ambiguous situations also encourage factions to compete in militancy, ideological purity, utopian demands and boldness of actions (Ehrmann, 1968; Krusius-Ahrenberg, 1958), making it difficult for representatives to present their organizations outwards. Thus, the effects of ambiguity depend strongly upon the level of intraorganizational trust and conflict.

THE FUTURE?

This analysis should comfort those who fear that liberal democracies are heading for a corporatist era where integrated organizational participation replaces parties, electoral systems, and legislatures. Integrated participation is attractive only for some organizations, for some policies, in some situations. Specifically, organizations are unlikely to make major changes in their environments through this form of coordination. Increasing complexity and ambiguity may make integrated participation less attractive. This analysis also should comfort those who fear that integrated participation results in co-optation of organizations by the state, loss of freedom of association and organizational self-governance, and helpless individuals facing a powerful state. Typically, organizations have refused integrated participation where their ideological purity and self-governance have been threatened. Structures of integrated participation supplement rather than replace other forms of participation. The multitude of forms of participation and coordination in Western societies reflect functional differentiation, as well as patterns of power. Prescriptive and descriptive theories of democracy have so far not been able to comprehend this complexity.

Notes

* This chapter is a slightly edited version of an article which first appeared in Paul G. Nystrom and William H. Starbuck (eds.), Handbook of Organizational Design, vol. 2, pp. 492–516 (New York: Oxford University press, 1981).

The end product has benefited from the criticism, comments, advice, information, and questions of Michael D. Cohen, Lewis A. Dexter, Morten Egeberg, Kjell Eliassen, Jostein Gaasemyr, Finn Holmer Hoven, Stein Kuhnle, Gerhard Lehmbruch, Per Lægreid, Jorolv Moren, Paul C. Nystrom, Jeremy J. Richardson, Stein Rokkan, Paul Roness, Don S. Schwerin, Philippe C. Schmitter, Joan Dunbar, Lars Svåsand, and Harald Sætren. The author also acknowledge the invaluable help of Ester Nilsen and Reidun Tvedt who have prepared several drafts of this chapter. Special thanks are in order to James G. March and William H. Starbuck, who have generously put at the author's disposal time, scholarship, and friendship.

6

STILL PEACEFUL COEXISTENCE AND REVOLUTION IN SLOW MOTION?*

Political systems have to make a variety of decisions, each calling for a different strategy and organizational structure. Over time policy styles develop: the process by which policies are formulated and implemented acquire certain characteristics, reflecting to some extent typical problems and issues (Thompson and Tuden, 1959). The predominant policy styles in Norway since 1945 have been problem-solving, bargaining and self-governance. Crucial to these routine policy-making styles is that most elements are predetermined: *(a) who* will be making a decision; each feasible choice set involving only a few people; *(b) what* the agenda is and the relevant problems, goals and solutions; *(c) how* the decisions should be made; and *(d) why* outcomes should be accepted and considered legitimate. Within such constraints, outcomes will seldom deviate significantly from earlier results. The image is one of order, incrementalism and compromise. A modern welfare state has been built without agonizing conflicts. Norway has moved from being one of the poorest to one of the richest countries in Europe – a "revolution in slow motion" (Larssen, 1973) – while retaining peaceful coexsistence between major groups.

There are, however, deviations from the routine policy-making styles; mobilization and confrontation occasionally occur. These styles involve many, and sometimes unexpected, participants; conflicting definitions of problems, goals and solutions; disagreement on pertinent procedures and arenas; absence of legitimacy; and sometimes the imposition of significant policy changes.

This chapter discusses some of the conditions for the use of the different styles. First, policy style characteristics are specified in more detail, and we present some theoretical idea about how policy styles may be linked to societal cleavages, the political organization of social groups and the organization of policy-making institutions. Secondly, we specify the Norwegian setting in terms of major cleavages and the resources mobilized by different politically organized interests. Thirdly, we describe the apparatus for routine policy-making and compare it with more "irregular" policy-making in terms of participants, issues, values, procedures, results and legitimacy. Finally, we discuss some of the possibilities and constraints for managing the use of policy-making styles.

POLICY STYLES: CAUSES AND MOTIVES

The structure and standard operating procedures of the state reflect the outcomes of previous political struggles, and we would expect political organization and policy styles to be influenced by societal cleavages (how people are divided into long-lasting factions), and by the resources mobilized. We should not, however, expect a simple causal structure. There is the usual inertia: the longer certain cleavages have dominated a system and been "frozen" into the political-administrative structure, the more likely that they will remain important even after "obsolescence". Organizing always implies selecting. Some conflicts, issues and groups are organized *into* politics, while others are "organized out" (Schattschneider, 1960). The ways in which a political system copes with cleavages influence the bases of the cleavages and the development of conflicts. This impact is twofold: through substantive outputs – or the imposing of burdens and awarding of benefits to various interests; and through the procedures and styles employed.

The emphasis on style has always been an important aspect of political governance. We often assume that people accept a policy because they accept the legitimacy of the preceding political process. Hence, we may challenge the idea that styles and processes should be linked primarily to substantive outputs – in other words, who gets what. Styles should also be related to *social outcomes* like *(a)* who thinks and feels what as a result of the process (redistribution of trust, friendship, alienation, distribution of credit or blame, redefinition of interests and truth); *(b)* who is competent for what as a result of the experience, information and so on, gained through the process; and *(c)* who does what as a result of the process (for example, mobilization, apathy, joining or leaving parties and interest organizations, forming citizens' initiatives or revolutionary armies, and so on), and potential effects of such actions on the pattern of cleavages and conflicts in society (Cohen et al., 1972; March and Olsen, 1976).

Anticipated social outcomes may provide motives for choice between policy styles, supplementing motives stemming from anticipated substantive outputs and causal factors related to cleavage structures. And they suggest important dimensions for a typology of policy styles. A typology of policy styles should indicate who the participants are – the role of the citizens, elected representatives and experts – as well as their agendas, the level of conflict, their strategies, and the substantive outputs and the social outcomes.

Organizing means providing arenas and choice opportunities, and regulating the access of participants, problems and solutions to these arenas and choices. The decision structure indicates which participants may (or have to) attend an arena or a choice. We are interested in the number and stability of participants – whether choices are made by a few representatives and experts, or whether there is mass mobilization and unconventional participation. Likewise, the access structure indicates which problems and solutions may attend an arena or a choice opportunity. We are interested in the number and stability of goals and causal theories, and the extent of any conflicts. The level of conflict is often related to attempts by groups to redress the power balance by changing the decision and access structures, and thus the activation patterns and the definition of issues. We are interested in when such strategies are used, as compared with when choices are made through analysis and search behavior, "sounding out" and attempts to achieve a compromise (Olsen, 1972a; Schattschneider, 1960; Thompson and McEwan, 1958). Finally, a typology of policy styles should consider results. Substantive outputs may be discussed in terms of whether there are clearcut winners/losers, or a sharing of benefits and costs, as well as whether policies are incrementalistic or constitute basic changes. Social outcomes may be related to legitimacy, and the unifying or polarizing effects on people's attitudes and behavior as well as the development of citizens' political potential and to gains in their effectiveness, knowledge and policy understanding. Table 6.1 summarizes some of the main characteristics and hypothesized correlates of five policy styles.[1]

The comparatively limited use of styles like mobilization and confrontation may be linked to factors such as size, homogeneity and history. Norway is a small and fairly homogeneous country. In modern Norwegian history consensus and peaceful coexistence, rather than dissensus, have prevailed (Torgersen, 1970). Here, however, we are primarily interested in variations in policy styles *within* this general framework. In the section below we indicate the setting of Norwegian public policy-making in terms of the cleavage structure and the politically organized resources behind various interests.

CLEAVAGES AND POLITICALLY ORGANIZED GROUPS

Cleavages

The best specified model of the Norwegian cleavage structure has been developed by students of the party system and electoral behavior (Valen and Rokkan, 1974). They describe cleavages as a product of complex historical processes and a sequence of conflicts triggered by waves of mobilization since the 1880s (figure 6.1).

First, *geography,* a territorial conflict where two distinct peripheries (the south-west and the north) mobilized against the center. Secondly, *culture,* where three dimensions have dominated: *(a)* the conflict about linguistic policy, between the defenders of the established central stan-

Table 6.1: *Policy styles – characteristics and correlates.*

Style	Structure		Level of conflict	Strategy	Results	
	Decision	Access			Substantive output	Social outcome
Problem-Solving (entrepreneurial)	Single decision-maker or a few experts	Agenda given with a few well-defined goals, well-understood means-ends connections	Consensus-objectives, norms, or standards shared, at least at some level; differences over subgoals can be mediated by reference to common goals by testing subgoals for consistency with other objectives	Analysis, identify a solution that satisfies shared criteria; enlarge resources; search for new alternatives; rationalistic and empirical; study problems carefully; reduce uncertainty about causal structures	All winners, no losers; incrementalism	Integration, goodwill and trust building; little competence building, except for the few participants; legitimacy related to cost-benefit analysis, and to beliefs in professional competence
Bargaining	A few recognized spokesmen for well-defined interests	Few, well-defined and stable interests, goals and causal theories	Agreement without persuasion; live with conflicts; disagreement about goals, but goals are bargainable within established rules of the game (arenas and procedural rules)	Pragmatic compromises and 'contacts'; gamesmanship and use of resources, sanctions, threats, offers and promises; no participant can unilaterally force through a decision; coalition building	Sharing more than winners/losers; distributional quantitative outputs; incrementalism	Some strain on the power and status system, but a possibility for longterm trust building; little competence building, except for the few participants; legitimacy related to pareto-optimal solutions or from widespread acceptance of both the postulates of politics, and the distribution of power within the system
Self-Governance	Several separated and autonomous decision-making centers with different participants; geographic or functional groups with self-governance; within each arena a few participants	Different definitions of problems, goals and solutions; within each arena a few well-defined and stable interests, goals and causal theories	Implicit or explicit contracts of mutual non-interference and adherence to common rules of peaceful coexistence; different rules and processes within each unit	Conflict avoidance through local rationality and low degree of non-agreement between units; spontaneous adaptation between units	Different solutions in different units; each choice supposedly affects a limited part of the population	Little strain in the power and status system; acceptance of cultural variation at the expense of national standards; more people are trained, and competence such as local knowledge is used; legitimacy related to axioms of self-governance

Table 6.1: *(Continued)*

Style	Structure				Results	
	Decision	Access	Level of conflict	Strategy	Substantive output	Social outcome
Mobilization	The arena of bargaining is not considered fixed; new participants are mobilized or activate themselves during a policy process	The agenda is not considered fixed; new problems, goals and solutions introduced during a policy process	Fairly high level of conflict; disagreement over goals and causal theories as well as over procedural rules of the game	Power struggle; activate followers; redefine issues; attacks on the management and legitimacy of the process; little agreement about who are experts	Winners or losers – all or nothing; potential for significant changes and renewal	Strong strains on power and status system; reduced trust between groups; increased trust within each group, more people get political experience and training, legitimacy related to direct democracy and people's right to self-governance
Confrontation	The arena of bargaining is not considered fixed; new participants are mobilized or activate themselves during a policy process	The agenda is not considered fixed: new problems, goals, and solutions introduced during a policy process	Very high level of conflict, total disagreement over goals and causal theories as well as over procedural rules of the game	Power struggle; protests, civil disobedience, use of physical power in open, violent confrontations	Winners or losers – all or nothing, potential for very significant changes and renewal	Extreme stress on the power and status system, alienation, lack of trust between groups, increased trust within groups, many people get experience and training, potential for changed 'consciousness' and level of activation, legitimization related to basic personal or group norms concerning the operation and structure of the policy

192

dard (*riksmål*) and the protagonists of the rural counter-language (*nynorsk*); (*b*) the conflict about moral legislation, particularly the control with the production and consumption of alcohol; and (*c*) the struggle for the control of the church, now basically a contrast between the active Christians, mostly orthodox Lutherans closely attached to lay religious bodies, and the great majority of religiously indifferent citizens.[2] Thirdly, *economy,* also with three dimensions: (*a*) the rural-urban conflict in the commodity market – a battle between market oriented farmers and the various urban and consumer interests, for the control of prices and subsidies; (*b*) the rural class struggle of laborers, smallholders and fishermen against local notables and the urban establishment; and (*c*) the industrial class struggle of the unionized working class against owners and employers.

Figure 6.1: *The Valen–Rokkan model (1974) of the Norwegian cleavage structure.*

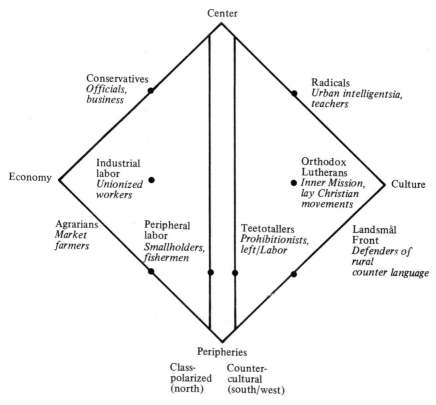

7 - Organized democracy.

Norwegian policy-making takes place within this established cleavage structure. New issues have evoked shifting cleavages, but in the twentieth century there is a distinct trend. One aspect is the increasing salience of economic cleavages, especially between unionized industrial workers and employers. Another aspect is the transformation of class conflict into class co-operation.

The sequence of cleavages is important, and so is the level of conflict. Up until 1918 traditional issues on cultural policy proved distinctly more divisive than the new issues of class conflict (Rokkan, 1966: 79). Following the electoral success of the socialists in 1927, the principal division has been between socialists and non-socialists, with an increasing emphasis on economic issues. But gradually class confrontation was transformed into class cooperation (Seim, 1972). 1945–1965 is a distinctive period in Norwegian political history, characterized by social change, political stability and an unusual degree of consensus on public tasks and goals (Bergh and Pharo, 1977; Bull, 1979). In 1945 all political parties presented a joint platform: the country was to be rebuilt after the war, and the problems of the 1920s and the 1930s – unemployment and poverty – had to be solved. Economic modernization was the key word – a belief in solving the problems through growth, industrialization and mass education. Growth presupposed peace in the labor market, and explicit and implicit contracts of peaceful coexistence – if not consensus – among the major interests contrasted the class struggle of the 1920s and 1930s.

The emphasis on economics, modernization and class cooperation has affected the saliency of other cleavages. It was widely believed that the rational use of the country's resources presupposed industrialization, urbanization, formal education and geographic mobility. Regional differences became less relevant. And with labor and employers as the major poles, cultural conflicts lost some of their saliency. Institutional arrangements for resolving such conflicts developed, and there were comparatively few confrontations over issues like religion, alcohol, or language.

Thus, styles of confrontation and mobilization may be preferred by groups who are concerned with other cleavages than the dominant one, and by groups who believe more in class conflict than class cooperation. First, we consider which cleavages and issues concern ordinary people. Is the Valen-Rokkan model adequate when extending the analysis from the development of the party system to other political structures and behavior? Has the welfare state itself caused new divisions in society (Kuhnle, 1980; Valen, 1981)?

Table 6.2 indicates that in the mid-1970s most people still perceived economic cleavages and issues as the most important.[3] Some use class terminology, others refer to tension between employers and employees, and still others use party terminology – socialists/non-socialists. At the same time the increase in the number of pensioned people and the costs of the welfare state, as well as the growing expectations of pensioners, cause 14 per cent to cite tensions between the working and the non-working parts of the population. The conservationist movement and its criticisms of the economic growth ideology, as well as the local/central conflict, are reflected even stronger in the data.

Table 6.2: *Evaluation of the importance of various cleavages and divisions: by the population, elected officials and employees in economic-producer organizations, and civil servants in the ministries 1975–76 (percentages).*

Type of cleavage/ divisions between:	Population	Economic-producer organizations		Civil servants in the ministries
		Elected officials	Employees	
Economy:				
Social classes	35 ⎫	39 ⎫	35 ⎫	44 ⎫
Employers/employees........	30 ⎪	71 ⎪	66 ⎪	62 ⎪
Blue-and white-collar workers.................	11 ⎬ 76	32 ⎬ 92	21 ⎬ 91	20 ⎬ 86
Employed-pensioned	14 ⎪	36 ⎪	28 ⎪	26 ⎪
Socialists/non-socialists.......	39 ⎭	74 ⎭	73 ⎭	59 ⎭
Ecology:				
Economic growth vs environmentalism	25	71	63	54
Geography:				
Center/periphery............	28 ⎫	64 ⎫	56 ⎫	64 ⎫
Rural/urban residents	13 ⎬ 41	39 ⎬ 75	40 ⎬ 67	44 ⎬ 73
Different regions	11 ⎭	32 ⎭	22 ⎭	23 ⎭
Culture:				
Religious people/others	17 ⎫	22 ⎫	14 ⎫	21 ⎫
Teetotallers/others	18 ⎬ 33	19 ⎬ 36	19 ⎬ 27	14 ⎬ 32
Different language groups .... (bokmål–nynorsk)	11 ⎭	14 ⎭	13 ⎭	15 ⎭
Demography:				
Women/men..............	13 ⎫ 31	35 ⎫ 61	25 ⎫ 51	27 ⎫ 61
Young/middle-aged..........	23 ⎭	48 ⎭	40 ⎭	50 ⎭
Meritocracy:				
Groups with different levels of education	25 ⎫	47 ⎫	44 ⎫	50 ⎫
Experts – common people	21 ⎬ 45	58 ⎬ 82	53 ⎬ 69	49 ⎬ 70
Public employees – clients	14 ⎭	53 ⎭	39 ⎭	29 ⎭
No. of respondents	(2 084)	(444)	(509)	(756)
No. of non-respondents	(119)	(31)	(27)	(28)

195

The traditional cultural cleavages still prevail for 11–18 percent. In addition comes tension between the sexes and between generations – groups that did not count directly in the structuring of the party system (Valen and Rokkan, 1974: 364). Also, large groups are concerned with divisions linked to meritocracy: experts, bureaucrats and people with high formal education, on the one hand; ordinary people and the clients of public bureaucracies, on the other. These are potential cleavages made more conspicuous by the growth of the welfare state.

We conclude that the economic divisions have a dominating position, but that Norway – as perceived by the man in the street – clearly has a pluralistic cleavage structure. The likelihood that some of these divisions should provide a basis for mobilization and confrontation, depends on the politically organized resources linked to the various groups, and on the responsiveness of political institutions – their ability and willingness to accommodate the concerns of various groups in terms of effective problem-solving and conflict resolution.

Politically organized resources

The present emphasis on economic issues is reflected in the mobilization of resources behind various interests. Around 1920 the prohibitionists could, for instance, claim by far the largest organized membership in the country, about twice that of the trade unions (Nilson, 1978: 179). And several political parties were in many ways instruments of the temperance movements.

The Norwegian party system, like the (perceived) cleavage structure, is pluralistic. But since 1945 the Labor Party and the Conservatives have been the most important parties in terms of votes, members, economic resources and seats in the *Storting* (Parliament). The main tendency has been that the Labor Party and the Conservatives are at opposite poles on issues within the advanced corporate urban economy, while they tend to take the same side in territorial-cultural conflicts. Their positions are very similar on the level of support for the primary economy, and they do not differ much in their reactions to the religious activism of the Christian People's Party. Territorial-cultural variables seem to prevail in differentiating the parties of the middle from those of the left and the right, while a set of functional-economic variables helps contrast the socialists from the conservatives (Rokkan, 1966: 103; Valen and Rokkan, 1974: 335).

The resource concentration around economic cleavages is strengthened because economic interest groups today control more politically relevant resources than any other type of interest group – as well as more resources than the political parties. Approximately 70 per cent of the

Norwegian population (15 years and older) are members of one or more interest organizations. Only humanitarian and recreational associations can compete with economic interest organizations in terms of membership, and the former are rarely involved in politics. Cultural associations

Table 6.3: *Support for various types of organizations in the Norwegian population in 1975. Percentages. (Number of respondents = 2 203)*

Type of organization	Total membership as a proportion of adult population (15 years and above)	Proportion of members who regard the organization the most important one[1]	Proportion of the population who think the influence of an organization			
			Is big	Is small	Should be bigger	Should be smaller
Federation of Trade Unions (LO)	18	64	60	2	6	16
Unions and professional associations outside LO	9	73	13	11	5	2
Organizations for people employed in agriculture, forestry, fisheries	5	59	26	11	14	4
Employers' associations and organizations in industry, commerce and shipping	5[2]	24	50	11	6	18
Housewives' associations ...	4	31	–	–	–	–
Pensioners' associations ...	3	43	3	30	22	1
Students' associations	4	12	9	14	4	7
Consumer groups	9	10	17	9	4	4
Environmental associations	–	–	9	13	24	3
Humanitarian associations	17	28	7	13	20	1
Religious associations.....	9	57	16	19	8	7
Teetotallers' associations ...	2	19	9	24	9	6
Language associations	2	3	3	27	2	4
Youth associations	5	39	7	14	10	1
Women's liberation associations	2	50	7	16	11	5
Sports clubs	17	37 }	4	20	11	1
Hobby clubs and recreational associations	14	27 }				
Automobile associations ..	12	15	–	–	–	–
Neighborhood associations	10	20	4	14	14	1

[1] This question was asked of those with multiple memberships. The numbers represent the percentage of those with multiple memberships who say the organization in focus is most important for themselves.

[2] This number is too high. The correct number is about 2 percent. The question is probably misunderstood by some respondents, and this explains why only 24 percent say this membership is the most important for them.

–: question not asked.

today mobilize relatively few citizens (table 6.3). Religious associations may be an exception – but even their membership is modest given that 95 percent of the population belongs to the state church. The importance of economic organizations also emerges when people with multiple organizational memberships are asked to judge which one is the most important (table 6.3).

Table 6.4: *Number of organizations and their administrative resources at the central offices at the national level, by type of organization in 1976.*

Type of organization:	Number of organizations	Percentage with own secretariat	Number of employees
Economic-producer organizations			
Primary sector	56	61	810
Industry	118	37	305
Norwegian Confederation of Industries	57	24	170
Norwegian Federation of Crafts	25	44	50
Others	36	50	85
Trade	107	29	320
Federation of Norwegian Commercial Associations	61	33	150
Others	46	29	170
Banking, insurance and transportation	61	49	715
Employers' associations	59	25	550
Norwegian Employers' Association	40	40	290
Others	19	27	260
Employees	206	45	990
Federation of Trade Unions	42	81	550
Others	164	38	440
Other organizations	369	47	1 245
Students'	8	87	25
Pensioners'	3	0	0
Youth	9	89	80
Women	4	75	10
Language	7	43	10
Teetotallers'	18	61	50
Religious	58	64	260
Environmentalists'	7	57	20
Humanitarian	64	53	345
Athletics and recreational	85	47	355
International cooperation, culture and professional associations not focussed on employee interests	106	24	90

Source: Moren et al. (1976).

The tendency is reinforced when the administrative resources of different organized interests are considered (table 6.4).[4] It is primarily economic interests which have administrative staffs of a size that make them a potential counterweight to public bureaucracies. The size of the staffs is strongly correlated with economic and other resources (Hallenstvedt, 1979; Moren et al., 1976), and the ability of such organizations to disrupt the economic system is a significant political resource.

A somewhat different pattern is seen in the responses to questions about which organized groups ought to have more or less influence upon the development of Norwegian society. While a majority of the population has no opinion about this question, or they are satisfied with the present distribution of power, those who do want changes have a clear idea of how influence should be redistributed. The most resourceful and (perceived) influential organizations – economic interests in the secondary and tertiary economies – should have less power. Likewise, there is a tendency to want more influence for those who are considered less powerful (table 6.3).

The conclusion is that most politically relevant resources are linked to economic cleavages. Still, the pluralism of the cleavage structure is reflected in a multiparty system and in a well-developed system of interest organizations. While the resources of parties and organizations emphasizing non-economic tensions are modest, some of them have a significant number of "identifiers" in the population. These identifiers may be mobilized under certain circumstances, for example, if political institutions do not respond to and accommodate such interests.

POLITICAL INSTITUTIONS AND POLICY-MAKING STYLES

Possibly the most important change in the macro-political organization of Western societies, has been the interpenetration of governmental agencies and organized interests in society. The locus of public policy-making has moved from the parliamentary arena to the corporative-functional arena; political parties have been deprived of their hegemony as the intermediary link between the people and government; and styles of problem solving, bargaining, and self-governance have become predominant (chapter 5). Heisler and Kvavik (1974) argued that Norway is the archetype of the "Europeal polity"-model – that is, a modern welfare state which has institutionalized a stable political process which (using the categories of table 6.1) is characterized by:

(a) *a decision structure*, where the influence of the general public can be said to have been effectively removed from decision-making; a decline in the role of the parliaments, ideological parties and elections; the co-optation of organized groups – so that virtually all have access to government. Administrative agencies have come into focus – the co-optation of organized groups has been accompanied by the development of a new type of policy-making structure, essentially a network of committees, as an extension of the formal governmental bureaucracy; a delegation to administrative subsystems where highly organized sectors enjoy substantial self-governance, with the groups most affected by public policies wielding considerable control over distinctive issue areas.

(b) *an access structure,* where broad ideological issues have vanished and the agenda is dominated by more technical issues; high task and goal consensus; and causal theories provided by recognized experts, and thus –

(c) *a low level of conflict.*

(d) *strategies* characterized by analysis, rational argumentation, compromises and bargaining, and little emphasis of politization and mass appeals based on clashing ideologies; lack of competition and emphasis on security and the avoidance of uncertainty – in general strategies presupposing trust rather than hostility and suspicion, and emphasizing the need to reach decisions by consensus rather than one actor imposing a solution on the rest.

(e) *substantive outcomes,* where all interests are accommodated to some extent – the substantive result of policy-making is to produce "sharers" more than winners and losers. The test of a good decision is not so much some objective rationality, but that as many as possible (of the significant parties) agree to it. The *social outcome* is that the trust among the elites is preserved and developed. The elites have a vested interest in the continued successful operation of the structure, while ordinary people are primarily interested in who gets what – not in participation and how things are done. Thus, they receive little political training and education. The lack of public debate deprives the political process of the renewal generated by disputation and competition. The political system does not receive inputs from groups not represented in the corporative-functional policy-making structure, and it is less able to adjust swiftly to environmental changes. Intra (political) systemic phenomena provide better clues for understanding the political process than do environmental factors.

Many of the features emphasized by Heisler and Kvavik are well documented in the literature. In Norway organizations have legitimate and institutionalized rights to participate in all phases of governmental policy-making as representatives of specific interests (chapter 5). There are group-government interactions like delegation of public authority to interest organizations; the remiss system, whereby interested organizations are invited to comment on public policies before they are presented to the Storting or implemented; and the well-developed informal, day-to-day consultations with organized interests and groups. The level of conflict is low. And both participants and citizens report a fairly widespread satisfaction with the outcomes of public policy-making processes (NOU 1982: 3).

There are, however, variations in policy-making styles across issue areas, and ministries concerned with economic policy-making are most likely to develop a cooptive structure. The fact is even more evident in the selectivity of the system concerning which groups are coopted. Civil servants and the leaders of the economic-producer organizations perceive a pluralistic cleavage structure (table 6.2), but the corporative-functional system does not accommodate or permit participation for all interests – not even for all organized interests. Thus, we need to study whether interests not participating in this arena are active in other arenas, and if they in this way make the policy-making more dynamic. The corporative-functional system is in certain respects *status quo* oriented. However, it is not isolated from other policy-making arenas. In order to understand the dynamics of the system and the use of mobilization and confrontation, we consider the selectivity of different policy arenas and the ways in which the arenas are interconnected.

Selectivity and arena interaction
Economic-producer interests, especially large, powerful business and employers' associations, along with organizations in agriculture and fisheries, labor unions, and the associations of various professions, dominate the committee structure – with more than 90 per cent of the representatives from organized interests. In 1979 the Federation of Trade Unions, together with its component unions, was represented in 270 committees. Likewise, the Confederation of Industries participated in approximately 100, and the Norwegian Employers' Association in seventy committees. In contrast, promotional interests cultural, humanitarian, and the like – were represented in only sixty-seven committees, that is 8 per cent of the total at the national level. Religious interests were represented in six committees; youth, sports and recreational interests in fourteen; and humanitarian interests in twenty-eight committees (St. meld. no. 7, 1979–80).

While a majority of the national organizations have contact with the ministries, the great majority is *not* directly represented in the committee system (Christensen and Egeberg, 1979; Egeberg, 1981). Neither are all such organizations represented through established peak organizations. Table 6.4 indicates that a large number of national economic-producer organizations are not members of the major peak organizations in their sector.

The economic-producer organizations' dominance is also found in the workings of the remiss system, where economic organizations receive five times as many remisses as non-economic organizations (Egeberg, 1981); in contacts with policy-making centers like the Cabinet and the ministries; as well as the judgments of civil servants of the influence of various organized interests (chapters 3 and 4; Lægreid and Olsen, 1978).

The conclusion is that the corporative-functional policy-making system is primarily centered on economic cleavages, and that access is provided mainly to resourceful economic-producer groups. Other groups and cleavages may be absent because they are excluded, or because they choose not to participate. Integrated organizational participation in public policy-making has costs as well as benefits, and sometimes the costs may exceed the benefits to the interest organizations (chapter 5).

The corporative-functional arena is also selective in terms of problems that can be solved and conflicts that can be coped with. It is used more often for specific, limited issues than for broad, general issues. The reluctance to accept permanent integrated participation where general principles – like the structuring of the economy, and especially the right of private ownership and the "free bargaining rights" of the economic organizations – are at stake, contrasts with the widespread willingness of Norwegian organizations to participate on committees dealing with specific, limited problems. The result is a specialized system of representation where organizations participate at, or below the ministerial level (chapter 5).

The description of the corporative-functional arena contrasts with descriptions of other phases of Norwegian political history where the contest for power has generated mass mobilization into politics; where the conditions for political activity has changed and set the scene for new alignments and new cleavages. These have been periods where the system has lost its equilibrium, and each party has pressed to bring in new allies and tried out new alliances (Rokkan, 1966: 76). In comparison descriptions of the corporative-functional system are static, and often it is assumed that the policy-making processes of that system also dominate other arenas and blunt the edges of ideological conflict. This may, however, be to generalize from a very special period (1945–65) in Norwegian political history and to underestimate the extent to which the workings of the corporative-functional arena depend on a larger configuration of political forces and institutions.

The development of the corporative-functional system was not opposed by political parties. On the contrary, the idea of "democratic corporatism" – economic planning based on a corporate structure – was launched before the Second World War and developed in London and

Stockholm during the war on the initiative of leaders of the Labor Party and the Federation of Trade Unions. The new policy-making structure was to cooperate closely with political parties and other democratic institutions (Bergh and Pharo, 1977: 38). While the original plans were never implemented, the history of the corporative-functional policy-making system illustrates the strong links between political parties and economic-producer groups in Norway, and the integrating role of the political parties.

A study of 475 elected leaders and 536 administrators in national economic-producer organizations shows that more than half of the former and nearly half of the latter have held office in a political party or represented a political party in public office. The study also shows that specific parties have their strongholds in different organizations: the Labor Party in the Federation of Trade Unions, the Conservatives in the employers' organizations, and the Center Party (former Agrarians) in the farm organizations (Gaasemyr, 1979). The Labor Party and the Federation of Trade Unions have more formalized cooperation than do other parties and economic-producer organizations. However, there is no doubt that the same specific interests and causes are argued both by parties and organizations.

The corporative-functional policy-making system also operates within a context where the majority of Cabinet members have held party membership (and most often party office) for decades; where the press traditionally has been strongly linked to political parties; and where political parties spend a lot of time and effort developing their platforms.

Thus, one characteristic of the Norwegian policy-making system is that there is a considerable interaction and overlap in terms of leadership in the corporative-functional and the territorial-electoral channel. In addition, the law of anticipated reactions is a prime form of coordination. The influence of the Storting is often manifested not by active participation in policy processes, but by how its interests and views are taken into account in advance by other participants in the policy process. Neither bureaucrats nor economic-producer organizations view the Storting as a rubber-stamp institution, or view the political parties as insignificant (chapters 2 and 3).

In certain respects political parties, elected bodies and the public have recently improved their position *vis-à-vis* the corporative-functional policy-making system. The change in 1961 from one-party, majority governments to coalition or minority governments enhanced the importance of the Storting in coalition building and bargaining in the policy process. During the 1970s the tensions between the political parties increased, new parties were founded, and in the Storting the number of dissenting votes in committees more than doubled from 1972–3 to 1974–7 (Rommetvedt, 1980). At the same time, public funds were used to strengthen the political parties, and the new instability of voters (Valen, 1981) required the parties to take heed of public opinion. More policy-making functions are delegated to elected bodies at the regional or local level, rather than to administrative and thus corporative-functional units. More critical mass media, backed by the Right to Information Act on Administrative Affairs 1970, has reduced the possibility for the corporative-functional elite to operate "without the constraints of constant public surveillance" (Kvavik, 1976: 95).

These tendencies illustrate the limitations of the corporative-functional system and its policy styles. They are reflected in a number of significant policy-making decisions: the Norwegian decision not to join the European Common Market; the democratization of business banks; the introduction of free abortion; energy policy-making, such as the decision not to develop nuclear power, and the decision to build a hydroelectric power plant on the Alta River; the introduction of the principle that farmers' incomes should equal that of industrial workers; decentralization of policy-making functions to regional and local authorities; the decision to store military equipment for U.S. Marines in Norway; the introduction of a fifteen month-long price and income freeze in 1978.

None of these policy decisions were launched and settled within the corporative-functional arena alone. Some were handled entirely outside this arena. Others involved a complex interaction between several policy arenas and a mobilization of a large number of citizens. Furthermore, the corporative-functional system shows signs of stagnation. The period following the Second World War brought a wave of committees, but since the 1960s the expansion has been modest. Since the mid-1950s, when postwar reconstruction was drawing to an end, there has been a levelling off in the number of governmental committees with organizational representatives. And presently the Conservative government is making an attempt to reduce the number of public committees.

What, then, are the conditions under which the standard operating procedures of the policy-making system break down and citizens refuse to accept policies arrived at through this system?

Mobilization and confrontation

The standard operating procedures of a polity reflect certain stable interests, goals and cleavages, causal theories, power and alliances. Are those resorting to styles of mobilization and confrontation citizens who are excluded from routine policy-making; citizens who try to compensate their lack of formal positions by a high level of activity? Are they trying to transform the institutional context, within which policies are made, by bringing in new participants, issues, definitions and rules of the game?

The study of citizens' initiatives showed that there is a strong connection between the organization of routine policy-making and the occurrence of collective protests organized outside established political institutions (chapter 1). With few exceptions such initiatives are triggered by public policy decisions. And the fact that nearly half of the population, 15 years of age or above, has participated, is a warning of the potential inadequacies of the territorial-electoral and the corporative-functional systems.

The exclusion argument is more relevant for issues and cleavages than for participants. Citizens' initiatives seldom activate people with few political resources. Most likely to be mobilized are the political losers. They participate in routine policy-making processes but are unable to achieve a majority for their view. Another active group is the "politically unwilling" – people who do not want permanent engagement in parties and interest organizations, but who have the necessary (individual) resources to protest if their immediate interests are at stake.

Styles of mobilization and confrontation are frequently used to focus issues given scant attention in routine politics. Citizens' initiatives in several respects represent an opposition to the "Establishment" organized around economic cleavages, superior in organizational and political party resources, and with an institutionalized right to participate in public policy-making. Issues pertaining to economic production and distribution seldom set off citizens' initiatives. Issues of life style, norms and moral principles are emphasized.

However, citizens' initiatives are ideologically heterogeneous. They are issue oriented more than system oriented. They do not reflect a general lack of confidence in government or in political institutions. They are a nuisance more than a threat to the leaders, and their legitimacy in the population is fairly high. In most cases there is no dramatic difference between "regular" and "irregular" politics.

The level of conflict is low in irregular policy-making, as it is in routine policy-making. Citizens' initiatives appeal to public opinion. The strategy is to gain sympathy among ordinary citizens by evoking their sense of fairness, equity and justice. Civil disobedience is infrequent, and physical violence is extremely rare (Olsen, 1981). In modern times Norway has never experienced civil war, armed insurrection, and the like. For most participants in citizens' initiatives the goal is to achieve a specific outcome on a specific policy, not to achieve major transformations of the polity, the socio-economic system, or changes in the territory of the state.

Leaders of citizens' initiatives are also concerned with the social outcomes of conflicts. They might want to alter the pattern of loyalties and support given different parties or organizations. But most of the time they are careful not to provoke hostilities and antagonism that may be difficult to heal, and compromises are achieved fairly often. Even in the confrontation over the building of a hydroelectric power plant on the Alta River, which involved hunger strikes, road blocks, occupation of the prime minister's office, use of explosives, and the arrest of several hundred protesters (chapter 1), there was a touch of "Norwegian style". A few days before the police action was to start, TV was able to get the leader of the police operations and the leader of the demonstrators together. Over a cup of coffee and some cookies the two spoke calmly about the prospects for the conflict. Both hoped the other party would give in. They promised to do their best to prevent violence, and expressed their understanding for the other party. When the Alta initiative was dissolved, a major argument was that continued activity would lead to the use of more violent means, a development the protesters did not want.

The Norwegian data indicate that use of different policy styles might reflect a functional differentiation between styles and institutions as well as power differentials. Styles of confrontation and mobilization and the use of citizens' initiatives supplement the styles of routine policy-making. They remind us about the limitations of ballots and organizational membership as signals of peoples' preferences on single issues, and about the limitations of making collective, political decisions through problem solving, bargaining, and self governance.

The differences between citizens' initiatives and the policy-making style of the corporative-functional system is particularly striking: Spontaneity and flexibility are emphasized rather than certainty and predictability; ideological identity, symbolic-expressive behavior and publicity rather than compromises behind closed doors; freedom from responsibility for public policies rather than official recognition; and activity and control by members and participants rather than leader autonomy. The result is a policy style that might provide new directions and a new sense of purpose for public policy issues, identities, and alignments, as a counterweight to the status quo orientation of the corporative-functional system.

The development of the corporative-functional system, with its emphasis on economic issues, has been in accordance with what the majority of the population has perceived as the most significant cleavages in Norwegian society. The development of this policy-making structure has also been consistent with the distribution of politically organized resources in society. The use of styles of confrontation and mobilization represent attempts to call attention to other cleavages, issues, values, and causal theories. And these styles have provided the losers in routine politics with an opportunity of appeal to the public.

So far, the fairly frequent use of styles of mobilization and the more rare styles of confrontation, have not changed the way most Norwegians feel: a common sense of identity, a fairly high legitimacy of policy-making institutions and of the present distribution of burdens and benefits. Does, then, the Alta case, with its many elements of confrontation, mark a change in Norwegian policy-making, away from peaceful coexistence and revolution in slow motion? Have the corporative-functional policy-making styles – based on the cooperation between stable power blocs organized around economic cleavages – been a finite phase? Have they been an institutional solution to the economic problems of the 1920s and the 1930s and the experiences with styles of confrontation and class conflict in that period? Will Norway experience a shift in power and new stable coalitions around other cleavages than the economic ones? Will there be a new equilibrium through changed participation rights for groups and access rights for issues and cleavages? Or will the future bring confrontations between issue-oriented, unstable coalitions?

Among the many factors affecting future trends, we offer some speculations about the role of political design: the degree to which policy-makers can affect future policy-making styles through a choice of institutional solutions.

POLITICAL INSTITUTIONS: DESIGN OR DEVELOPMENT

The more the public agenda grows in size and complexity, the more the most important role for political leaders will be to manage the policy process, not to make specific policy choices. Political leaders have to become organizers. They may try to affect the access structures, that is, to manage the agenda of various policy-making bodies, the issues, problems and solutions given access. They may try to affect the decision structure, that is, which participants are allowed to take part as well as the interaction between them by influencing the "rules of the game". They may try to manage the timing of policy decisions and thus the context (in terms of participants and issues) in which a choice is made. And they may try to create new policy-making arenas or to dismantle established ones. The policy styles used will depend on their ability to control the ways in which streams of participants, problems, solutions and choice opportunities flow together or are kept apart through organizational means.

It is not obvious that political leaders have much freedom to design and manage the policy-making structures and processes (Mill, 1962). Hopes for a firm theoretical basis for institutional design have been mostly unfulfilled (March and Olsen, 1982; Seidman, 1980; Szanton, 1981). In matters of polity building innovation is rare and slow. Successful innovations have usually been accidental rather than results of conscious design

(Sait, 1938; Sartori 1968). Organizational patterns also reflect power structures, and today governments have to strike a balance between a more complex matrix of competing interests than hitherto (Richardson and Jordan, 1979). It is possible that policy styles are the outcome of such a complex set of interactions that they may be difficult to change in a desired fashion (Richardson, 1982).

To some degree studies of administrative reorganization in Norway support such a pessimistic conclusion. We are left with the impression that considerable structural change has occurred since 1945, but largely unrelated to any consistent design on the part of the leadership. Political leaders are not very interested in governing by organizational means, their objectives are often ambiguous or conflicting and means-ends relations are not well understood. In addition the chances of a successful implementation are limited by the interests of civil servants as well as by organized clients (Roness, 1979; Sætren, 1983).

Administrative issues are directed by the heterogeneous Ministry of Consumer Affairs and Government Administration, where the political leaders usually take most interest in issues like prices, salaries and problems related to sexual equality, families and children. In 1979 a new Ministry of Coordination of Planning was established. However, the resources of this ministry were very modest; its leaders were advocating planning as a pedagogical exercise, and in the fall of 1981 the ministry was abolished by the new conservative government.

Thus, we should not look for a "master-designer". But neither should we conclude that adaptation and design do not take place. Organizations monitor their environment. They routinely try to make sense of experience, and they try to adapt goals, expectations, competences, and decision rules on the basis of that experience. In favorable times they accumulate slack resources which may work as a reservoir of unexploited opportunities when the environment turns less benign (Cyert and March, 1963; March, 1981b; March and Olsen, 1976). Three possible strategies should be mentioned: *ejection of issues from the agenda, cooptation of groups* and *cooptation of causes or interests*. Political leaders may try to get rid of problems and conflicts they cannot cope with through routine policy-making processes and styles. Or they may try to coopt the groups, causes, or interests which make routine processes break down and initiate the use of styles like mobilization and confrontation.

Ejection

Decentralization is (among other things) a technique for getting rid of difficult policy choices. Central authorities avoid a dilemma when they transfer to local authorities problems like how kindergartens should be organized and what role Christian values should have.

208

In Norway decentralization has for some time been a highly valued goal, but opinions differ as to the degree to which such goals have been successfully implemented. Decentralization creates a resource problem for the authorities to whom the decisions are decentralized. There are strong norms for equal treatment wherever one lives in the country, and whenever local policy-makers adopt different solutions, it is fairly easy for minorities to appeal to national authorities through questions in the Storting, delegations to the ministries, or through the mass media. Thus, we may expect problems and decisions to bounce up and down the system (Gustafsson and Richardson, 1979).

An alternative to decentralization is to give functional groups more self-governance. Such groups may prefer self-governance, sometimes supported by public money, rather than pursuing their aims in the political system. An example is religious groups which want to reduce state interference in the affairs of the state church, or to dissolve the state church. The state monopoly on TV and radio broadcasting is under attack. And the planning vs market debate has been revived, with a demand for letting market forces operate more independent of governmental, selective intervention. As public funds have become more scarce, economic-producer groups have also advocated less state interference in negotiations on wages and salaries.

While it has become more accepted that many problems cannot be solved through government, no major party wants drastic changes in the public agenda. The Conservatives argue for less public interference, but they have voted for most elements in the present welfare state. In general, the main tendency is a more complex public agenda aiming at "a qualitatively better society", rather than the ejection of problems and conflicts (Bratbak, 1981a). It is unlikely that policy styles will be affected in major ways through transferring decisions from the public to the private sector. Decentralization to local public policy-makers is more likely, but we expect cooptation to be more significant than ejection.

Cooptation of groups

Norwegian government has done more to increase participation rights than to reduce the public agenda. For instance, it has been explicit policy to increase the proportion of women on public committees; females have increased their participation in political parties, the Storting and local councils, and more women are recruited to higher positions in the civil service (Hernes, 1982; Skard, 1980).

The tendency is that groups which so far have been absent from, or marginal in, the corporative-functional system are coopted: artists, pensioned people, Lapps, the handicapped, and so on – sometimes not without problems. The new law on public administration (*Forvaltnings-*

loven) also states that affected groups should be heard before policies are set, and a proposed law on public planning provides for wider participation by affected neighborhood groups (NOU 1977: 1). Experiments with such participation has taken place within highway planning (Baldersheim, 1979). And the establishing of neighborhood councils (*bydelsutvalg*) also tends to coopt and accommodate groups which earlier have resorted to irregular politics (Stokkeland, 1976).

Civil servants in the ministries view the committee network as manageable. They report that they generally control when committees should be established and how the agenda should be determined. They have less control of who should be recruited to such committees (Egeberg, 1981).

Cooptation of causes

The political-administrative leadership also has the option of coopting causes and interests without coopting representatives of these interests. Causes and interests are built into the administrative structure. Sometimes institutions articulate interests, even if those affected do not participate (Egeberg, 1978). Other times administrative agencies supplement and form coalitions with coopted groups.

One solution is ombudsmen. The ombudsmen for civil affairs, military personnel and consumer affairs have been supplemented with one for sexual equality, and one for children, and several new ombudsmen have been suggested. It may also be argued that the Consumer Council in many ways functions like an ombuds institution. And the civil servants in the Ministry of Environment may give more political leverage to the environmentalists than do their own participation in the corporative-functional structure or through the remiss institution. Civil servants often defend the interests of strongly organized groups, but they may also be the defenders of weak, unorganized groups unable to represent themselves (Hoem, 1976). Generally, "new" interests related (and often created by) public services, credit arrangements and so on, are weakly organized and their interests are primarily protected by the professions and institutions providing the services.

The limits of cooptation

Cooptation is no miracle cure. For organizations, integrated participation in government has costs in terms of loss of freedom to act spontaneously, loss of ideological identity, responsibility for public policies and loss of control of organizational leaders by members (chapter 5). Likewise, there are costs for government. Government may find itself responding to social conflicts by incorporating interests and cleavages in its own policy-making structure, and the accumulation of mutually exclusive obligations may paralyze it from taking action (Schwerin, 1980). Policy sectors may become overcrowded, but in Norway the government has tried to counteract this tendency by linking participation rights to mergers of interest organizations, or to the formation of new peak organizations. The result has been a "structural rationalization" of interest organizations (Egeberg et al., 1978).

The willingness of organized interests to become coopted and the ability of government to coopt relevant interests without becoming immobilized is linked to the level of conflict in society, the political organization of interests, the resources available and the design of political institutions. Our interpretation of the present Norwegian situations is that styles of mobilization and confrontation will also be used in the future, but styles of problem-solving, bargaining and self-governance will dominate. The main tendency will still be peaceful coexistence and revolution in slow motion. The Norwegian situation will be influenced by a long tradition of political compromises and by the awareness of the importance of the social outcomes as well as the substantive outcomes of decisions; by the fact that most (but not all) interests are organized; by the willingness of citizens' initiatives to avoid violence; and by a certain ability to adapt political institutions to new circumstances. Certainly, there are limits to what can be achieved by organizational means, but those limits are not given. They may be stretched through more knowledge about the conditions for and the actual effects of various organizational forms in public policy-making.

Notes

* This chapter relies extensively on a paper which was written together with Paul G. Roness and Harald Sætren, and published in J. J. Richardson (ed.), Policy Styles in Western Europe (London: Allen & Unwin, 1982).
  The authors want to thank Morten Egeberg, Martin Heisler, Jeremy J. Richardson, Lars Svåsand, Ulf Torgersen, Reidun Tvedt and Mariann Vågenes for advice and help.

[1] The purpose of table 6.1 is only to illustrate some dimensions (March and Simon, 1958; March and Olsen, 1976; Olsen, 1972b; 1978). Majority decisions through voting procedures have elements of several styles, for instance, the decision and the access structures are often highly regulated. There are conflicts over substance but not procedures. Strategies depend (among other things) on the availability of stable, organized parties. Majority decisions may to some degree take into consideration the interests of the minority, and thus affect the social outcome of the process.

[2] Commenting on an earlier draft of this chapter, both Lars Svåsand and Ulf Torgersen suggested alternative ways of categorizing the actors in religious conflicts.

[3] The questions differed somewhat from the population to the three elite groups. Thus, the ranking of cleavages/divisions is more important than the percentage responding to each. The question to the population was: "In discussions of society and politics we often hear different statements as to the most important divisions or cleavages in this country. This card lists several such cleavages/divisions. Which of these do you consider the most

significant one, that is, the one which creates the most important conflicts in our society today?" The next question was: "If you were to cite some other important cleavages/ divisions in today's society, which then would you mention? Are there any you feel are important and of great significance?" The table reports those who have answered one of these two questions. (The respondents were also asked to mention cleavages/divisions of little significance.) For the three elite groups the introduction was identical to the one for the population, but they were asked to evaluate each cleavage/division on a five-point scale – very important, somewhat important, so-so, somewhat unimportant and very unimportant. The table reports those who say a cleavage/division is very or somewhat important. These differences are due to the economic costs of using the latter technique in the survey of the population.

[4] The categorization used involves several problems both in terms of what should constitute an interest organization, and how each organization should be classified. We have made use of the stated objective of an organization. Fiftysix organizations in "productivity and technical affairs" and sixtyone in research and services are excluded, because their primary goal is not interest mediation. Some economic-producer organizations are members both of the Norwegian Employers' Association, and of industrial or trade associations. These are doublecounted, which gives six organizations and ten employees too many in the industry category, three and ten respectively, too many in the trade category and nineteen and 115 too many in the employers' category, compared to the categories used by Moren et al. (1976). The figure for religious organization employees is somewhat too small, because we do not have exact numbers for the Salvation Army, the Norwegian Mission Alliance and the Norwegian Lutheran Inner Mission Society. However, none of these discrepancies should change any of the trends in the material or the conlusions.

BIBLIOGRAPHY

Adams, J. Stacy 1976, "The structure and dynamics of behavior in organizational boundary roles." In Marvin D. Dunnette (ed.), Handbook of Industrial and Organizational Psychology: 1175–1199. Chicago: Rand McNally.

Allison, Graham T. 1971, Essence of Decision. Boston: Little, Brown.

Almond, Gabriel A. 1958, "A comparative study of interest groups and the political process." American Political Science Review, 52: 270–282.

Almond, Gabriel A., and Verba, Sidney 1963, The Civic Culture. Princeton, N.J.: Princeton University Press.

Andenæs, Johs. 1964, "Parlamentarisme, jus og statsvitenskap." Lov og rett,: 55–56.

– 1978, "Stortingets kontroll med regjering og forvaltning. Stortingets eget syn." Jussens Venner, :1–18.

Andersen, Svein S. 1980, Styring og protest. En studie av kjernekraftplanleggingen i Norge 1972–1975. Oslo: Project on Energy and Society, Report No. 3.

Arrow, Kenneth J. 1974, The Limits of Organization. New York: Norton.

Aubert, Vilhelm 1969, "Some social functions of legislation." In V. Aubert (ed.), Sociology and Law: 116–127. Baltimore: Penguin.

– 1976, Rettens sosiale funksjon. Oslo: Universitetsforlaget.

Auerbach, Arnold J. 1969, "Confrontation and administrative response." Public Administration Review, 29: 639–646.

Bacharach, Samuel B. and Edward J. Lawler 1980, Power and Politics in Organizations. San Francisco: Jossey-Bass.

Baerwald, Hans H. 1979, "Committees in the Japanese diet." In John D. Lees and Malcolm Shaw (eds.), Committees in Legislatures: A Comparative Analysis: 327–360. Durham, NC: Duke University Press.

Bagehot, Walter 1966, The English Constitution. Ithaca, N.Y.: Cornell University Press.

Bailey, Samuel 1835, The Rationale of Political Representation. London: Hunter.

Baldersheim, Harald 1979, Organisasjonsformer i offentlig planlegging. Bergen: Report to the Ministry of Consumer Affairs and Government Administration.

Balutis, Alan P. 1975, "Legislative Staffing: A review of current trends." In J.J. Heaphey and A.P. Balutis (eds.), Legislative Staffing: A Comparative Perspective. London: Sage.

Barnard, Chester 1938, The Function of the Executive. Cambridge: Harvard University Press.

Barnes, Samuel H., and Kaase, Max 1979, Political Action: Mass Participation in Five Western Democracies. London: Sage.

Barth, Fredrik 1966, Models of Social Organization. London: Royal Anthropological Institute of Great Britain and Ireland.

Bates, Robert H. 1970, "Input structures, output functions and systems capacity: a study of the Mineworkers' Union of Zambia." Journal of Politics, 32: 898–928.

Bauer, Raymond A., Pool, Ithiel de Sola, and Dexter, Lewis Anthony 1963, American Business and Public Policy. New York: Atherton Press.

Beard, Charles A., and Lewis, John D. 1932, "Representative government in evolution." American Political Science Review, (2): 223–240.

Beer, Samuel H. 1958, "Group representation in Britain and the United States." Annals of the American Academy of Political and Social Science, 319: 130–140.

  – 1965, British Politics in the Collectivist Age. New York: Knopf.

Bell, Daniel 1976, The Cultural Contradictions of Capitalism. New York: Basic Books.

Benewick, Robert, and Smith, Trevor 1972, Direct Action and Democratic Politics. London: Allen and Unwin.

Bentham, Jeremy 1838, "An essay on political tactics." In Works II: 299–373. Edinburgh: William Tait.

Bentley, Arthur F. 1967, The Process of Government. Cambridge, Mass.: Harvard University Press.

Benum, Edgeir 1979, Sentraladministrasjonens historie 1845–1884. Oslo: Universitetsforlaget.

Berger, Suzanne 1979, "Politics and antipolitics in Western Europe in the seventies." Daedalus, Winter: 27–50.

Berggrav, Dag 1978, "Regjeringen i arbeid." Oslo: unpublished lecture.

Bergh, Trond 1977, "Some preliminary notes on quantitative economic planning and the use of economists in government." Oslo: mimeo.

Bergh, Trond, and Pharo, Helge Ø. 1977, Vekst og velstand. Oslo: Universitetsforlaget.

Bernstein, Marver H. 1955, Regulating Business by Independent Commission. Princeton, N.J.: Princeton University Press.

Bjurulf, Bo, and Glans, Ingemar 1976, "Från tvåblocksystem till faktionalisering: Partigruppers och ledamoters röstning i norske Stortinget 1969–1974." Statsvetenskapeleg Tidsskrift, (3): 231–252.

Bjørklund, Tor 1976, Ad hoc-bevegelser. Working paper, Institutt for samfunnsforskning, University of Oslo.

  – 1981, 'De vikarierende argumenter. Om sivil ulydighet i norsk etterkrigshistorie." In Bernt Hagtvet (ed.), Den vanskelige ulydigheten: 126–140. Oslo: Pax.

Blankenship, L. Vaughn, and Elling, Ray H. 1962, "Organizational support and community power structure: the hospital." Journal of Health and Human Behavior, 3: 257–268.

Bloch, Kristian 1963, Kongens råd. Oslo: Universitetsforlaget.

Blondel, Jean 1973, Comparative Legislatures. Englewood Cliffs, N.J.: Prentice Hall.

Bradley, Joseph Francis 1965, The Role of Trade Associations and Professional Business Societies in America. University Park: Pennsylvania State University Press.

214

Bratbak, Berit 1981a, Fra gjenreising til "et kvalitativt bedre samfunn". Working paper, Institute of Public Administration and Organization Theory, University of Bergen.

- 1981b, Politisk lederskap: Rekrutteringspraksis og karrieremønster. Mimeo, Institute of Public Administration and Organization Theory, University of Bergen.

- 1982, Noen kommentarer til surveymateriale om folks holdninger til Regjeringen. Working paper, Institute of Public Administration and Organization Theory, University of Bergen.

Bratbak, Berit, and Olsen, Johan P. 1980, "Departement og opinion: Tilbakeføring av informasjon om virkninger av offentlige tiltak." In Johan P. Olsen (ed.): Meninger og makt: 86–167. Bergen: Universitetsforlaget.

Bratland, Per 1965, Hvem har makt i Norge? Oslo: Aschehoug.

Brautaset, Tarald O. 1973, Industrien og organisasjonene. Dissertation (hovedoppgave), University of Oslo.

Brautaset, Tarald O., and Dovland, Tor-Inge 1974, "Organisasjonenes formelle representasjon, litt om omfang og forutsetninger." In Jorolv Moren (ed.), Den kollegiale forvaltning. Oslo: Universitetsforlaget.

Brinch, Chr. 1975, "Embetsstandens stilling truet." Aftenposten (Oslo), August 2.

Brown, David S. 1972, "The management of advisory committees: an assignment for the '70's." Public Administration Review, 32: 334–342.

Brunvand, Olav 1973, Fra samspill til sammenbrudd. Oslo: Tiden.

Buksti, Jacob A. 1974, Et enigt landbrug? Århus: Universitetsforlaget i Århus.

Buksti, Jacob A., and Johansen, Lars Nørby 1978, Variations in Organizational Participation in Government. The Case of Denmark. Working paper, University of Århus and European University Institute, Firenze.

Bull, Edvard 1979, Norge i den rike verden. Oslo: Cappelen.

Bull, Trygve 1980, For å si det som det var. Oslo: Cappelen.

Campbell, Colin, and Clark, Harold 1980, "Conspectus." In Harold Clark et al., Parliament, Policy and Representation. Toronto: Methuen.

Campbell, Colin, and Szablowski, George J. 1979, The Super-Bureaucrats. Toronto: Macmillan of Canada.

Carter, April 1973, Direct Action and Liberal Democracy. London: Routledge and Kegan Paul.

Castberg, Frede 1945, Den utøvende makt. Bergen: Grieg.

Castles, Francis G. 1969, "Business and government: a typology of pressure group activity." Political Studies, 17: 160–176.

Chapman, Richard A. 1973, The Role of Commissions in Policy Making. London: Allen and Unwin.

Child, John 1977, Organizational Design and Performance: Contingency Theory and Beyond. In Elmer H. Burack and Anant R. Negandhi (eds.) Organization Design: Theoretical Perspectives and Empirical Findings, pp. 169–183, Kent: Kent State University Press.

Christensen, Jørgen Grønnegaard 1978, Normene for samspillet mellem den danske centraladministration og interesseorganisationerne i centraladministrativt perspektiv. Working paper, University of Århus.

Christensen, Søren 1976, "Decision-making and socialization." In James G. March and Johan P. Olsen (eds.), Ambiguity and Choice in Organizations: 351–385. Bergen: Universitetsforlaget.

Christensen, Tom 1978, Ekstern effektivitet og internt demokrati. Working paper, University of Tromsø.

Christensen, Tom, and Egeberg, Morten 1979, "Organized group-government relations in Norway: On the structured selection of participants, problems, solutions and choice opportunities." Scandinavian Political Studies, 3(2): 239–260.

Clark, Harold et al. 1980, Parliament, Policy and Representation. Toronto: Methuen.

Clark, Peter B., and Wilson, James Q. 1961, "Incentive systems: a theory of organizations." Administrative Science Quarterly, 6: 129–166.

Cohen, Michael D., and March, James G. 1974, Leadership and Ambiguity: The American College President. New York: McGraw-Hill.

Cohen, Michael D., March, James G., and Olsen, Johan P. 1972, "A garbage can model of organizational choice." Administrative Science Quarterly, 17: 1–25.

Coleman, James S. 1957, Community Conflict. Glencoe, Ill.: Free Press.

Coser, Lewis A. 1956, The Functions of Social Conflict, Glencoe, Ill.: Free Press.

Crick, Bernhard 1964, The Reform of Parliament. London: Weidenfeld and Nicolson.

Crozier, Michel 1964, The Bureaucratic Phenomenon. Chicago: University of Chicago Press.

– 1974, The Stalled Society. New York: Viking Press.

– 1982, Strategies for Change: The Future of French Society. Cambridge, Mass.: MIT Press.

Crozier, Michel, Huntington, Samuel P., and Watanuki, Joji 1975, The Crises of Democracy: Report on the Governability of Democracies to the Trilateral Commission. New York: New York University Press.

Curtis, Russel L., jr., and Zurcher, Louis A., jr. 1973, "Stable resources of protest movements: The multi-organizational field." Social Forces, 52(1): 53–61.

Cyert, Richard M., and March, James G. 1963, A Behavioral Theory of the Firm. Englewood Cliffs, N.J.: Prentice-Hall.

Dahl, Robert A. 1961, Who Governs? New Haven, Conn.: Yale University Press.

– 1966, Political Oppositions in Western Democracies. New Haven, Conn.: Yale University Press.

– 1973, Regimes and Oppositions. New Haven, Conn.: Yale University Press.

Dahl, Robert A., and Lindblom, Charles E. 1953, Politics, Economics and Welfare. New York: Harper and Row.

Dahrendorf, Ralf 1979, Life Chances. Chicago: University of Chicago Press.

Damgaard, Erik 1980, Folkets veje i dansk politik. København: Schultz.

Danielsen, Rolf 1964, Det norske Storting gjennom 150 år, vol. 2. Oslo: Gyldendal.

Daly, Lawrence 1969, "Protest and disturbance in the trade union movement." Political Quarterly, 40: 447–453.

Debes, Jan 1961, Realiteter og illusjoner i statsadministrasjonen. Oslo: Universitetsforlaget.

– 1978, Statsadministrasjonen. Oslo: NKS-forlaget.

Demerath, Nicolas J., III, and Thiessen, Victor 1966, "On spitting against the wind: organizational precariousness and American irreligion." American Journal of Sociology, 71: 674–687.

Dexter, Lewis Anthony 1969, How Organizations are Represented in Washington. Indianapolis: Bobbs-Merrill.

– 1978, How other organizations influence government. Working paper, University of Maryland, Baltimore.

Drewry, Gavin 1972, "Political parties and members of parliament." In Robert Benewick and Trevor Smith, Direct Action and Democratic Politics. London: Allen and Unwin.

Easton, David 1965, A System Analysis of Political Life.New York: Wiley.

Eckhoff, Torstein 1976, "Regjeringens adgang til å avskjedige embetsmenn." In Torstein Eckhoff, Retten og samfunnet. Oslo: Tanum-Norli.

– 1978, Forvaltningsrett. Oslo: Tanum.

Eckhoff, Torstein, and Jacobsen, Knut Dahl 1960, Rationality and Responsibility in Administrative and Judicial Decision-Making. Copenhagen: Munksgaard.

Eckstein, Harry 1960, Pressure Group Politics. London: Allen and Unwin.

– 1966, Division and Cohesion in Democracy: A Study of Norway. Princeton, N.J.: Princeton University Press.

– 1979, On the "Science of the State." In Stephen R. Graubard (ed.): The State, pp. 1–20. New York: Norton.

Edelman, Murray 1964, The Symbolic Uses of Politics. Chicago: University of Illinois Press.

Edwards, John N., and Booth, Alan 1973, Social Participation in Urban Society. Cambridge, Mass.: Schenckman.

Egeberg, Morten 1978, "Institusjonell pluralisme som interesseartikulerende system." Tidsskrift for samfunnsforskning, 19: 42–54.

– 1981, Stat og organisasjoner. Oslo: Universitetsforlaget.

Egeberg, Morten, Olsen, Johan P., and Roness, Paul G. 1980, "Opposisjon og opinion." In Johan P. Olsen (ed.), Meninger og makt. 55–85. Bergen: Universitetsforlaget.

Egeberg, Morten, Olsen, Johan P., and Sætren, Harald 1978, "Organisasjonssamfunnet og den segmenterte stat." In Johan P. Olsen (ed.), Politisk organisering; 115–142. Bergen: Universitetsforlaget.

Ehrmann, Henry W. 1968, Politics in France. Boston: Little, Brown.

– 1971, "Interest groups and the bureaucracy in western democracies." In Mattei Dogan and Richard Rose (eds.), European Politics :333–353. Boston: Little, Brown.

Eide, Kjell 1978, "A planner looks back." Oslo: manuscript.

Eldersveld, Samuel J. 1958, "American interest groups: a survey of research and some implications for theory and method." In Henry W. Ehrmann (ed.), Interest Groups on Four Continents: 173–196. Pittsburgh: University of Pittsburgh Press.

Elvander, Nils 1966, Interesseorganisationerna i dagens Sverige. Lund: CWK Gleerup Bokförlag.

– 1972, "The politics of taxation in Sweden 1954–1970: a study of the functions of parties and organizations." Scandinavian Political Studies, 7: 63–82.

– 1974, "Interest groups in Sweden." Annals of the American Academy of Political and Social Science, 413: 27–43.

Enerstvedt, Regi 1967, "Toppskiktet i næringslivet – politisk deltakelse og partipreferanse 1890–1940." Tidsskrift for samfunnsforskning, :269–291.

Eschen, Donal von, Kirk, Jerome, and Pinard, Maurice 1971, "The organizational substructure of disorderly politics." Social Forces, (4):529–544.

Etzioni, Amitai 1964, Modern Organizations. Englewood Cliffs, N.J.: Prentice-Hall.

Eulau, Heinz 1967, "Changing views of representation." In Ithiel de Sola Pool, Contemporary Political Science: Toward Empirical Theory: 53–85. New York: McGraw Hill.

Eulau, Heinz, and Hinckley, Kathrine 1966, "Legislative institutions and processes." In James A. Robinson (ed.), Political Science Annual, (1):85–189.

Eulau, Heinz, and Karpe, Paul D. 1977, "The puzzle of representation: Specifying components of responsiveness." Legislative Studies Quarterly, 233–254.

Eulau, Heinz, and Prewitt, Kenneth 1973, Labyrinths of Democracy: Adaptation Linkages, Representation, and Policies in Urban Politics. Indianapolis, Ind.: Bobbs-Merrill.

Eulau, Heinz, and Wahlke, John C. 1978, The Politics of Representation. Beverly Hills, Calif.: Sage.

Evan, William M. 1966, "The organization-set: toward a theory of inter-organizational relations." In James D. Thompson (ed.), Approaches to Organizational Design : 174–191. Pittsburgh: University of Pittsburgh Press.

Evang, Karl 1974a, "Får vi snart orden på statssekretærene . . .?" Aftenposten (Oslo), October 21.

– 1974b, "En 'sideregjering' uten konstitusjonelt ansvar." Aftenposten (Oslo), October 22 and 23.

Feldman, Martha S., and March, James G. 1981, "Information as signal and symbol." Administrative Science Quarterly, (26): 171–186.

Fenno, Richard F., Jr. 1973, Congressmen in Committees. Boston: Little, Brown.

Finer, Samuel E. 1958, Anonymous Empire. London: Pall Mall Press.

– 1973, "The political power of organized labor." Government and Opposition, 8: 391–406.

Finstad, Hans Chr. 1970, Fra dragkamp til samspill. Oslo: Lutherstiftelsen.

Fivelsdal, Egil 1978, Embedsmandsperspektiver på samspillet mellem de økonomiske interesseorganisationer og centraladministrationen. Working paper, Handelshøjskolen i København.

Follesø, Gunnar 1975, Nasjonalisering og hva så? Unpublished dissertation, Institute of Public Administration and Organization Theory, University of Bergen.

Fox, Harrison W., and Hammon, Susan 1977, Congressional Staffs: The Invisible Force in American Lawmaking. New York: Free Press.

Franks, C.E.S. 1971, "The dilemma of the standing committees in the Canadian House of Commons." Canadian Journal of Political Science, (4): 461–476.

Freedman, James O. 1978, Crises and Legitimacy. Cambridge: Cambridge University Press.

Freeman, Jo 1975, The Politics of Women's Liberation. New York: McKay.

Friedrich, Carl J. 1937, Constitutional Government and Politics. New York: Harper.

Froman, Lewis A., Jr. 1968, "Organization theory and the explanation of important characteristics of Congress." The American Political Science Review, (62): 518–526.

Gaasemyr, Jostein 1979, Organisasjonsbyråkrati og korporativisme. Bergen: Universitetsforlaget.

Gamson, William A. 1968, "Stable unrepresentation in American society". American Behavioral Scientist, 12: 15–20.

– 1975, The Strategy of Social Protest. Homewood, Ill.: Dorsey.

Gerhardsen, Einar 1971, Samarbeid og strid. Oslo: Tiden.

– 1978, Mennesker og politikk. Oslo: Tiden.

Gerlach, Luther P., and Hine, Virginia H. 1970, People, Power, Change. Movements of Social Transformation. Indianapolis: Bobbs-Merrill.

Gerth, H.H. and Mills, C. Wright 1970, From Max Weber. London: Routledge & Kegan Paul.

Gidlund, Janerik 1978, Aktiongrupper och lokala partier. Temporära politiske organisationer i Sverige 1965–1975. Umeå: CWK Gleerup.

Gilb, Corinne Lathrop 1968, Hidden Hierarchies. New York: Harper and Row.

Gjedrem, Njål 1975, Landbruksdepartementet og omgivelsene. Dissertation (hovedoppgave), University of Bergen.

Gleditsch, Nils Petter, Hartmann, Åke, and Naustdalslid, Jon 1971, Mardøla-aksjonen. Oslo: PRIO, mimeo.

Gleditsch, Nils Petter, and Hellevik, Ottar 1973, "The Common Market decision in Norway: a clash between direct and indirect democracy." Scandinavian Political Studies, 8: 227–235.

– 1977, Kampen om EF. Oslo: Pax.

Gleditsch, Nils Petter, Østerud, Øyvind, and Elster, Jon 1974, De utro tjenere. Oslo: Pax.

Glenn, James R., Jr. 1975, Chief Executive Time: An Empirical Study of the Time Allocation of American College and University Presidents. Ph.D. dissertation, Stanford University.

Graham, George 1967, 'Labor participation in management: a study of the National Coal Board." Political Quarterly, 38: 184–199.

Grant, Wyn, and Marsh, David 1977, The Confederation of British Industry. London: Hodder and Stoughton.

Greve, Tim 1964, Det norske Storting gjennom 150 år, vol. 3. Oslo: Gyldendal.

Grimsbo, Olav 1973, Ekspertise og konflikter i utredningsutvalg. Unpublished dissertation in political science, University of Oslo.

Groennings, Sven 1962, Cooperation Among Norway's Non-Socialist Parties. Unpublished Ph.D. thesis, Stanford University.

Grumm, John C. 1971, "The effects of legislative structure on legislative performance." In Richard I. Hofferbert and Ira Sharkansky (eds.), State and Urban Politics: Readings in Comparative Public Policy: 298–322.

Grøndahl, Kirsti 1979, Dagbladet, Oslo, January 20.

Grønlie, Tore 1973, Jern og politikk. Bergen: Universitetsforlaget.

Gundelach, Peter 1979, Græsrodsorganisationer – en organisationssociologisk analyse. Århus: manuscript.

Gustafsson, Gunnel, Jordan, Grant, and Richardson, Jeremy J. 1981, "The concept of policy style." In J.J. Richardson (ed.), Policy Styles in Western Europe. London: Allen and Unwin.

Gustafsson, Gunnel, and Richardson, Jeremy J. 1979, "Concepts of rationality and the policy process." European Journal of Political Research, 7: 415–436.

Gustavsen, Finn 1979, Kortene på bordet. Oslo: Gyldendal.

Habermas, Jürgen 1975, Legitimation Crisis. Boston: Beacon.

Hadenius, Axel 1978, "Ämbetsverkens styrelser." Statsvetenskaplig Tidsskrift, 81: 19–32.

Haga, Gjermund 1978, Avviklingsbonden og hans representanter. Oslo: Cultura.

Hagtvet, Bernt 1981, Den vanskelige ulydigheten. Oslo: Pax.

Hallenstvedt, Abraham 1979, Organisasjoner og sektorsamordning. Institutt for fiskerifag, University of Tromsø.

Hallenstvedt, Abraham, and Hoven, Finn Holmer 1974, De tusen komitéer. Kristiansand: Agder distriktshøyskoles skrifter.

Hallenstvedt, Abraham, Kalela, Aira, Kalela, Jaakko, and Lintonen, Raimo 1976, "Nordic transnational association network: structure and correlates." Journal of Voluntary Action Research, 5: 123–154.

Hallenstvedt, Abraham, and Moren, Jorolv 1975, "Det organiserte samfunn." In N.R. Ramsøy and M. Vaa (eds.), Det norske samfunn. Oslo: Gyldendal.

Hallenstvedt, Abraham, and Rønning, Rolf 1975, De frivillige foreninger: medlemmer og medlemsaktivitet. Working paper, University of Tromsø and Hedmark/Oppland Distriktshøyskole.

Hannan, Michael T., and Freeman, John 1977, "The population ecology of organizations." American Journal of Sociology, (82): 929–964.

Hansen, Guttorm 1978, "All makt i denne sal." Sosialøkonomen, :22–25.

Haugen, Vidar 1979, Det Norske Arbeiderparti 1940–45. Fra forbud til gjenreisning. Unpublished dissertation, University of Bergen.

Hayes, Denis A., and March, James G. 1970, The Normative Problem of University Governance. Working paper, Stanford University.

Headey, Bruce W. 1970, "Trade unions and national wage policies." Journal of Politics, 32: 407–443.

– 1974, British Cabinet Ministers. London: Allen and Unwin.

Heaphey, James J. 1975, "Legislative staffing: Organizational philosophical considerations." In J.J. Heaphey and Alan P. Balutis (eds.), Legislative Staffing: A Comparative Perspective. London: Sage.

Heckscher, Gunnar 1946, Staten och organisationerna. Stockholm: Kooperative Förbundets Bokförlag.

Heclo, Hugh 1973, "Presidential and prime ministerial selection." In Donald R. Matthews (ed.), Perspectives on Presidential Selection: 19–48. Washington, D.C: Brookings Institution.

- 1977, A Government of Strangers. Washington, D.C.: Brookings Institution.

- 1978, "Issue network and the executive establishment." In Anthony King (ed.), The New American Political System. Washington, D.C.: American Enterprise Institute.

Hedberg, Bo L.T., Nystrom, Paul C., and Starbuck, William H. 1976, "Camping on seesaws: Prescriptions for a self-designing organization." Administrative Science Quarterly, 21: 41–65.

Heisler, Martin O. 1974, Politics in Europe. New York: David McKay.

Heisler, Martin O., with the collaboration of Robert B. Kvavik 1974, "Patterns in European politics: The 'European polity'-model." In Martin O. Heisler (ed.), Politics in Europe. Structures and Processes in Some Post-Industrial Democracies: 27–89. New York: David McKay.

Helfgot, Joseph 1974, "Professional reform organizations and the symbolic representation of the poor." American Sociological Review, 39: 475–491.

Hellevik, Ottar 1969, Stortinget – en sosial elite? Oslo: Pax.

Hennis, Wilhelm 1971, "Reform of the Bundestag: The case for general debate." In Gerhard Loewenberg (ed.), Modern Parliaments: Change or Decline. Chicago/New York: Aldine/Atherton.

Hermerén, Henrik 1975, Regeringsbildningen i flerpartisystem. Lund: Studentlitteratur.

Hernes, Gudmund 1971, Interest, Influence and Cooptation: A Study of the Norwegian Parliament. Unpublished Ph.D. thesis, Johns Hopkins University.

- 1973, "Stortingets komitésystem og maktfordelingen i partigruppene." Tidsskrift for samfunnsforskning (14): 1–29.

- 1974, "Political resource transformation." Scandinavian Political Studies, :157–158.

- 1977, "Interests and the structure of influence." In W.O. Aydelotte (ed.), The History of Parliament. Princeton: Princeton University Press.

- 1978, "Det mediavridde samfunn." In G. Hernes (ed.), Forhandlingsøkonomi og blandingsadministrasjon. Bergen: Universitetsforlaget.

Hernes, Gudmund, and Martinussen, Willy 1980, Demokrati og politiske ressurser. Oslo: Universitetsforlaget (NOU 1980: 7).

Hernes, Helga Maria 1982, Staten – kvinner ingen adgang. Oslo: Universitetsforlaget.

Hernes, Helga Maria, and Voje, Kirsten 1980, "Women in the corporate channel in Norway: A process of natural exclusion?" Scandinavian Political Studies, 3(2): 163–186.

Herring, E. Pendelton 1929, Group Representation before Congress. Baltimore: Johns Hopkins Press.

Highley, John, Brofoss, Karl Erik and Grøholt, Knut 1975, "Top civil servants and the national budget in Norway." In Mattei Dogan (ed.), The Mandarins of Western Europe: 253–274. Los Angeles: Sage.

Hirschman, Albert O. 1970, Exit, Voice and Loyalty. Cambridge, Mass.: Harvard University Press.

Hoel, Einar 1972, Stortinget 1961–69 og organisasjonssamfunnet. Mimeo, Institute of Political Science, University of Oslo.

Hoem, Ragnhild 1976, Undersøkelse av høringsbehandlingen ved utferdigelse av forskrifter. Oslo: Report to the Ministry of Justice.

Holtzman, Abraham 1966, Interest Groups and Lobbying. New York: Mac-Millan.

Huitt, Ralph K. 1968, "Legislatures." In International Encyclopedia of the Social Sciences, vol. 9. New York: MacMillan and Free Press.

Huntington, Samuel P. and Jorge I. Domeniguez 1975, Political Development. In Fred I. Greenstein and Nelson W. Polsby (eds.) Handbook of Political Science, vol. 3: Macropolitical Theory, pp. 1–114. Reading, Mass.: Addison-Wesley.

Hvinden, Bjørn, et al. 1974, Grasrothåndbok. Oslo: Pax.

Inglehart, Ronald E. 1977, The Silent Revolution: Changing Values and Political Styles among Western Publics. Princeton: Princeton University Press.

- 1981, "Post-materialism in an environment of insecruity." American Political Science Review, 75(4): 880–900.

Jacobsen, Knut D. 1960, "Lojalitet, nøytralitet og faglig uavhengighet." Tidsskrift for samfunnsforskning, (1): 231–248.

- 1964, Teknisk hjelp og politisk struktur. Oslo: Universitetsforlaget.

- 1966, "Public administration under pressure: The role of the expert in the modernization of traditional agriculture." Scandinavian Political Studies, 1: 59–93.

- 1968, Ekspertenes deltakelse i den offentlige forvaltning. Paper presented at the Scandinavian Political Science Association's meeting in Helsinki.

Jarlov, Carsten, Johansen, Lars Nørby, and Kristensen, Ole P. 1976, The Danish Committee System. Working paper, University of Århus and University of Odense.

Johansen, Lars Nørby, and Kristensen, Ole P. 1978, Corporatist Traits in Denmark 1946–76. Working paper, European University Institute, Firenze and University of Århus.

Jørgensen, Klaus 1973, Atomvåbnenes rolle i dansk politikk. Odense: Odense Universitetsforlag.

Kaartvedt, Alf 1964, Det norske Storting gjennom 150 år, vol. 1. Oslo: Gyldendal.

Kamsvåg, Ragnar 1980, Høyre og den økonomiske politikken 1945–53. Unpublished dissertation in history, University of Oslo.

Karlsen, Jan Erik 1977, Hva skjer i fagbevegelsen? Oslo: Tiden.

Kaufman, Herbert 1956, "Emerging conflicts in the doctrine of public administration." American Political Science Review, (4): 1057–1073.

- 1969, "Administrative decentralization and political power." Public Administration Review, 29: 3–15.

- 1977, "Reflections on administrative reorganization." In Joseph A. Pechman (ed.), Setting National Priorities: The 1978 Budget. Washington, D.C.: Brookings Institution.

Key, Valdimer O. 1961, Public Opinion and American Democracy. New York: Knopf.

Kielland, Arne 1972, All makt? Dagbok fra Stortinget. Oslo: Pax.

Kimber, Richard, and Richardson, Jeremy J. 1974, "Some aspects of the T.U.C. and C.B.I. as pressure groups." In Richard Kimber and Jeremy J. Richardson (eds.), Pressure Groups in Britain :110–119. London: Dent.

King, Anthony 1975a, "Executives." In Fred I. Greenstein and Nelson W. Polsby (eds.), Handbook of Political Science, vol. 5, Governmental Institutions and Processes. Reading, Mass.: Addison-Wesley.

- 1975b, "Overload: Problems of governing in the 1970s." Political Studies, 23: 290–295.

Kjellberg, Francesco, et al. 1980, Forvaltning, byråkrati og den enkelte. Institute of Political Science, University of Oslo.

Kjellberg, Francesco, and Hansen, Tore 1979, Det kommunale hamskiftet. Oslo: Gyldendal.

Knudsen, John Chr. 1979, Nei til tvangsregulering. En analyse av politisk symbolbruk under drivgarnsfiskernes aksjon 1977. Thesis, Institute of Anthropology, University of Bergen.

Knutsen, Oddbjørn 1981, Barn av økonomisk depresjon og barn av økonomisk velstand: Partipreferanse i Norge i et generasjonsperspektiv. Oslo: Mimeo, Institute of Social Research.

Kohlmeier, Louis M., Jr. 1969, The Regulators. New York: Harper and Row.

Koht, Halvdan 1909, "Folkestyre." Samtiden, :469–478.

Kolbenstvedt, Marika, Strand, Arvid, and Østensen, Erik 1978, Lokale aksjonsgrupper. Oslo: Norsk institutt for by- og regionforskning.

Komarovsky, Mirra 1975, Sociology and Public Policy. New York: American Elsevier.

Kornhauser, William 1959, The Politics of Mass Society. Glencoe, Ill.: Free Press.

Korvald, Lars 1978, "Regjeringens virkemåte." Bergen: Unpublished lecture.

Kovak, Richard M. 1972, "Urban renewal controversies." Public Administration Review, 32: 359–372.

Kreiner, Kristian 1976, "Ideology and management in a garbage can situation." In James G. March and Johan P. Olsen (eds.), Ambiguity and Choice in Organizations: 156–173. Bergen: Universitetsforlaget.

Krusius-Ahrenberg, Lolo 1958, "The political power of economic and labor-market organizations: a dilemma of Finnish democracy." In Henry W. Ehrmann (ed.), Interest Groups on Four Continents :33–59. Pittsburgh: University of Pittsburgh Press.

Kuby, Thomas, and Marzahn, Christian 1977, "Lernen in Bürgerinitiativen gegen Atomlagen." Rotbuch: Kursbuch, 48: 153–174.

Kuhnle, Stein 1980, A Crisis of the Norwegian Welfare State? Mimeo, Institute of Sociology, University of Bergen.

Kvalø, Arnfinn 1968, Striden i Stortinget 1919–1952 om paragraf 57, 2. ledd i Grunnloven – 'bondeparagrafen'. Unpublished dissertation in history, University of Oslo.

Kvavik, Robert B. 1970, Interest Groups in Norway: A Study of Corporate Pluralism. Doctoral dissertation, Stanford University.

– 1974, "Interest groups in a 'cooptive' political system." In Martin O. Heisler (ed.), Politics In Europe. Structures and Processes in Some Post-Industrial Democracies: 27–89. New York: David McKay.

– 1976, Interest Groups in Norwegian Politics. Oslo: Universitetsforlaget.

Laasko, Markku 1981, "The distribution of power in the Scandinavian parliaments." Scandinavian Political Studies, :51–75.

Lafferty, William M. 1981, Participation and Democracy in Norway. Oslo: Universitetsforlaget.

Langslet, Lars Roar 1970, "Noen uskyldige ord om Stortinget." Nordisk Kontakt, (11): 621–624.

LaPalombara, Joseph 1964, Interest Groups in Italian Politics. Princeton, N.J.: Princeton University Press.

Larsen, Stein U., and Offerdal, Audun 1979, De få vi valgte. Bergen: Universitetsforlaget.

Larssen, Olav 1973, Den langsomme revolusjonen. Oslo: Aschehoug.

Laux, William E. 1968, "Agricultural interest groups in Danish politics: an examination of group frustration amidst political stability." Western Political Quarterly, 21: 436–455.

Lehmbruch, Gerhard 1974, Consociational Democracy, Class Conflict, and the New Corporatism. Working paper, University of Mannheim.

– 1977, "Liberal corporatism and party government." Comparative Political Studies, 10: 91–126.

Leiserson, Avery 1942, Administrative Regulations. Chicago: University of Chicago Press.

Levine, Sol, and White, Paul E. 1961, "Exchange as a conceptual framework for the study of interorganizational relationships." Administrative Science Quarterly, 5: 583–601.

Lie, Haakon 1975, . . . slik jeg ser det. Oslo: Tiden.

Lijphart, Arend 1968, The Politics of Accommodation. Berkeley: University of California Press.

– 1977, Democracy in Plural Societies. New Haven, Conn.: Yale University Press.

Lindberg, Leon N., et al. 1975, Stress and Contradiction in Modern Capitalism, Lexington, Mass.: Heath.

Lindblad, Ingemar, Wahlbäck, Krister, and Wicklund, Claes 1974, Politik i Norden (2. revid. uppl.). Stockholm: Aldus/Bonnier.

Lindblom, Charles E. 1965, The Intelligence of Democracy. New York: Free Press.

– 1977, Politics and Markets. New York: Basic Books.

Linz, Juan 1978, Crisis, Breakdown and Reequilibration. Baltimore: Johns Hopkins.

Lipset, Seymour Martin 1963, Political Man. Garden City, N.Y.: Doubleday.

Lipset, Seymour Martin, and Rokkan, Stein 1967, Party Systems and Voter Alignments. New York: Free Press.

Lipset, Seymour Martin, Trow, Martin A., and Coleman, James S. 1956, Union Democracy, Glencoe, Ill.: Free Press.

Lipsky, Michael 1968, "Protest as political resource." American Political Science Review, 62: 1144–58.

Litwak, Eugene, and Hylton, Lydia F. 1962, "Interorganizational analysis: a hypothesis on coordinating agencies." Administrative Science Quarterly, 6: 395–420.

Loewenberg, Gerhard 1971, Modern Parliaments: Change or Decline: Chicago: Aldine.

Loewenberg, Gerhard, and Patterson, Samuel C. 1979, Comparing Legislatures. Boston: Little, Brown.

Logue, John 1979, "The welfare state: Victim of its success." In Stephen R. Graubard (ed.), The State: 69–100. New York: Norton.

Lorentzen, Pål E. 1978, Undersøkelse om offentlighetsloven. Den offentlige forvaltning som informasjonskilde for pressen. Bergen: Discussion paper No. 74, Maktutredningen.

Lowery, David, and Siegelman, Lee 1981, "Understanding the tax revolt: Eight explanations." American Political Science Review, 75(4): 963–974.

Lowi, Theodore J. 1964, "American business, public policy, casestudies and political theory." World Politics, 16: 677–715.

– 1969, The End of Liberalism. New York: Norton.

– 1971, The Politics of Disorder. New York: Basic Books.

– 1972, "Four systems of policy, politics, and choice." Public Administration Review, 32: 298–310.

Lund, Steinar 1976, Sosialdepartementet og omgivelsene. Dissertation (hoved-oppgave), University of Bergen.

Lyng, John 1973, Vaktskifte. Oslo: Cappelen.

– 1978, Fra borgfred til politisk blåmandag. Oslo: Cappelen.

Lægreid, Per 1975, Tenestemenn i norske departement. Unpublished dissertation, Institute of Public Administration and Organization Theory, University of Bergen.

– 1980, Rekrutteringskriterier og karrierekontroll i norske departement. Mimeo, Institute of Public Administration and Organization Theory, University of Bergen.

Lægreid, Per, and Olsen, Johan P. 1978, Byråkrati og beslutninger. Bergen: Universitetsforlaget.

MacFarlane, L.J. 1971, Political Disobedience. London: MacMillan.

Madeley, J.T.S. 1977, "Scandinavian Christian democracy: Throwback or portent." European Journal of Political Research, 5: 267–286.

Mannheim, Karl 1949, Ideologia and Utopia. New York: Harcourt, Brace and World.

March, James G. 1962, The Business Firm as a Political Coalition. Journal of Politics, 24: 662–678.

– 1978, "Bounded rationality, ambiguity, and the engineering of choice." Bell Journal of Economics, 9: 587–608.

225

- 1980, How We Talk and How We Act: Administrative Theory and Administrative Life. Urbana, Ill.: Seventh David D. Henry Lecture.
- 1981a, "Decisions in organizations and theories of choice." In Andrew H. van de Ven and William F. Joyce (eds.), Perspectives on Organization Design and Behavior: 205–244. New York: Wiley.
- 1981b, "Footnotes to organizational change." Administrative Science Quarterly, 17(4): 563–577.

March, James G., and Olsen, Johan P. 1976, Ambiguity and Choice in Organizations. Bergen: Universitetsforlaget.
- 1982, Organizing Political Life: What Administrative Reorganization Tells Us About Governing. Paper presented at the International Political Science Association's World Congress, Rio de Janeiro, Brazil, August 9–14.

March, James G., and Sevon, Guje 1982, "Gossip, information, and decision making." To appear in Lee S. Sproull and Patric D. Larkey (eds.), Advances in Information Processing in Organizations, vol. 1. Greenwich, Conn.: JAI Press.

March, James G., and Simon, Herbert A. 1958, Organizations. New York: Wiley.

Marsh, Alan 1978, Protest and Political Consciousness. London: Sage.

Martinussen, Willy 1977, The Distant Democracy. New York: Wiley.
- 1978, Organisasjonssamfunnet og EF-striden. Trondheim: manuscript.

Maurseth, Per 1979, Sentraladministrasjonens historie 1814–1844. Oslo: Universitetsforlaget.

Mayntz, Renate 1980, German Federal Bureaucrats: A Functional Elite Between Politics and Administration. Paper presented at the Conference on the Role of Higher Civil Servants in Central Governments, Centro de Investigaciones Sociológicas, Madrid, Spain.

Mayntz, Renate, and Scharpf, Fritz W. 1975, Policy-making in the German Federal Bureaucracy. Amsterdam: Elsevier.

McConnell, Grant 1966, Private Power and American Democracy. New York: Knopf.

Meijer, Hans 1969, "Bureaucracy and policy formation in Sweden." Scandinavian Political Studies, 4: 103–116.

Melander, Karen Anette 1974, "Henvendelser til Stortinget." Unpublished dissertation in political science, University of Oslo.

Meyer, John W., and Rowan, Brian 1977, "Institutionalized organizations: formal structure as myth and ceremony." American Journal of Sociology, 83: 340–363.

Meyer, Marshall W. 1979, "Organizational structure as signaling." Pacific Sociological Review, (22): 481–500.

Michels, Robert 1949, Political Parties. Glencoe, Ill.: Free Press.

Milgram, Stanley, and Toch, Hans 1969, "Collective behaviour: Crowds and social movements." In Gardner Linzey and Elliot Aronsen (eds.), The Handbook of Social Psychology, vol. IV: 507–610. Reading, Mass.: Addison-Wesley.

Mill, John Stuart 1951, On Bentham and Coleridge. New York: Stewart.
- 1956 (1859), On Liberty. Indianapolis: Bobbs-Merrill (reprinted).

- 1962 (1861), Considerations on Representative Government. South Bend, Ind.: Gateway (reprinted).
Moren, Jorolv 1958, Organisasjonene og forvaltningen. Bergen: Garnæs Boktrykkeri.
- 1968, "Organization theory and the study of boards, councils, and commissions in public administration." Acta Sociologica, 11: 63–81.
- 1974, Den kollegiale forvaltning. Oslo: Universitetsforlaget.
Moren, Jorolv, Hallenstvedt, Abraham, Brautaset, Tarald O., and Dovland, Tor Inge 1972, Norske organisasjoner. Oslo: Tanum.
Moren, Jorolv, Hallenstvedt, Abraham, and Christensen, Tom 1976, Norske organisasjoner. Oslo: Tanum.
Mouritzen, Poul Erik, Poulsen, Niels Refslund, and Larsen, Finn Breinholt 1978, Borgerdeltagelse i græsrodsbevægelser. Århus: Politica.
Mulhollan, Daniel P. 1977, "An overview of lobbying by organizations." In U.S. Commission on the Operation of the Senate, Senators: Offices, Ethics, and Pressures: 157–192. Washington, D.C.: U.S. Government Printing Office.
Nadel, Mark V., and Rourke, Francis E. 1975, "Bureaucracies." In Fred I. Greenstein and Nelson W. Polsby (eds.), Handbook of Political Science, Vol. 5: 373–440. Reading, Mass.: Addison-Wesley.
Nedelmann, Birgitta, and Meier, Kurt G. 1977, "Theories of contemporary corporatism: static or dynamic?" Comparative Political Studies, 10: 39–60.
Nelkin, Dorothy, and Pollak, Michael 1981, The Atom Besieged: Extraparliamentary Dissent in France and Germany. Cambridge, Mass.: The MIT Press.
Neustadt, Richard E. 1969, "White House and Whitehall." In Anthony King (ed.), The British Prime Minister: A Reader. London: Macmillan.
- 1976, Presidential power. New York: Wiley.
Nie, Norman H., and Verba, Sidney 1975, "Political participation." In Fred I. Greenstein and Nelson W. Polsby (eds.), Handbook of Political Science, vol. 4: 1–74. Reading, Mass.: Addison-Wesley.
Nilson, Sten Sparre 1978, "Scandinavia." In David Butler and Austin Ranney (eds.), Referendums. A Comparative Study of Practice and Theory. Washington, D.C.: American Enterprise Institute.
Norbom, Jon 1971, "Den økonomisk-politiske beslutningsprosess." In Økonomi og politikk, skrift til Ole Myrvolls 60 års dag. Oslo: Aschehoug.
Nordahl, Konrad 1973, Gode arbeidsår. Oslo: Tiden.
Nordli, Odvar 1978, "Regjeringens virkemåte." Bergen: Unpublished lecture.
Nygaardsvold, Johan 1947, Kong Haakon 7 i samarbeid og samvær med Regjeringen. Oslo: Den norske forleggerforening.
Nystrom, Paul C. and William H. Starbuck (eds.) 1981, Handbook of Organizational Design, vol. 2. Remodeling Organizations and Their Environments. London: Oxford.
Næss, Arne 1964, Økologi, samfunn og livsstil. Oslo: Universitetsforlaget.
Oberschall, Anthony 1973, Social Conflict and Social Movement. Englewood Cliffs, N.J.: Prentice Hall.
Offe, Claus 1972, "Klassenherrschaft und Politisches System. Die Selektivität politischer Institutionen." In Strukturprobleme des Kapitalistischen Staates. Frankfurt: Suhrkamp.

Offerdal, Audun 1974, "Folkerøystinga om EF. Aktivitet blant veljarane." Statistiske analysar nr. 11. Oslo: Statistisk Sentralbyrå.

Olsen, Johan P. 1970, "Local budgeting: Decision making or ritual act?" Scandinavian Political Studies, (5): 85–118.

– 1972a, "'Voting', 'sounding out', and the governance of modern organizations." Acta Sociologica, 15: 267–283.

– 1972b, "Public policy making and theories of organizational choice." Scandinavian Political Studies, 7: 45–62.

– 1978, "Folkestyre, byråkrati og korporativisme." In Johan P. Olsen (ed.), Politisk organisering :13–114. Bergen: Universitetsforlaget.

– 1981, "Sivil ulydighet og politisk organisering." In Bernt Hagtvet (ed.), Den vanskelige ulydigheten. Oslo: Pax.

Olsen, Johan P., and Sætren, Harald 1980a, Aksjoner og demokrati. Bergen: Universitetsforlaget.

– 1980b, "Massemedier, eliter og menigmann." In Johan P. Olsen (ed.), Meninger og makt: 13–54. Bergen: Universitetsforlaget.

Panitch, Leo 1977, "The development of corporatism in liberal democracies." Comparative Political Studies, 10: 61–90.

Parkin, Frank 1968, Middle Class Radicalism. Manchester: Manchester University Press.

Paynter, Will 1970, "Trade unions and government." Political Quarterly, 41: 444–454.

Peabody, R.L. and Rourke, F.E. 1965, "Public bureaucracies." In James G. March (ed.), Handbook of Organizations: 802–837. Chicago: Rand McNally.

Pennock, J. Roland 1979, Democratic Political Theory. Princeton, N.J.: Princeton University Press.

Pestoff, Victor Alexis 1977, Voluntary Associations and Nordic Party Systems. Stockholm: University of Stockholm, Department of Political Science.

Peterson, Eric A. 1977, Interest Group Incorporation in Sweden. A Summary of Arguments and Findings. Working paper, Yale University.

Peterson, Paul E. 1970, "Forms of representation: participation of the poor in the community action program." American Political Science Review, 64: 491–507.

– 1971, "British interest group theory reexamined." Comparative Politics, 3: 381–402.

Pfeffer, Jeffrey 1981, Power in Organizations. London: Pitman.

Pfeffer, Jeffrey, and Salancik, Gerald R. 1978, The External Control of Organizations. New York: Harper and Row.

Polsby, Nelson W. 1975, "Legislatures." In Fred I. Greenstein and Nelson W. Polsby (eds.), Handbook of Political Science. Reading, Mass.: Addison-Wesley.

Putnam, Robert D. 1973, "The political attitudes of senior civil servants in Britain, Germany and Italy." British Journal of Political Science, 3: 257–290.

Richardson, Jeremy J. 1982, Policy Styles in Western Europe. London: Allen & Unwin.

Richardson, Jeremy J., and Jordan, G.A. 1979, Governing Under Pressure. Oxford: Martin Robertson.

Riedel, James A. 1972, "Citizen participation: myths and realities." Public Administration Review, 32: 211–220.

Rodenstein, Marianne 1978, Bürgerinitiativen und politisches System. Lahn-Giessen: Focus.

Rokkan, Stein 1966, "Norway: numerical democracy and corporate pluralism." In Robert A. Dahl (ed.), Political Oppositions in Western Democracies: 70–115. New Haven, Conn.: Yale University Press.

–   1970, Citizens, Elections, Parties. Oslo: Universitetsforlaget.

Rokkan, Stein, and Campbell, Angus 1960, "Citizen participation in political life: Norway and the United States of America." International Social Science Journal, 12(1): 69–99.

Rommetvedt, Hilmar 1980, Sprikende staur eller laftet tømmer? En analyse av partiavstander i Stortinget som grunnlag for borgerlig samarbeid 1945–77. Unpublished dissertation, Institute of Political Science, University of Oslo.

Roness, Paul G. 1979, Reorganisering av departementa. Bergen: Universitetsforlaget.

–   1981, "Politisk lederskap gjennom oppretting av departement." Paper presented at the Nordisk Statsvitenskapelig kongress, Åbo, Finland.

Rose, Richard 1969, "Dynamic tendencies in the authority of regimes." World Politics, 21(4): 602–628.

–   1980, Challenge to Governance. Beverly Hills: Sage.

Rothschild, Joseph 1977, "Observations on political legitimacy in contemporary Europe." Political Science Quarterly, 92(3): 487–501.

Ruin, Olof 1974, "Towards a corporate society? Participatory democracy and corporativism: the case of Sweden." Scandinavian Political Studies, 9: 171–184.

Rønbeck, Sissel 1979, Bergens Tidende, December 12.

Sait, Edward McChesney 1938, Political Institutions – A Preface. New York: Appleton-Century-Crofts.

Salisbury, Robert A. 1975, "Interest groups." In Fred I. Greenstein and Nelson W. Polsby (eds.), Handbook of Political Science, vol. 4: 171–228. Reading, Mass.: Addison-Wesley.

Salisbury, Robert H., and Shepsle, K.A. 1981, "Congressional staff: Turnover and the ties-that-bind." American Political Science Review, (2): 381–396.

Sartori, Giovanni 1968, "Democracy." In International Fncyclopedia of the Social Sciences, vol. 4: 112–121.

Schaar, John H. 1981, Legitimacy in the Modern State. New Brunswick, N.J.: Transaction Books.

Scharpf, Fritz W. 1977, Does Organization Matter? Task Structure and Interaction in the Ministerial Bureaucracy. In Elmer H. Burack and Anant R. Negandhi (eds.), Organization Design: Theoretical Perspectives and Empirical Findings, pp. 149–167. Kent: Kent State University Press.

Schattschneider, E.E. 1935, Politics, Pressures and the Tariff. New York: Prentice-Hall.

–   1960, The Semisovereign People. New York: Holt, Rinehart and Winston.

Schelling, Thomas C. 1960, The Strategy of Conflict. Cambridge, Mass.: Harvard University Press.

Schmitter, Phillippe C. 1974, "Still the century of corporatism." Review of Politics, 36: 85–131.

– 1977, "Modes of interest intermediation and models of societal change in western Europe." Comparative Political Studies, 10: 7–38.

Schwerin, Don S. 1980, The Limits of Organization as a Response to Wage-Price Problems. In Richard Rose (ed.), Challenge to Governance: 71–104. Beverly Hills: Sage.

Scott, W. Richard 1981, Organizations: Rational, Natural and Open Systems. Englewood Cliffs, NJ: Prentice-Hall.

Sears, David O. 1975, "Political socialization." In Fred I. Greenstein and Nelson W. Polsby (eds.), Handbook of Political Science, vol. 2: 93–136. Reading, Mass.: Addison-Wesley.

Seidman, Harold 1980, Politics, Position and Power. New York: Oxford University Press.

Seim, Jardar 1972, Hvordan Hovedavtalen av 1935 ble til. Staten, organisasjonene og arbeidsfreden 1930–35. Oslo: Tiden.

Seip, Jens A. 1963, Fra embetsmannsstat til ettpartistat og andre esseys. Oslo: Universitetsforlaget.

– 1974, Utsikt over Norges historie. Oslo: Gyldendal.

– 1981, Utsikt over Norges historie. Annen del. Tidsrommet 1850–1884. Oslo: Gyldendal.

Sejersted, Francis 1979, "Rettsstaten og den selvdestruerende makt." In Rune Slagstad (ed.), Om staten. Oslo: Pax.

Self, Peter, and Storing, Herbert J. 1962, The State and the Farmer. London: Allen and Unwin.

Seligman, Lester G. 1968, "Leadership: Political aspects." In David L. Sills (ed.), International Encyclopedia of the Social Sciences, vol. 12. New York: Macmillan and Free Press.

Selle, Per 1981, Stortingskomitéene 1814–1981. Bergen: Maktutredningen, Discussion paper.

Shonfield, Andrew 1965, Modern Capitalism. London: Oxford University Press.

Simon, Herbert A. 1957, Administrative Behavior, (2nd ed.). New York: MacMillan.

Simpson, Richard L., and Gulley, William H. 1962, "Goals, environmental pressures, and organizational characteristics." American Sociological Review, 27: 344–351.

Sisson, Richard, and Snowiss, Leo 1979, "Legislative viability and political development." In Joel Smith and Lloyd D. Musolf (eds.), Legislatures in Development. Durham, NC: Duke University Press.

Skard, Torild 1980, Utvalgt til Stortinget. Oslo: Gyldendal.

– 1981, Hverdag på Løvebakken. Oslo: Gyldendal.

Solstad, Arve 1969, "The Norwegian coalition system." Scandinavian Political Studies, 4: 160–67.

Solumsmoen, Olav 1962–63, "Regjeringens arbeidsform i Sverige og Norge." Administrasjonsnytt (Oslo): 4–10.

Solumsmoen, Olav and Larssen, Olav 1967, Med Einar Gerhardsen gjennom 20 år. Oslo: Tiden.

Solvang, Bernt K. 1972, LO og forvaltningen – en studie av LO's medlemskap i det offentlige komitésystem. Dissertation (magistergrad), University of Oslo.

Sorel, Georges 1950, Reflections on Violence. Glencoe, Ill.: Free Press.

Spitz, David 1954, "Democracy and the problem of civil disobedience." American Political Science Review, 48: 386–403.

Starbuck, William H. 1965, "Organizational growth and development." In James G. March (ed.), Handbook of Organizations: 451–533. Chicago: Rand McNally.

– 1976, "Organizations and their environment." In Marvin D. Dunnette (ed.), Handbook of Industrial and Organizational Psychology: 1069–1123. Chicago: Rand McNally.

– 1982, "Congealing oil: Inventing ideologies to justify acting ideologies out." Journal of Management Studies, 19(1): 3–27.

Starbuck, William H., Greve, Arnt, and Hedberg, Bo L.T. 1978, "Responding to crises." Journal of Business Administration, 9(2): 111–137.

Stavang, Per 1964, Parlamentarisme og maktbalanse. Oslo: Universitetsforlaget.

Steen, Sverre 1958, "Ole Gabriel Ueland og bondepolitikken." In Sverre Steen, Tusen års norsk historie. Oslo: Cappelen.

Stinchcombe, Arthur L. 1965, "Social structure and organizations." In James G. March (ed.), Handbook of Organizations: 142–193. Chicago: Rand McNally.

– 1968, Constructing Social Theories. New York: Harcourt.

– 1974, Creating Efficient Industrial Administration. New York: Academic Press.

Stokkeland, Harald 1976, Etablering av bydelsutvalg i Oslo. Dissertation, Institute of Political Science, University of Oslo.

Strand, Torodd 1978, "Staten og kommunane: Standardisering, hjelp og sjølvhjelp." In J. P. Olsen (ed.), Politisk organisering: 143–184. Bergen: Universitetsforlaget.

Strange, John H. 1972, "The impact of citizen participation on public administration." Public Administration Review, 32: 457–470.

Strøm, Kåre 1982, Minority Government and Majority Rule. Dissertation in progress, Stanford University.

Stø, Eivind 1974, "Stortingsvalg som legitimering." Tidsskrift for samfunnsforskning, (15): 209–232.

– 1978, De frivillige organisasjonenes representasjon og deltakelse i norsk forbrukerpolitikk. Oslo: Fondet for markeds- og forbrukerforskning, Working paper.

Suleiman, Ezra N. 1974, Politics, Power and Bureaucracy in France. Princeton, N.J.: Princeton University Press.

Sullivan, William M. 1979, "Shifting loyalties. Critical theory and the problem of legitimacy." Polity, 12(2): 253–272.

Sundar, Egil 1979, "Skifte bør skje brått." Aftenposten (Oslo), May 19, 1979.

Szanton, Peter 1981, Federal Reorganization: What Have We Learned? Chatham, N.J.: Chatham House.

Sætren, Harald 1983, Iverksetting av offentlig politikk: Utflytting av statsinstitusjoner fra Oslo. Bergen: Universitetsforlaget, forthcoming.

Sørebø, Herbjørn 1971, Slik sprakk koalisjonen. Oslo: Det norske samlaget.

Talbot, Ross B., and Hadwiger, Don F. 1968, The Policy Process in American Agriculture. San Francisco: Chandler.

Tangenes, Bjørn 1978, Ad hoc-aksjon som politisk deltakelsesform. En studie av sykehussaken i Sogn og Fjordane. Dissertation (hovedoppgave), Institute of Public Administration and Organization Theory, University of Bergen.

Taylor, Charles L., and Hudson, Michael C. 1972, World Handbook of Political and Social Indicators. New Haven, Conn.: Yale University Press.

Thompson, James D. 1962, "Organizations and output transactions." American Journal of Sociology, 68: 309–324.

– 1967, Organizations in Action. New York: McGraw-Hill.

– 1974, "Technology, polity, and societal development." Administrative Science Quarterly, 19: 6–21.

Thompson, James D., and McEwan, W. J. 1958, "Organizational goals and environment: Goal setting as an interaction process." American Sociological Review, 23: 23–31.

Thompson, James D., and Tuden, Arthur 1959, "Strategies, structure and processes of organizational decision." In James D. Thompson, Peter W. Hawkes, Buford H. Junker, and Arthur Tuden (eds.), Comparative Studies in Administration. Pittsburgh: University of Pittsburgh Press.

Tilly, Charles 1975, "Revolutions and collective violence." In Fred I. Greenstein and Nelson W. Polsby (eds.), Handbook of Political Science, vol. 3: 483–556. Reading, Mass.: Addison-Wesley.

– 1982, British Conflicts, 1828–1831. CRSO Working Paper No. 255, University of Michigan.

Tingsten, Herbert 1966, "De norska regeringskriserna 1963." In Herbert Tingsten, Från ideer til idyll. Stockholm: Norstedt.

Tocqueville, Alexis de 1945, Democracy in America. New York: Knopf.

Torgersen, Rolf N. 1948a, "Flere departementer?" Verdens Gang (Oslo), November 22, 1948.

– 1948b, "Regjeringsformer: Konsentrasjon av den utøvende makt?" Verdens Gang (Oslo), November 23, 1948.

Torgersen, Ulf 1968, 'De politiske institusjonene." In N. Rogoff Ramsøy (ed.), Det norske samfunn. Oslo: Gyldendal.

– 1970, "The trend towards political consensus." In Erik Allardt and Stein Rokkan (eds.), Mass Politics: 93–104. New York/London: Free Press/Collier-MacMillan.

Torp, Olav 1946–1981, Stortinget i navn og tall. Oslo: Universitetsforlaget.

Trice, Harrison M. et al. 1969, "The role of ceremonials in organizational behavior." Industrial and Labor Relations Review, (23): 40–51.

Truman, David B. 1951, The Governmental Process. New York: Knopf.

Turk, Herman, and Lefcowitz, Myron J. 1962, "Towards a theory of representation between groups." Social Forces, 40: 337–341.

Tønnesson, Kåre D. 1965, "Et departement med det rette hjertelag for nærings-livets vel." Historisk Tidsskrift. 44: 1–16.

United States, President 1977, Federal Advisory Committees. Fifth Annual Report. Washington, D.C.: U.S. Government Printing Office.

Valen, Henry 1973, "'No' to EEC." Scandinavian Political Studies, 8: 214–226.

– 1974, "The recruitment of parliamentary nominees in Norway." Scandinavian Political Studies, :214–226.

– 1976, "Norway: The local elections of September 1975." Scandinavian Political Studies, 11: 168–184.

– 1978, EF-standpunkt: Politisk påvirkning og sosial struktur. Oslo: manuscript.

– 1981, Valg og politikk. Oslo: NKS-forlaget.

Valen, Henry, and Katz, Daniel 1964, Political Parties in Norway. Oslo: Universitetsforlaget.

Valen, Henry, and Rokkan, Stein 1974, "Conflict structure and mass politics in a European periphery." In Richard Rose (ed.), Electoral Behavior: A Comparative Handbook: 315–370. New York/London: Free Press/Collier-MacMillan.

Vassbotten, O. Joh. 1935, "Stortingets arbeid med lovene." In Ragnar Knoph (ed.), Loven og lovgivningsmakten: 86–132. Oslo: Stenersen.

Vassbotn, Per 1971, Lekkasje og forlis. Oslo: Cappelen.

Verba, Sidney, and Nie, Norman H. 1972, Participation in America. New York: Harper & Row.

Verney, Douglas V. 1957, Parliamentary Reform in Sweden 1866–1921. Oxford: Clarendon.

Vidich, Arthur J., and Glassman, Ronald M. 1979, Conflict and Control: Challenge to Legitimacy of Modern Governments. Beverly Hills: Sage.

Wahlke, John C. 1971, "Policy demands and system support: The role of the represented." British Journal of Political Science, (1): 271–290.

Wahlke, John C. et al., 1962, The Legislative System: Explorations in Legislative Behavior. New York: Wiley.

Wale, Torbjørn 1972, Fjerde statsmakt eller annen partimakt. Unpublished dissertation in political science, University of Oslo.

Walton, Richard E., and McKersie, Robert B. 1965, A Behavioral Theory of Labor Negotiations. New York: McGraw-Hill.

Weber, Max 1924, "Der Sozialismus." In Gesammelte Aufsätze zur Soziologie und Sozialpolitik. Tübingen.

– 1946, "Politics as a vocation." In H.H. Gerth and C. Wright Mills, From Max Weber: 77–128, London: Routledge and Kegan (reprinted).

– 1968, 1978, Economy and Society. New York: Bedminster Press.

Weiler, Hans N. 1981, Compensatory Legitimation in Educational Policy: Legalization, Expertise, and Participation in Comparative Perspective. Paper to the Tenth European Conference on Comparative Education, Geneva, September 20–23, 1981.

Weiner, Stephen S. 1976, "Participation, deadlines, and choice." In James G. March and Johan P. Olsen (eds.), Ambiguity and Choice in Organizations: 225–250. Bergen: Universitetsforlaget.

Wheeler, Christopher 1975, White-Collar Power. Urbana: University of Illinois Press.

Wheeler, Harvey 1975, Constitutionalism. In Fred. I. Greenstein and Nelson W. Polsby (eds.), Handbook of Political Science vol. 5, Governmental Institutions and Processes, pp. 1–91. Reading, Mass.: Addison-Wesley.

Wilson, Graham K. 1977, Special Interests and Policymaking. New York: Wiley.

– 1978, Why the United States is not Corporatist. Working paper, University of Essex.

Wilson, James Q. 1961, "The strategy of protest: problems of negro civic action." Journal of Conflict Resolution, 5: 291–303.

– 1973, Political Organizations. New York: Basic Books.

Wilson, Woodrow 1956 (1885), Congressional Government. New York: Meridian.

Windmuller, John P. 1969, Labor Relations in the Netherlands. Ithaca, N.Y.: Cornell University Press.

Winsnes, A.H. (ed.) 1942, Nansens røst. Oslo: Dybwad.

Wolfe, Alan 1977, The Limits of Legitimacy: Political Contradictions of Contemporary Capitalism. New York: Free Press.

Wolin, Sheldon 1960, Politics and Vision. Boston: Little, Brown.

Wolman, Harold 1972, "Organization theory and community action agencies." Public Administration Review, 32: 33–42.

Wootton, Graham 1970, Interest-groups. Englewood Cliffs, N.J.: Prentice-Hall.

Zald, Mayer N., and Ash, Roberta 1966, "Social movement organizations: growth, decay, and change." Social Forces, 44: 327–341.

Zoffer, H.J. 1976, "Introduction." In Ralph H. Kilman, Louis R. Pondy, and Dennis P. Slevin (eds.): The Management of Organizational Design. Amsterdam: North Holland.

Østerud, Øyvind 1979, Det planlagte samfunn. Oslo: Gyldendal.

Øystese, Ole 1974, "Statens verdigrunnlag i et pluralistisk samfunn." Kirke og kultur, 79: 544–560.

– 1980, Staten i en skjebnetime. Oslo: Lunde.

Aasland, Tertit 1963, "Representantenes deltakelse i stortingsdebattene." Tidsskrift for samfunnsforskning, (3): 163–176.

Public documents

The book contains a number of references to Norwegian public documents. *St. meld.* signifies a report to the Storting from a ministry; *St. prp./Ot. prp.* – a proposition to the Storting from a ministry; *Innst. S.* – a recommendation from a Storting committee to the Storting; *Dok.* – a presentation to the Storting of a type or by an institution not covered by the documents listed above; *Forh. i St./St.tid.* refers to the minutes from the debates in the Storting; and *NOU* signifies an official recommendation from a public committee or sometimes from individuals (year and number in the series is denoted 19xx:xx).

INDEX

(see also *Corporative-functional channel, Economic-producer organizations, Interest organizations*) 30, 32, 33, 35, 44, 90, 148 ff., 202
- access 149, 151, 152, 153, 155, 158, 175, 176
- autonomy 153, 156, 157, 158, 161, 162, 174, 183, 185, 206
- benefits/costs of 33, 152, 153, 154, 157–165, 170, 183, 184, 185, 186, 202
- certainty 33, 158, 159, 164, 183, 184, 206
- conditions for 148, 155, 164, 168, 169, 170, 174, 187
- contact patterns 149, 152, 156, 163
- cooptation/governmental control (see also *Cooptation*) 148, 152, 158, 162, 187, 210, 211
- discretion of representatives 162, 163, 164, 173, 176, 183, 184, 186
- exclusion 151, 152, 155
- external efficiency 161, 162, 163, 184, 186
- functions, effects, impact 150, 158, 160, 161, 162, 173, 174
- ideological identity 33, 158, 160, 161, 164, 170, 179, 183, 184, 185, 186, 187, 206, 210
- legitimacy 152, 157, 161, 164, 166, 167, 168, 174, 184, 185, 186
- member control 33, 150, 154, 158, 161, 162, 163, 164, 170, 185, 186, 206, 210
- reluctance to participate 83, 152, 153, 169, 177, 178, 185, 186, 202
- representativeness 180, 181, 183
- responsibility 33, 152, 158, 161, 163, 164, 170, 183, 184, 186, 206, 210
- spontaneity, flexibility 33, 158, 159, 163, 164, 206
- types of issues 162, 165, 176, 177, 178, 179, 183, 184, 185, 186, 202
- types of organizations 168, 170, 171, 172, 173, 174, 175, 176, 184, 185
- types of participation 155, 156, 157, 166, 167, 175, 176, 183
- types of societies 166, 170–174, 178, 181, 182, 183

Interest organizations (see also *Corporative-functional channel, Economic-producer organizations, Integrated organizational participation*) 10, 14, 15, 17, 19, 20, 28, 29, 30, 32, 33, 34, 42, 49, 54, 55, 60, 67, 68, 69, 70, 72, 79, 82, 91, 101, 104, 109, 115, 117, 122, 129, 144, 165, 189, 201, 202, 211, 212
- contact pattern 69, 70, 78, 83, 90, 95, 96, 127, 139, 140, 142
- impact 70, 96, 108, 109, 110, 111, 112, 120, 161, 168, 174, 197
- participation by 22, 32, 33, 68, 70, 79, 87, 89, 109, 114, 116, 117, 124, 125, 133, 135, 137, 139, 143, 147, 148 ff., 200, 201
- participants 22, 28, 35, 197
- resources 131, 156, 157, 160, 161, 188, 196, 198, 199

Interpretation (political) 39, 40, 41, 45, 47, 49, 50, 51, 57, 64, 65, 72, 73, 75, 186

Intraorganizational structures, see *Structures*

Jacobsen, K. D. 45, 70, 123, 125, 147, 156
Jarolv, C. 156, 166
Johansen, L. N. 150, 156, 162, 166, 169, 171, 172
Jordan, G. 34, 67, 208
Jørgensen, K. 34

Kaartvedt, A. 43
Kaase, M. 29, 36
Kalela, A. 166
Kalela, J. 166
Kamsvåg, R. 76
Karlsen, J. E. 181
Karpe, P. D. 39
Katz, D. 51, 53, 64, 65
Kaufman, H. 45, 57, 152
Key, V. O. 149
Kielland, A. 48, 67, 71

241